Migration of Labour in India

T0298602

Migration – both within and between countries – is increasingly one of the world's most important policy issues. The faster the Indian economy grows, the larger will be the geographical redistribution of the workforce from localities of low to those of high employment growth. Thus, territorial mobility is fundamental both to realizing the full economic potential of India's people and to allowing the population to escape from rural poverty.

The book analyses the decisive factors in labour migration. Based upon a thorough and robust examination of migrants to three slum localities of Delhi stretching over four decades, the author examines why people migrate, the circumstances of their decision and their experience at their destination. He investigates the myths of urban policy – that "rural development" will reduce migration to the cities, that "growth poles" can be created to divert migrant flows, and that government has the power to influence significantly migration scales and directions while pursuing essentially unpredictable market-driven economic growth.

Testing the essential theoretical basis for urban policy in India, the book is of interest to academics studying migration of labour and urbanization, and those interested in South Asian Studies.

Himmat Singh Ratnoo teaches in the Department of Economics at Maharshi Dayanand University, India. His research interests include migration and urbanization.

Routledge Contemporary South Asia Series

For a full list of titles in this series, please visit www.routledge.com

108 Islamic NGOs in Bangladesh
Development, Piety and Neoliberal Governmentality
Mohammad Musfequs Salehin

109 Ethics in Governance in India
Bidyut Chakrabarty

110 Popular Hindi Cinema
Aesthetic Formations of the Seen and Unseen
Ronie Parciack

111 Activist Documentary Film in Pakistan
The Emergence of a Cinema of Accountability
Rahat Imran

112 Culture, Health and Development in South Asia
Arsenic Poisoning in Bangladesh
M. Saiful Islam

113 India's Approach to Development Cooperation
Edited by Sachin Chaturvedi and Anthea Mulakala

114 Education and Society in Bhutan
Tradition and modernisation
Chelsea M. Robles

115 Sri Lanka's Global Factory Workers
(Un) Disciplined Desires and Sexual Struggles
in a Post-Colonial Society
Sandya Hewamanne

116 Migration of Labour in India
The squatter settlements of Delhi
Himmat Singh Ratnoo

Migration of Labour in India
The squatter settlements of Delhi

Himmat Singh Ratnoo

Foreword by Nigel Harris

Routledge
Taylor & Francis Group

LONDON AND NEW YORK

First published 2017 by Routledge

2 Park Square, Milton Park, Abingdon, Oxfordshire OX14 4RN

52 Vanderbilt Avenue, New York, NY 10017

Routledge is an imprint of the Taylor & Francis Group, an informa business

First issued in paperback 2019

British Library Cataloguing in Publication Data
A catalogue record for this book is available from the British Library

Library of Congress Cataloging-in-Publication Data
Names: Ratnoo, Himmat Singh, author.
Title: Migration of labour in India : the squatter settlements of Delhi / Himmat Singh Ratnoo.
Description: Abingdon, Oxon ; New York, NY : Routledge, 2016. | Series: Routledge contemporary South Asia series ; 116 | Includes bibliographical references and index.
Identifiers: LCCN 2016004652 | ISBN 9781138962736 (hardback) | ISBN 9781315659220 (ebook)
Subjects: LCSH: Migrant labor—India. | Labor mobility—India. | Rural-urban migration—India. | Urbanization—India. | Migration, Internal—India.
Classification: LCC HD5856.I4 R37 2016 | DDC 331.5/440954—dc23
LC record available at http://lccn.loc.gov/2016004652

ISBN: 978-1-138-96273-6 (hbk)
ISBN: 978-0-367-87520-6 (pbk)

Typeset in Times New Roman
by Apex CoVantage, LLC

For Balubai

And in loving memory of

Chandi Dan ji
Karian Devi
Deenu
Dhanpati Devi
Dr Mahadev Prasad Saha
Professor Surajbhan
Narpat Lal Bhati

Contents

List of maps   x

List of maps x
List of figures xi
List of tables xiii
Foreword xvi
Preface xvii
Acknowledgments xviii
Glossary xxii
Abbreviations xxiii

1 Introduction: background and organisation of the case study   1

Introduction 1
Theoretical and analytical background of the case study 2
Problem 13
Empirical backdrop of the case study 13
Hypotheses 15
Choice of Delhi for the case study 15
Generalising nature of the present case study 15
Structure of the book 16
References 18

2 Method in the sample survey   23

Introduction 23
Why only the squatter settlements? 23
The process of sample selection 24
The survey 27
*Retracing the criterion migrants after 17 years for a resurvey
   in 2009 27*
References 28

3   Socio-economic status of migrants before migration   29

Introduction 29
A test on the area explanation of migration 30
Occupational status and employment 32
Assessment of economic position in the agricultural context 41
Socio-economic indicators of status 48
Migrants' economic and social position 50
Qualitative analysis of the socioeconomic position 52
Conclusion 54
References 56

**4   Channels of information, job expectation and the process
of migration**   57

Introduction 57
Pre-migration urban visits, contacts, information and advice 57
*Pre-migration knowledge of vacancies and chances to get work
    in Delhi 62*
*Attitudinal patterns of families towards migration to Delhi:
    an evidence of family strategy 63*
*Patterns of job search, waiting and support in the urban labour
    market 65*
Jobs in Delhi 72
Why not work in the village? 80
Additional observations on the process of migration 82
Conclusion 86
References 87

**5   Retrospective on the process of migration two
decades later**   88

Introduction 88
Whereabouts in 2009 88
Occupational status and mobility of the respondents 91
What has changed in the jobs? 99
How are new jobs different from the old ones? 100
Change in skill 101
Regarding those who were nonworkers in 2009 102
*A retrospective on the process of migration by those who stayed
    in Delhi 102*
Conclusion 104
References 104

6 Discovering and characterising groups of migrants 105
Introduction 105
Clustering analysis 105
Groups emerging from the clustering exercise 106
Significance of differences between groups 106
Conclusion 110
References 110

7 Who stays and who returns? 111
Introduction 111
The concept and illustration of the decision-tree method 111
*The decision-tree model with respect to the 'stay or return'
    dichotomy 113*
*Analysis of the dynamics of 'stay or return' on the basis of
    knowledge gained from the decision tree 114*
Conclusion 116
References 117

8 Conclusion 118
References 127

*Appendix A: Empirical backdrop of starting the present
    longitudinal study in the early 1990s: a detailed note on
    then-prevalent interpretation of inter-State rural to urban
    migration in India* 131
*Appendix B: Methodological details of the sample surveys and
    demographic profile of the criteria migrants* 137
Appendix C: Ownership, leasing-in and leasing-out of land 147
Appendix D: Occupational moves at the sub-sectoral level 153
*Appendix E: Methodological details relating to data-mining
    techniques applied in Chapter 6 and Chapter 7* 156
Appendix F: Statistical tables 163
Appendix G: Details relating to the reduced dataset 193
*Appendix H: The four questionnaires and a letter format used
    during different stages of the study* 204
Index 231

Maps

2.1 Location of squatter settlements where sample survey
was conducted 26
3.1 Area of high out-migration: North and Central Bihar and Eastern
Uttar Pradesh 31

Figures

3.1	Percentage distribution of the migrants by economic status and by area of origin	32
3.2	Classes by occupation	34
3.3	Hiring basis in the pre-migration job	35
3.4	First main 'reason group' for stopping the pre-migration job	38
3.5	Unemployed for any time before migration	38
3.6	Duration of unemployment	39
3.7	Levels of employment	40
3.8	Operational holdings by size groups	43
3.9	Operational holdings by tenurial status	43
3.10	Number of harvests in the year before migration	44
3.11	Proportion of agricultural output sold	45
3.12	Fulfilling food requirements in the off-season	46
3.13	Livelihood compared with others	51
3.14	Classification of families by economic position	53
4.1	Distribution of migrants by pre-migration visits to Delhi	58
4.2	Reasons for visiting often	59
4.3	Purpose of pre-migration visit: percentage distribution of the one-time visitors	60
4.4	Family attitude to migration	64
4.5	Job search start time	66
4.6	Waiting time	67
4.7	First 'methods of support' group during the waiting period	69
4.8	First 'channel of recruitment' (grouped) to the first job in Delhi	71
4.9	Channels of recruitment – an index of their effectiveness	72
4.10	Sectors of migrants' entry into the urban labour market	73
4.11	Methods of payment in the first job	74
4.12	Percentage distribution of migrants by the duration of the first job (months)	75
4.13	First reason (group) for ending the first job in Delhi	77
4.14	Sectors of the second job	79
4.15	Sectors of the third job	79
4.16	The most important reason for migration	84

5.1	All the criteria migrants in 2009	89
5.2	The living and traced criteria migrants in 2009	90
5.3	Sector-wise distribution of migrants' first jobs and current jobs	92
5.4	Occupational mobility in the construction sector	93
5.5	Occupational mobility in the service sector	94
5.6	Occupational mobility in the factory sector	94
5.7	Occupational mobility in the shopkeeping/shop workers sector	95
5.8	Occupational mobility in the sector category 'others'	95
5.9	Sub-sectors of the construction sector: percentage distribution of first jobs and current jobs	96
5.10	Sub-sectors of the service sector: percentage distribution of first jobs and current jobs	96
5.11	Sub-sectors of the factory sector: percentage distribution of first jobs and current jobs	97
5.12	Sub-sectors of the shopkeeping/shop-workers sector: percentage distribution of first jobs and current jobs	98
5.13	Sub-sectors of the 'others' sector: percentage distribution of first jobs and current jobs	98
5.14	The most important reason for migration	103
6.1	Characterization of migrants	109
7.1	Illustration of a decision tree	112
7.2	Decision tree created for the decision to stay or return	114
C1	Ownership distribution of cultivable land (in acres)	148
C2	Extent of cultivable land	148
C3	Distribution of single-plot cultivable holdings	149
C4	Size distribution of single plots of leased-in land	151
C5	Extent of irrigation in the leased-in land	151

Tables

3.1	Main job of the criteria migrants before migration	33
3.2	Reasons for leaving the pre-migration job	36
3.3	Months of employment in the year before migration	40
3.4	Percentage distribution of operational holdings by tenurial status and size groups	42
3.5	Months of food from own harvest	46
3.6	Percentage distribution of respondents by the percentage of income from different sources	47
3.7	Percentage distribution of respondents by number of animals owned	48
3.8	Percentage distribution of the respondents by ownership of certain durable items	50
4.1	The method of support during the waiting period in Delhi	68
4.2	The methods used for searching for the first job in Delhi	69
4.3	The channels of recruitment for the first job in Delhi	70
4.4	The index of effectiveness of the various channels of recruitment in getting the first job in Delhi	70
4.5	The main reasons for ending the first job in Delhi	76
4.6	Reasons for not preferring to live in the village	80
4.7	Reasons for not doing a similar job in the village	82
4.8	Most important reason for migration	83
4.9	The most important reason of migration (criteria migrants)	83
5.1	Change in the nature of the same jobs between 2009 and 1992	99
5.2	Difference in the nature of work between 2009 and 1992	100
6.1	List of variables with similar modal values for the two groups	107
6.2	List of variables with dissimilar modal values for the two groups	108
A-1.1	Lifetime internal male migrants as a percentage of the internal male population in the States and Union Territories of India – 1961, 1971, 1981	163
A-1.2	Male migrants of different categories as a percentage of the total internal male migrants – 1961, 1971, 1981	167

A-1.3   Lifetime inter-State male migrants from rural and urban
          areas (per cent) and their growth rates – 1971–1981   171
A-1.4   Lifetime inter-State male net migrants and the decadal rates
          1971–1981   172
A-1.5   Areas of high out-migration as specified by Mohan (1982:
          42)   172
A-2.1   Population of *jhuggie jhonpari* clusters (squatter settlements)
          in different parts of Delhi   173
A-2.2   Percentage of criteria migrants from different squatter
          settlements   173
A-2.3   The percentage distribution of criteria migrants among
          census blocks and the migrant proportion   173
A-2.4   Percentage distribution of the phase I interviews with the
          criteria migrants by day of the week   174
A-2.5   Phase II interview in the forenoon or afternoon   174
A-2.6   Interview duration in minutes (Phase II)   174
A-2.7   Age at the time of the interview in 1992   175
A-2.8   Years of schooling   175
A-2.9   Marital status   175
A-2.10   Total duration of stay in Delhi (in months)   175
A-2.11   Years since migration   176
A-2.12   The distribution of the criteria migrants by calendar month
          of arrival in Delhi   176
A-2.13   Calendar year of arrival in Delhi   176
A-2.14   Age at arrival in Delhi   177
A-2.15   Type of place of last residence   177
A-2.16   State of birth   177
A-2.17   Percentage distribution of criteria migrants by State of
          last residence   178
A-3.1   Duration of unemployment for those unemployed before
          migration   178
A-3.2   Duration of underemployment for those underemployed
          before migration (in days)   178
A-3.3   Percentage distribution of respondents by the amount of total
          and cultivable land owned (acres)   179
A-3.4   Leased-in land (in acres)   179
A-3.5   Size of single plot of leased-in land (acres)   179
A-3.6   Percentage of leased-in to owned cultivable land   180
A-4.1   Calendar month of pre-migration visit   180
A-4.2   Calendar year of pre-migration visit   180
A-4.3   Length of stay during pre-migration visit (in days)   180
A-4.4   First job in Delhi   181
A-4.5   Total duration of first job (in months)   181
A-4.6   Second job in Delhi   182
A-4.7   Third job in Delhi   182

A-4.8	Fourth job in Delhi	183
A-5.1	Reason for death (all sources used)	183
A-5.2	Locality during migrant resurvey in 2009	183
A-5.3	Main activity of the respondents	183
A-5.4	Cross-tabulation of the sectors of the first city jobs with the sectors of the current city jobs	184
A-5.5	Kind of study or work learned	185
A-6.1	Data and cluster norms from k-means clustering	186
D1	Occupational moves at the sub-sectoral level	153
E1	The values of silhouette widths for different values of k	157
E2	Attributes used for the decision tree	158
E3	Ranking of variables using the gain ratio attribute evaluation method	161
E4	Decision rules induced with respect to the decision to stay or return	162
G1	List of variables in the reduced dataset	194

Foreword

Migration – both within and between countries – is increasingly one of the world's most important policy issues. The faster the Indian economy grows, the larger will be the geographical redistribution of the workforce from localities of low employment growth to those of high employment growth. Thus, territorial mobility is fundamental, both to realising the full economic potential of India's people and to allowing the millions to escape from the cruelty and stunted expectations of rural poverty.

Yet these truisms – and the policy reactions they should promote (facilitating movement and protecting the migrants) – are still often disputed. Migrants in this version are not rational adults choosing the most sensible option, but part of a blind torrent of lemmings, driven out of rural poverty to self-destruction in city slums. The fear engendered by the movement of population (and its "pressures") supersedes a concern with people.

Dr Himmat Singh Ratnoo's theme in this work is therefore of profound importance for India's future. Based upon a thorough and robust examination of migrants to three slum localities of Delhi stretching over four decades – why people migrate, the circumstances of their decision and their experience at their destination. It is thus also a rich exposure of the myths of urban policy – that "rural development" will reduce migration to the cities and that "growth poles" can be created to divert migrant flows – indeed that government has the power to influence significantly migration scales and directions while pursuing essentially unpredictable market-driven economic growth.

The core of the work is a dense study of migration to three localities (with an excellent follow-up study twenty years later of those migrants who could be traced) in order to test the essential theoretical basis for much urban policy. Methodologically, the work is thorough and rigorous, a model for "evidence-based policy making".

It is an honour and a privilege to be asked to introduce this substantial and well-written work.

Nigel Harris
University College London

Preface

There is a tale of my own migration and return migration behind this book. In 1992, as a part of my doctoral studies, I carried out a sample survey of inter-State rural migrants in the squatter settlements of Delhi. I was awarded a PhD by the University of London in 1994, and there were a few offers for publication of the results. On completion of my PhD, I returned to my teaching job in an Indian university, as that was a condition of the Commonwealth Academic Staff Scholarship on which I went to England. Over the next two decades, a la Charlie Chaplin in *Modern Times*, I have been an active, often dissenting, voice in Indian academic governance, which brought to me in ample measure the kind of rewards that generally follow. My interest in rural to urban migration persisted, of course, and in 2009 I retraced the migrant respondents of my 1992 fieldwork and interviewed the ones I could find in Delhi after a gap of seventeen years. The humble purpose of this book is to report, without any further delay, the results of this longitudinal empirical research based on a generalising case study started in the early 1990s.

I wish this book reaches whoever it could be of any interest to and await feedback and exchange.

Acknowledgments

I owe a lot to many people. With my socially and economically backward background, it was imperative that I found help at critical stages of my life and career, and I have. Because it is not possible to mention by name the many people who have influenced my thoughts and emotions while undertaking this research, I offer my gratitude (and apologies!) to all those with whom I have discussed *Migration of Labour in India* over the years, and also to all those with whom I have shared problems that life has a tendency to throw up. I specifically acknowledge the following from my head and heart.

I thank Nigel Harris, who, as my doctoral supervisor, inspired this project with his critical and insightful comments, with courage of conviction for a beautiful and cosmopolitan world and insistence that I organise my thoughts on migration and urbanisation in consonance with facts. I am grateful to my MPhil supervisor Professor Amitabh Kundu, who introduced me to this area of study and to Nigel.

During my doctoral phase, dialogue with Fabio Scatolin was continuous and most fruitful. I had the benefit of discussions with Moha Abdullah, Gabriel Porcila, Liang Yeh Chein, Jeoffery Nsemukila, Tayfun Atay, Sanjay Sharma and Pragati Mohapatra. I received psychological back-up from Rajinder, Joginder, Anjali, Anna, Guy, Leo, Beata, Iqbal, Rupinder, Swapna and Khanindra. From across the seas, the late Dr Mahadev Prasad Saha, Sukhbir Kaur, Surinder Kumar, Satvir Dahiya and Ajay Divakaran kept my spirits up with warmth and reassurance. Discussions with Professor Amitabh Kundu, Dr Sapna Mukhopadhyaya, Dr Promila Suri, Navsharan Singh and Atul Sood were helpful in considering issues that came up during sample selection. Professor Devendra Gupta of the Institute of Economic Growth; Mr K.S. Natrajan, Mr M.S. Bhati, Mrs Veena Dixit and Mr Ansari of the Census of India; Sadashivam, K. Srirangan and Chandu Bhutia of the Delhi Development Authority (DDA); Mr P.K. Chopra, Mrs Sangita Verma, Mr Y.P. Sharma and Shivakant of the Slum Wing of the DDA were very helpful in listening to my problems with sample selection. At times, Rishikant, Sunit, Rais, Arvind, Kunna and my brother Gopal shared my logistic worries. The late Deenu and Dr Surat Singh were my solace after day's work. My friends Tej Narain and Satdev shared all my problems and enthused me greatly at all times. Due to the support from my parents-in-law, the late Dhanpati Devi and Mr Satpal Dahiya I could do my fieldwork without worry.

It has been a rough landing back in India after the doctoral studies in England, and I have passed through tough times. Numerous strong-willed friends have kept my sanity intact with love and comradeship, and it's hard to name all of them. However, I would like to specifically thank a few of them without whom I would not have survived: Satvir Dahiya, Manmohan, Shubha, Pradeep Kasni, Inderjit, Jagmati, Manjeet, Taj Manchanda, Bhupendra Yadav, Rajinder Chaudhary, Surinder Kumar, Ram Babu Bhagat, Dinesh Pratap Singh, Mercy and Thomas Joseph, Pushpendra Jugtawat, Seema Baghel, Harish Kumar, Pradipta Chaudhury, Anita Dagar, Vinod Varma, Baldeo Singh and Dalbir Singh. My thanks to Bhupen, Munin, Sobha Barhath, Purshottam Pancholi, Sultan Tyagi, Bhairon Dutt Joshi, Sachidanand Sinha, Rahul Ramagundam and Naresh Hoshiarpuria. My long and often action-packed association with the teachers' movement in India afforded a close and fearless look at the running of Indian academics, and I would like to thank the Maharshi Dayanand University Teachers' Association (MDUTA), the All India Federation of University and College Teachers' Organisations (AIFUCTO) and all my companions from the movement.

Pardeep Kumar, Anil Panikkar and Dushyant always cheered me up from the depths of despair and have been consistently understanding of my inner voice. Dr Chhaya Lamba not only gave me homeopathic medicine for the neuralgia that struck me while I was preparing this manuscript, she mindfully helped me to complete it. Advocate Mr Naveen Kumar Singhal, who often stands up for legal and constitutional rights, touched my heart through expression of his support for realisation of my academic dreams.

In 2008, I started thinking of ways to recover, revive and follow up on my research work and to communicate it. It has taken this long to actually reach a point where completion of the process appears to be in sight. All sorts of difficulties cropped up. My nephew-in-law and friend Parikshit Charan understood it all and stood by me, in all ways, in all its aspects and at all times. At crucial moments – when I had nearly given up or when I wanted to move ahead and needed a nod – in times good and bad – Parikshit sahib was always at hand to solace me through his admirable qualities of head and heart. He was involved in all planning, programming, scheduling and reviews to see a happy end for this project. The best thing was that we could laugh at things under all circumstances. My niece Vipin and Parikshit sahib looked after me by appreciating and understanding my educational and cultural needs; providing an affectionate, caring and congenial atmosphere wherein I could find inner peace; and by encouraging me to complete it all.

This book would not have been possible without the cooperation, trust and affection with which the residents of squatter settlements gave me the stories of their migration to Delhi. The hundreds of names cannot be mentioned here, but I would like to put on record the initial help of Satyapal Singhal, Sushil Kumar, Shamim Khan, Jeet Ram, Satvir Singh, Niranjan Chacha and Pradip Sarakar in navigating the serpentine lanes of my field sites. Sukh Ram Laurik and Ram Dular helped me in organising the pre-testing of the questionnaires. The respondents whom I could interview again two decades later were both amazed at and forgiving of my absence during the intervening period – some wondered if I was going to do a further resurvey a few decades down the line! Shamim Khan and Satvir Singh made me feel so much at home that my bond with the labouring classes feels strengthened.

I particularly thank Maharshi Dayanand University, Rohtak, for nominating me for the Commonwealth Academic Staff Scholarship; the University Grants Commission of India for recommending my name; and the Association of Commonwealth Universities for providing me scholarship for doctoral research. I am grateful to the Graduate School of the University College London and the Mountbatten Memorial Fund for providing two months' maintenance each. I thank my colleagues of the Department of Economics of the Maharshi Dayanand University for coping with the burden of my absence. I also thank the Nansen Village for providing me with a congenial environment during my stay in London.

I thank the Indian Council of Social Science Research that awarded me a fellowship for two years and the Jawaharlal Nehru University, New Delhi, and the Chaudhary Charan Singh Haryana Agricultural University, Hisar, for their affiliation and the Maharshi Dayanand University for granting me leave. I am most grateful to Professor Arjun Singh Rana of the Department of Agricultural Economics, CCS Haryana Agricultural University, Hisar, who readily took me under his wings, placed complete faith in me and gave unconditional love and unstinted support when I needed it. Mahalaya Chatterjee and Sumit Dahiya have been very kind in providing suggestions and encouragement to communicate my research. Mahabir Jaglan has always been a friend in need and he lovingly helped me with maps. Mr Amarnath Pathak provided technical assistance when the tables and figures needed some reworking.

When I was a little boy in a Thar village, my father Chandi Dan ji taught me to believe in myself, value dignity and keep alive the spirit of questioning and dissent and the courage of conviction, and my mother Balubai tried to keep me on track. My eldest brother Suresh helped me as a friend to dream but to stay grounded at the same time. My brothers Rajendra and Hari and sisters Indubai, Shushila and Sumitra stood by me. My family understood my decisions even while they disagreed. I am grateful to my teachers in various villages and towns of India who constantly showed me the next step.

My wife Saroj and son Vigyan shared every moment of joy and worry that this longitudinal research has entailed. In fact, throughout the history of our mutual association, all three of us have been trying to live together and get educated together. At the time of my first fieldwork in 1992, Saroj was learning computing and now she specialises in computational intelligence. Apart from the personal and social strings that bind us both, she provided in-depth aid and advice in the use of data-mining techniques in Chapters 6 and 7 of this book. Master Vigyan was two when we went to England for my doctoral studies; he accompanied me back to India when I came for the first fieldwork in Delhi, and as a child he pretended to be doing all that followed: processing, presentation and thesis writing. Today Vigyan is studying to be an economic historian, and I am very proud to state for the record how lovingly and wisely he helped and encouraged me to revise an earlier draft of the book manuscript while I was getting restive under the weight of my circumstances. When Vigyan was a little boy, one of the first things he learned to say was, "What are friends for?" Nothing surpasses friendship indeed.

Finally, I am grateful to the two anonymous referees for their helpful comments and to Routledge for accepting this book. It has been a pleasure to work with Dorothea Schaefter, the Senior Editor of Asian Studies at Routledge, and the team consisting of Jillian Morrison and Sophie Iddamalgoda. I am grateful to Lisa MacCoy and Christopher Mathews at Apex CoVantage for the thoughtful copyediting.

Glossary

Anna	A currency unit formerly used in India and Pakistan; equal to 1/16 of a rupee
Basti	A slum locality inhabited by poor people
Beldari	A labourer's job, usually as an unskilled construction worker
Chakkar	Trouble
Chowk	Market square
Jhuggie	Slum dwelling of a squatter
Jhuggie-jhonpari	Squatter settlement
Kanoon	Law
Karigar	Skilled worker
Kothiwala	Bungalow resident
Labour chowk	Market square where daily-wage workers gather to be hired
Majoori	Wage labour
Mazdoor	An unskilled labourer
Namaskar	A term of greeting in India
Naukari	A service job or employment in the formal sector
Panchayat	Village council
Poorbia	Term used by the natives of north India for migrants from Eastern Uttar Pradesh and Bihar, meaning 'Easterner'
Poorvanchal	A geographic region of northern India, which comprises the eastern end of the State of Uttar Pradesh
Poorvanchali	A person hailing from the Poorvanchal region of India
Poorvee	Easterner
Raya	Advice or opinion
Sarpanch	Head of the village council
Shri	A title meaning Mister
Tehsil	An administrative unit smaller than a district
Vilayat	A term meaning foreign country

Abbreviations

CART	Classification and Regression Tree
CHAID	Chi-squared Automatic Interaction Detection
DDA	Delhi Development Authority
FDI	Foreign Direct Investment
FLPH	Foreign Languages Publishing House
GNP	Gross National Product
GOI	Government of India
IDSMT	Integrated Development of Small and Medium Towns
IOM	International Organisation for Migration
ISSP	International Social Survey Programme
LDC	Less Developed Country
MNREGA	Mahatma Gandhi National Rural Employment Guarantee Act
NCR	National Capital Region
NCU	National Commission on Urbanisation
POB	Place of Birth
POLR	Place of Last Residence
SDP	State Domestic Product
TB	Tuberculosis
TCPO	Town and Country Planning Organisation
TRO	Total Relative Deprivation
UIDSSMT	Urban Infrastructure Development Scheme for Small and Medium Towns
UN	United Nations
UN ECOSOC	United Nations Economic and Social Council
UNFPA	United Nations Fund for Population Activities

1 Introduction

Background and organisation of the case study

Introduction

The development of theories of migration, particularly the ones pertaining to developing countries of the past century, appears to be a cyclical journey of moving away from and then back to 'the basics of the classics' – from a delinking from classical political economy, to bewilderment at the speed of urbanisation during the middle of the twentieth century, to being lost in the wilderness amongst land–man ratios and population densities and absorption capacities evoked by geographers and demographers, to a point finally where scholars seem to be rediscovering the utility of applying modern means of research to the modern-day migration of labour within the frameworks of classical and Marxist political economy. Some of the examples of the latter trend include Ellis and Harris (2004), Stark (2006) and Breman (2010). The movement towards embracing the holistic and classical approach is also reflected in the fact that labour migration is being studied to bring out more and more common elements that apply equally to the movement of labour within the boundaries and to those across boundaries (Lall, Selod and Shalizi, 2006; Stark, 2006; Stark, Micevska and Mycielski, 2009).

The present study uses methods that are anchored to the understandings of labour migration as reflected in the writings of classical and Marxist political economists and fuses these with modern techniques within an integrated social science approach. The study aims at empirically finding the decisive factor in labour migration through a generalising case study. It critically examines the pivotal role of demand for labour through the following main themes: the role of relative deprivation in rural areas of origin and the mechanisms of information, advice and job searches in the process of rural to urban migration of labour, as well as the sequence, importance and manner in which variables determine the question of who stays and who returns. The primary dataset covers different time points in the processes of migration and return migration spanning four decades and has been collected from hundreds of representative migrants via two rounds of fieldwork nearly two decades apart. Analysis of this panel data forms the backbone of the current work.

To lay the contextual foundation for our results, this first chapter states the research problem of this study in light of the theoretical and analytical background, the empirical backdrop when this longitudinal study was being planned in 1991 and hypotheses that emerged and why Delhi was chosen for the case study. The second section contains a review of some important studies that have analysed the mechanics of rural to urban migration of labour. The review includes classical and Marxist writings and models of migration that have vastly influenced the popular and at times populist conventional wisdom on rural to urban migration in developing countries as studies that also depart from the conventional wisdom. The third section introduces the research problem emerging from the literature. The fourth section refers to a general picture of inter-State rural to urban migration in India at the time this case study was being designed. The fifth section states the hypotheses of the study. The next section considers the relevance of a case study of Delhi. The seventh section describes the nature of the present study as a generalising case study. The final section lays out the structure of the book.

Theoretical and analytical background of the case study

Debates on employment and labour transfer have roots in the great works of classical economics, and as with other economic theories, there is value in exploring the insights that are relevant to us in modern economics.[1] Accordingly, the first sub-section is concerned with the development of ideas on rural to urban migration of labour in classical economic writings. Then we turn our attention to a review of the traditional theories of migration that came to the fore in the second half of the twentieth century and continue to dominate current academic debates in the field. The next sub-section reviews the studies that depart from the traditional pessimistic view and support a move back towards a holistic and optimistic view that is closer to the classical and Marxist understanding of labour migration under capitalism.

The evolution of classical ideas on labour transfer

In a sense, the historical inevitability of the transfer of labour from rural to urban regions and from agriculture to industry is an old conclusion. Early post-mercantilist economic writers appreciated the significance of class differentiation in rural areas that comes with the transition to capitalism, and they underlined the low value of skills in the countryside compared with urban areas. A case in point is David Hume's comment on the marginal life of the landless peasant in

> rude unpolished nations, where the arts are neglected, all labour bestowed on the cultivation of the ground . . . [Vassals and tenants] are necessarily dependent, and fitted for slavery and subjugation; *especially where they possess no riches, and are not valued for their knowledge in agriculture*, as must be always the case where arts are neglected.
>
> (Hume in Rotwein, ed., 1955: 28, emphasis mine)

Hume's eighteenth-century counterpart Adam Smith took this further. He recognised the potential for migration from the areas of low costs of reproduction of labour to the areas where the costs are higher, saying that

> it appears evidently from the experience that a man is of all sorts of luggage the most difficult to be transported. If the labouring poor, therefore, can maintain their families in those parts of the kingdom where the price of labour is the lowest, they must be in affluence where it is highest.
>
> (Smith in Skinner, ed., 1970: 178)

With regard to the rate of accumulation (and not the stage of accumulation) determining wages and, by implication, the demand for labour, Smith was a true predecessor to Karl Marx. He argued that it is not the actual greatness of national wealth, but its continual increase, which occasions a rise in the wages of labour. It is not, accordingly, in the richest countries, but in the most thriving, or in those growing richest the fastest, that wages are highest. Smith illustrated this point in the context of England and North America, saying,

> England is certainly, in the present times, a much richer country than any part of North America. The wages of labour, however, are much higher in North America than in any part of England . . . it is in the progressive state, while the society is advancing to the further acquisition, rather than when it has acquired its full complement of riches that the condition of the labouring poor, the great body of the people, seem to be the happiest and the most comfortable.
>
> (Smith in Skinner, ed., 1970: 172)

David Ricardo developed the theory of capital accumulation further by adding a technological dimension to it. He demonstrated that, with technological changes, the rate and pattern of accumulation will change and consequently the demand for labour will also change. Ricardo was thus able to make a crucial inference about the cyclical nature of production under capitalism and its serious implications for labour demand. Illustrating the problem of unemployment arising out of the decline in labour demand due to the replacement of labour by capital, Ricardo stated the following:

> All I wish to prove, is that the discovery and use of machinery may be attended with a diminution of gross product; and whenever it is the case, it will be injurious to the labouring class, as some of their number will be thrown out of employment, and population will become redundant, compared with the funds which are to employ it.
>
> (Ricardo in Sraffa and Dobb, ed., 1951: 390)

Karl Marx took forward Ricardo's idea that capital accumulation changes the very nature of demand for labour and makes it cyclical. The accumulation of capital and its relation to the growth of the relative surplus population are two key elements in Marx's analysis of rural to urban migration. Marx found the seeds of the growth of capital accumulation and relative surplus population in the transition from pre-capitalist economic formations (Marx in Hobsbawm, ed., 1965). He argued that the development of the classes of owners and of the proletariat is a logical corollary of the transformation of all existing property into commercial and industrial capital (Marx in Hobsbawm, ed., 1965, p. 30). Thus appears a 'doubly free' mass of living labour power on the labour market, that is, "Free from the old relations of clientship, villeinage or service, but also free from all goods and chattels, from every real and objective form of existence, free from all property" (Marx in Hobsbawm, ed., 1965, p. 111). The role of capital in the accumulation of labour and its instruments at given points is seen as the main element of accumulation of capital (Marx in Hobsbawm, ed., 1965, pp. 111–112).

Smith and Marx both recognised that the growth of accumulation and its rapidity give rise to increases in productivity, which allows a smaller quantity of labour to produce a greater quantity of output – the composition of capital therefore changes in favour of its constant portion. Here, Marx makes a distinction between the two stages of capitalistic accumulation, that is, concentration and centralisation (Marx in Progress, Moscow edition, 1954). The first stage of capital accumulation involves concentrating the means of production and command over labour, and at this stage individual capitals fiercely guard their independence against each other. According to Marx, the second stage of capital accumulation (the stage of centralisation) is marked by the concentration of capital that is already formed, destruction of independence of individual capitals, 'expropriation of capitalist by capitalist' and transformation of many small capitals into a few large capitals (Marx in Progress, Moscow edition, 1954, p. 586). The stage of centralisation extends and speeds up the revolutions in the technical composition of capital, which in turn result in an absolute reduction in the demand for labour (Marx in Progress, Moscow edition, 1954, p. 588). Because this stage is marked by sudden expansions and contractions of economic activity, it needs a disposable industrial reserve army which makes possible suddenly throwing great masses of workers at the decisive points without injury to the scale of production. Its function is to ensure that demand for labour can be met independently of the increase in population. According to Marx, "The industrial reserve army, during the periods of stagnation and average propensity, weighs down the active labour-army; during the periods of over-production and paroxysm, it holds its pretensions in check" (Marx in Progress, Moscow edition, 1954, 598).

In this framework, the relative surplus population, or industrial reserve army, is a pivot point upon which the law of demand and supply of labour works, and it is a potential factor of mobility. It can take different forms, but apart from the acute form (during crisis) and chronic form (during dull times), it always has three forms – namely, floating surplus population, latent surplus population and stagnant surplus population (Marx in Progress, Moscow edition, 1954, pp. 600–603.) The form of the relative surplus population that is most relevant in understanding the process of rural to urban migration of labour in this framework is latent surplus population so the discussion here will focus on that.

Marx postulated that with the introduction of capitalistic production into agriculture, the demand for an agricultural labouring population falls absolutely. Even while accumulation continues, this repulsion is not compensated by greater attraction, as is the case with nonagricultural industries. One part of the agricultural population is therefore constantly on the point of passing over into the urban or manufacturing proletariat and on the lookout for circumstances favourable to this transformation. This constantly flowing source of a relative surplus population presupposes in the country itself that there is a constant latent surplus population, which becomes evident only when outlets open. Lenin (in FLPH, Moscow edition, 1956: 551–599) applied this framework to study the development of capitalism in Russia, and in that context, he used variables like land ownership status of cultivators, ownership of animals and implements, the availability of grain all year around and employment in nonagricultural occupations to measure the latent reserve army.

The classical and Marxist ideas on rural to urban migration are intertwined with the development of capitalism, the role of accumulation and the related aspect of the growth of labour demand, on the one hand, and the creation of a mass of 'free labourers', on the other. In other words, the concentration of economic activities in urban areas, as well as the reorganisations of these activities, lead to increases in urban demand for labour, which in turn necessitates a rural-urban transfer of labour. A reading of classical and Marxist writings remains an insightful theoretical tool for scholars of rural to urban migration, but we now move on to discuss traditional models of migration that are more popular in academic parlance.

W.A. Lewis (1954) was among the first to consider rural to urban migration in the context of the developing countries of the second half of the twentieth century, and the model he developed remains at the core of migration theory today.[2] His model visualised the economy as consisting of two sectors: the traditional rural subsistence sector which is characterised by zero or very low productivity surplus labour, and the high-productivity modern industrial sector which attracts the surplus labour. The primary focus is on the process of labour transfer, as well as on growth of employment in the modern sector, both of which are brought about by the growth of output in the modern sector. The speed at which these occur is given by the rate of capital accumulation in the modern sector, which in turn depends on the excess of modern-sector profits over wages, assuming that all capitalists reinvest all profits. The level of wages in the modern sector is taken as constant – being determined at a fixed premium over a constant subsistence level of wages in the traditional sector. At a constant urban wage, the supply of rural labour is considered perfectly elastic. According to the Lewis model, the rural-urban wage differential allows urban areas to attract unlimited supplies of labour from the countryside. The Lewis model, like most of the models of economic development of the 1950s, took accumulation as the key constraint on economic transformation. As in the case of classical and Marxist writings, its recognition of the demand-pull forces in the shape of elastic response to favourable employment conditions was reflected in a positive optimism towards rural to urban migration.

In the context of such theories that largely viewed rural to urban migration of labour in a positive light, we now look at some of the prominently negative and pessimistic views on rural to urban migration of labour.

The traditional pessimistic models of migration

Hoselitz (1953, 1955, 1957) was the first to offer the evidence that ratios of industrial employment to urban population were small in contemporary developing nations – Asia in particular – compared with developed countries in the late nineteenth and early twentieth centuries. Hoselitz's original finding encouraged the perception of urban services as 'unproductive activities' and mainly a response to migrant-swollen labour supplies. The belief in Hoselitz's (1962: 169) proposition that rural migration is caused by "sheer excess of human resources on land" and "population pressure" has lingered longer. The essence of Hoselitz's ideas is that the agglomeration of population occurs on grounds of "economically irrational" motivations. According to him, migration is not "provoked" by increasing demand for labour in urban concerns, but rather by considerations "outside the sphere of resource allocation and use". The term 'push migration' became part of the popular parlance because it seemed simple and it was appealing to describe migration as flight from misery. Thus, Lee (1966) followed Hoselitz in saying the magnitude of net stream (i.e., stream minus counter-stream) is directly related to the preponderance of minus factors at origin – that is, origin 'push' factors are more important than destination 'pull' factors. Hoselitz (1962) used the term 'over-urbanisation' to convey the idea of urbanisation outpacing industrialisation. Bairoch (1975: 150) supported Hoselitz's finding, saying that "[t]he degree of urbanisation in under-developed countries was the same in 1960 as it had been in Europe in 1880–85 when the latter's percentage of working population engaged in manufacturing was twice that of the less developed countries". On the basis of World Bank data from the 1960s, Berry and Sabot (1984: 106) reached the same conclusion and stated that "[w]hereas at the turn of the century the industrializing European nations absorbed almost half of their incremental labour force into industry each year, today the developing countries absorb less than 30 per cent of their additional workers into industry". Even the authors who had earlier followed an optimistic classical framework started turning negative and pessimistic in their assessment of rural to urban migration in the context of developing countries. For example, in a later writing Lewis, even while reasserting the salient points of the model he gave in 1954, also talked of "over-urbanisation" of the developing countries (Lewis, 1988: 14). Lewis emphasised that disguised unemployment, diminishing returns and rate of growth of the urban population in developing countries are greater than those in the developed countries during the end of the nineteenth century. According to Lewis, development raises the rate of natural increase in a population in a less developed country (LDC) and if the land–labour ratio is unfavourable, the land absorbs more labour – by subdivision of family farms or otherwise. At some point the diminishing returns drive young men off the farms into the towns, if that is where development is occurring. Lewis supported his conclusion of 'over-urbanisation' with the observation that 4.5 per cent per annum growth of urban population in the LDCs of the 1960s and 1970s was higher than the 3.5 per cent for Australia and the United States at the end of the nineteenth century. Some authors have contradicted this assertion by Lewis (Williamson, 1988b: 24–30).

Opponents of the over-urbanisation thesis argued that Third World cities could not be expected to replicate the employment patterns of the nineteenth century. For example, unlike in the nineteenth century, twentieth-century urban areas had higher levels of social services and greater potential employment in the formal and informal sectors of the growing cities' construction industries (Williamson, 1988a: 426). Based on assessment of the industrial employment trends between 1950 and 1970, Preston (1979) did not find deterioration in industry/urban ratio (meant to compare the share of industry in production to the share of urban area in population) in the Third World as a whole. In fact, in the largest of the developing regions – Middle South Asia, including India – the ratio had risen. The opposition to the Hoselitz thesis was backed up by evidence from later studies (Williamson, 1988a: 439–441; Lall, Selod and Shalizi, 2006). Migrants did not appear to be dominating urban service employment (Yap, 1977: 255). It was difficult to argue that wages are relatively low in the urban service sector, including the urban informal sector (Yap, 1977; Papola, 1981; Kannappan, 1985). Mazumdar (1976) questioned the understanding that urban informal sectors are a point of entry for the in-migrant any more than for the city-born. Oucho and Gould (1993: 275) observe that urbanisation in Africa has been independent of industrialisation. Fay and Opal (1999: 28) observed that in a significant number of countries, urbanisation has taken place even during periods of economic stagnation or decline. Dyson (2011: 41) reviewed a wide range of demographic data, particularly the data on mortality, from different parts of the world to clarify why urbanisation is outpacing industrialisation. Fox (2013: 72) has argued with evidence that "urbanisation and urban growth are also intrinsically associated with demographic processes that can become de-linked from economic ones".

In fact, some recent studies tend to break this belief in the over-urbanisation thesis through synthesis of the demographic and economic research and explanation of the urbanisation-industrialisation gap by way of a change in the demographic situation, particularly in terms of the declines in mortality rates (Dyson, 2011; Fox, 2011; Fox, 2013).

The two-sector model of Harris and Todaro (1970) was an important development in the poverty theory of migration that was inherent in the idea of over-urbanisation. Harris and Todaro (1970) refined their migration theory through their two-sector model, arguing that migration proceeds in response to the urban-rural differences in expected earnings, which, they postulate, arise out of the provision of politically determined minimum wages in urban areas, with the employment rate acting as an equilibrating force. This model was based on an earlier model by Todaro, which was primarily concerned with the formulation of a theory of urban unemployment in the developing countries (Todaro, 1969). Todaro (1976: 25) also talked of an 'empirically testable model' to explain what he saw as a contradiction during the 1960s – large and even increasing rural-urban migration in many countries, in spite of rising levels of urban unemployment and under-employment. He concluded that in the decision to migrate, the individual has to balance the probabilities and risks of being unemployed for a considerable period against a positive wage differential.

Todaro argued that rural-urban migration itself must act as the ultimate equili-brating force with the assumption of the downward inflexibility of urban wages. In this case, the modern industrial sector is assumed to be noncompetitive, so wages are institutionally determined at well above the opportunity cost of labour. But entry to it is restricted. Despite a very low chance of finding employment in this sector, its relative attractiveness prompts rural-urban migration. The rate of migration to the urban sector depends on the relation between two values: the present value of the expected stream of future net income from urban employ-ment, and the present value of the expected stream of future net income from rural employment. If the present value of the expected stream of future net income from urban employment is higher than the present value of the expected stream of future net income from rural employment, it is beneficial to migrate. The for-mer depends on the probability of successful entry into preferred employment in successive time periods. The length of the queue of migrants waiting for formal sector employment and the present value are inversely related. The length of the queue is the equilibrator of the present values of the two streams of urban and rural future earnings. While waiting, migrants are willing to accept wages below their opportunity cost in the expectation of future compensation after entry into the high wage sector.

The most striking result of such a model is its rigorous demonstration that migration in excess of growth of urban job opportunities is not only privately rational from an income-maximising point of view, but will continue as long as rural-urban income differentials exist.

A decade later Todaro (1980: 362) had not changed his view:

> On the contrary, migration today is being increasingly viewed as the major contributing factor to the ubiquitous phenomenon of urban surplus labour and as a force that continues to exacerbate already serious urban unemployment problems caused by growing economic and structural imbalances between urban and rural areas.

The conclusions to emerge from this model are that migrants earn lower incomes than nonmigrants, and migrants have a higher incidence of unemploy-ment. It implies that wages are lower in informal sector[3] employment than in industrial employment. It also implies that migrants earn less in the cities when they first arrive than they earned in the rural areas they left. Introducing a dynamic and productive informal sector in place of a stagnant and unproductive informed sector that was assumed by the Harris–Todaro model, Bhattacharya (1993: 244) concluded that in this situation, rural to urban migration does not result in urban unemployment.

However, there are several serious criticisms of the Todaro model. Each of the five critical assumptions that led to its dramatic results seems vague, or at least deserves far more research (Williamson, 1988a: 445–448).

First, job allocation rules are unlikely to follow the simple lottery mechanism of the Todaro model (Willis, 1980: 396). There is no role for investment in job search in the Todaro model except the decision to migrate. The evidence from the Third World suggests that unskilled migrants do not make long job searches and that overt urban unemployment is a characteristic of the skilled rather than the unskilled (Yap, 1976, 1977; Papola, 1981). It has led to the development of two-stream migration models that acknowledge the importance of labour heterogeneity (Fields, 1975; Fallon, 1983; Cole and Sanders, 1985). Bhattacharya (2015: 3) refers to empirical evidence to suggest that

> an overwhelmingly large number of migrants from the rural to the urban area migrate to the informal sector and without any thoughts of obtaining jobs in the formal sector; further that there is very little job search activity by the migrant workers in the informal sector.

The results from a study on self-employment and queuing for wage work in Chile indicate that the Chilean labour market is heterogonous with wage work, voluntary self-employment and involuntary self-employment (Contreras, Gillmore, and Puentes, 2015). It implies that the Todaro model of dual markets might be too extreme in the light of this Latin American study. Second, wages do clear the labour market and they are responsive to demand and supply. Third, there has been little proof in support of the modern-sector rigid wage assumption (Montgomery, 1985). In fact, Breman (2010) finds wages in the formal sector to be rather flexible in the case of China. Fourth, the issue of discount rates and rational migrants needs explanation. Under assumptions of the Todaro model, Cole and Sanders (1985: 485) ask the question 'how long a time horizon would a potential migrant have to have before present values were equated?' and they conclude that "[i]f one must assume very long time horizons, in some cases more than 50 years, an alternative explanation of migration may be in order".[4] Fifth, and perhaps most important, the model abstracts from many additional influences on the potential migrant's decision. This is the thrust of much of Stark's work on risk aversion, relative deprivation and cooperative family games (Stark, 1991). In fact, an alternative framework based on relative deprivation seems to be taking shape (Stark, 2006; Stark, Micevska and Mycielski, 2009).

However, almost all governments in developing countries have often been unhappy with their migration trends. According to a study of 106 governments carried out during the late 1970s, three-quarters of them wanted to slow or reverse migration to cities as part of their strategy of decentralisation (UN ECOSOC, 1978: 27–28). Similar attitudes were reported by the 1981 survey of 126 governments (United Nations, 1984: 19). In recent years, a similar proportion of governments have been found to feel the need to devise policies to slow rural to urban migration. According to a United Nations report, among 185 countries for which data were available in 2013, 80 per cent of governments had policies to lower rural to urban migration, an increase from 38 per cent in 1996. [UN, 2013: 109].

Harris (1992: x–xvii) described the many threads of the case of 'urban bias' and 'over-urbanisation' that focus the responsibility for migration on the conditions in the areas of origin and thus are conveniently used to deny any responsibility of the urban destination for 'excess migration'. More recent studies not only question the validity of such beliefs, but have also shown that policies underpinned by these attitudes have the potential to do more harm than good. China is thought to have suffered losses in gross national product due to deficient agglomeration in urban areas due to its restrictions on city-ward migration (Au and Henderson, 2006). In addition, the migration restrictions in China have been found to be contributing to income inequality (Whalley and Zang, 2004; Breman, 2010). Lall, Selod and Shalizi (2006) and Fox (2011) describe how the message of the 'Todaro paradox' – that rural to urban migration exacerbates urban unemployment – encouraged many governments to implement policies aimed at restricting migration even though empirical validity of the Harris–Todaro model was far from established.

A departure from the conventional wisdom

There have been studies that provide a trail away from the conventional wisdom, which has largely viewed migration in a negative and pessimistic manner. This sub-section briefly reports these studies.

Buchanan (1966) and Banerjee (1986) were the earliest of the studies that challenged the dominant view in the context of India.

Buchanan (1966: 295) noted the recruitment efforts of Bombay mill owners and consequent development of the channels that were responsible for the predominance of migrants from Ratnagiri in Bombay. Crook (1993: 25–61) demonstrated the role of industry in selecting and encouraging migrants of a specific age, gender and background. He gave several illustrations to show how diversity in the composition of migrants corresponds with diversity in industrial structure.

Banerjee (1986) tried to see if those who migrated owned more or less land than the average or had different jobs. The amount of land migrants owned before migrating was compared with the land owned by people in the State of origin. This exercise was done for Punjab, Rajasthan and Uttar Pradesh. The study observed that the propensity to migrate to Delhi of those owning less than half an acre was lower than the migration propensity of households owning 10 acres or more. The study found that 26 per cent of the landless migrants in the sample were agricultural and farm labourers before they migrated. The occupations of the landless consisted of professional clerical workers, traders, artisans and service workers. The study found no evidence in support of the claim that it is the poorest who have the highest propensity to migrate. The study concluded that in the case of the landowners and the farm operators, the propensity to migrate first rises and then falls as farm size increases. However, the comparison of the land ownership of the migrants with the land ownership in the State of their origin as a whole implies certain unrealistic assumptions, such as the homogeneous quality of land and that the migrants are drawn equally from all parts of the State.

Relative deprivation as a condition of migration has been anchored to Marx's work on class differentiation in a capitalist society (Stark, 2006). It is a testimony to the insightful nature of classical and Marxist ideas that these continue to aid analysis even at a micro level (i.e., at the level of the individual migrant). The elements brought out through more elaborate migration research during the past quarter of a century challenge the premises, logic and conclusions of the pessimistic trends started by Hoselitz and Todaro (Stark, 1991; Lucas, 1997; Lall, Selod and Shalizi, 2006). In fact, one can discern a major change in the perspective of the migration models, particularly since the 1990s, as these have moved away from the redundant routine of explaining urban unemployment as in the Harris–Todaro scheme of things. There has been a greater emphasis on migrant selectivity, job search and the role of migration in rural development.

The issue of who migrates has been dealt with in terms of asymmetry of information, shortcomings of insurance and credit markets and relative deprivation. Katz and Stark (1984, 1986) bring up the issue of asymmetry of information and argue that as employers in the area of origin may be better informed about workers' productivity than the employers of the host region, it could be beneficial for the workers to 'signal' themselves to the employers of the host region by incurring some moderate fixed cost that they can afford. In this framework, those with high or low skill levels are more likely to migrate with to those with middle skill levels (Katz and Stark, 1987).

Another explanation put forward for the Todarian enigma – migration despite a small probability of high-wage formal sector employment – is that this process is driven by the desire for higher social status among rural residents and migrants (Stark, 1984, Katz and Stark, 1986). Similarly, repeat and return migration need not be seen in a negative light because these could be better understood as getting back to the area of origin after an optimal duration of time spent in the destination area (Dustman, 1997). The job search approach puts forth the positive externality on potential migrants through flow of information, advice and help by the earlier migrants (Carrington, Detragiache and Vishwanath, 1996).

There is a distinct trend in the literature to view migration as a social process rather than merely a matter of economic decision (de Haan, 1999; de Haan and Rogaly, 2002; Kothari, 2003). In fact, citing the examples of dockworkers of ports and Mumbai textile mills, Ellis and Harris (2004) describe migration patterns as related more closely to historical and cultural criteria than to short-term economic calculations. They also find the nature of implicit contracts between migrants and their resident families to be rooted in culture and society and consequently as varying substantially in different places according to these norms (Ellis and Harris, 2004: 9). In fact, a longitudinal social science approach to the question of rural to urban migration can also be discerned. Breman (1996, 2010), through sustained micro-research within a macro-framework with a social science approach, has not only refuted some of the basic assumptions of the prevalent dualistic models of labour migration, but also corroborated the key elements of the classical approach to the movement of labour from the countryside to the cities.

Marx (in International Publishers edition, 1976) describes how the working class compare their 'social position' to that of the capitalists and feel deprived even while their pleasures increase in a phase of rising productive capital and demand for labour and wages. He concludes that

> [o]ur wants and pleasures have their origin in society; we therefore measure them in relation to society; we do not measure them in relation to the objects which serve for their gratification. Since they are of a social nature, they are of a relative nature.
>
> Marx (in International Publishers edition, 1976: 22)

Duesenberry (1949) argued that individuals compare themselves with better-off groups. Whereas Borjas (1987) studied how migrants' attraction to different destinations is affected by income inequality there, Stark (1991) tried to study the effect of migrant remittances on inequality at the origin.

Stark (1991: 102–139, 371–395) synthesised these arguments and brought out how differential inducements to have family members sent out have their roots in relative deprivation expressed through interfamily comparison at the origin and how it is more productive to study the structure of incentives than migrant characteristics to understand migration *as well as* return migration. Stark (2006) and Stark, Micevska and Mycielski (2009) firmly base the breakthrough of the 'relative deprivation' thesis of migration on the theoretical work and evidence that support the view that individuals look up and not down while comparing themselves.

The 1995 International Social Survey Programme (ISSP) asked the question, inter alia, to nearly 28,000 individuals in 23 countries: "Would you be willing to move to another country to improve your work or living conditions?" Liebig and Sousa-Poza (2004) connected responses to this question to country data on inequality and concluded that "controlling for GNP per capita . . . the Gini coefficient always has a positive and highly significant impact [on the propensity to migrate]. A higher income inequality thus leads ceteris paribus to higher incentives to migrate" (Liebig and Sousa-Poza, 2004: 137). Stark (2006) proceeded to explain it analytically. Defining relative deprivation as "the proportion of those in the individual's group whose income[s] are higher than the individual's times their mean excess income" and summing up individual relative deprivations, he found it possible to arrive at total relative deprivation (TRD), which was found to be positively associated with the Gini coefficient. The 'conditional selectivity' idea of Borjas (1987) was that if the inequality in income distribution in the sending area was greater than that in the destination area, migrants will be chosen from the lower end of the income distribution. On the other hand, Stark (2006) argues that negative selectivity comes of income inequality at the origin by itself. The relative deprivation approach holds that negative selectivity will become more marked if income inequality at the origin increases and if no change in income distribution at the destination remains. Or that the worsening income distribution at the destination, with the origin income distribution remaining the same, will not diminish the inducement to migrate due to relative deprivation of the low-income members of the origin population. Stark, Micevska and Mycielski (2009) empirically show what Stark had postulated in his earlier analytical work (Stark, 2006), that is, the Gini coefficient and migration are positively related, holding constant the per capita income of the population.

Stark (2006) and Stark, Micevska and Mycielski (2009) thus further consolidate the integrated social science approach to migration that is, in principle, applicable to internal as well as international migration.

Problem

Whereas the classical and Marxist economists viewed urbanisation and migration within the logic and dynamics of the capitalistic development, the subsequent theories and experiences of Third World urbanisation have sparked an energetic debate. This section identifies the key questions that arise from previous sections and which shall be addressed in our own study.

The gist of our review of the dominant models of migration for developing countries of the second half of twentieth century (e.g., Hoselitz, Todaro) is that these models have exhibited a pessimist orientation by emphasising that the miserable conditions in the areas of origin in the countryside account for rural to urban migration in these countries (that is, a 'push' migration) and that urbanisation is out of proportion with the demand for labour (that is, 'over-urbanisation'). These dominant models of migration reflect the policy assumption that poverty in rural areas of developing countries drives people out. This assumption has resulted in a deflection of attention from the questions of key importance: Why is it that not all, or even most, of the poor living in the rural areas migrate to the cities and only a very small minority do? Of the overwhelming majority of the rural people who might be poor, how are the ones who migrate selected? And of all those who migrate, how are the ones who return selected?

In view of the importance of the debate on rural-urban migration for the critically important questions of economic development and urbanisation, it is surprising that few longitudinal micro-studies exist that address the question of 'recruitment versus expulsion' with a tight focus. The present study addresses this research problem.

Empirical backdrop of the case study

India is a prime example of developing countries that has been used to develop and advance ideas like over-urbanisation and push migration. The present section makes a brief reference to the most prevalent interpretations of the trends of inter-State rural to urban migration in India because these existed when the present study was conceptualised. The objective is to have a sense of a macro-empirical context to this primary micro-study of migration to Delhi. The section refers to a general picture of inter-State rural to urban migration in India in terms of conventional wisdom that forms the backdrop to this generalising case study of recruitment versus expulsion in rural to urban migration of labour. Because the study was planned, designed and started in the early 1990s, even though the details may not be of contemporary interest, it has historical value in helping to understand the argument of recruitment versus expulsion as a context to our study. Therefore, details of the empirical line-up of the expulsion argument in the Indian case have been provided in Appendix A and its supporting statistical tables in Appendix F.[5]

The States with a low proportion of migrants in the rural population and with greater out-migration from their rural as well as urban areas[6] are understood to have certain common features. These features include low availability of land per agricultural worker, higher share of net State domestic product originating in the primary sector, low productivity of agriculture and high rate of unemployment.[7] Apparently it is because of the combination of these factors that many feel that the rural push factor has been the common explanation for the areas of origin of the migrants.

The most common anxiety in many of the analyses of the level and pattern of rural to urban migration in India has generally been regarding employment growth. It has been noted that only a marginal decline has occurred in the dominance of the primary sector in the occupational structure of the workforce, despite a significant decline in its share in the net domestic product of India. The higher growth rates of income and employment in the tertiary sector compared with those in the secondary sector have been observed since the 1970s. It was interpreted as the failure of the secondary sector to generate additional employment (Rao, 1987; Papola, 2006). The informal sector is perceived as absorbing poor rural migrants in low-paying, low-productivity jobs. Mitra, Mukherji and Bose et al. (1980) thought that despite the concentration of investment in a few metropolitan nodes, proliferation of jobs in them is mostly of tertiary-sector, low-grade trade and services. Scarcity of land was thought to be 'pushing' the migrants out of the rural areas (Hoselitz, 1962: 169). Rural poverty was thought to be 'spilling over' into urban areas:

> The character of urban poverty is the consequence of the continuous migration of the rural poor into the urban areas in search of a livelihood, their failure to find adequate means to support themselves there and the resulting growth of pavement and slum life in the cities.
>
> Dandekar and Rath (1971: 35)

Migration was seen as a process that simply transformed rural poverty into urban poverty. It was thought that due to the limited job opportunities in the modern industrial sector, workers were being forced into the tertiary sector on unfavourable terms. These views have been very commonplace in much of the literature on migration in India. Mitra (1990) and Mallick (2012) can be cited as examples of this trend.

Within the highly out-migrating States of India, the geographically contiguous regions of North and Central Bihar and Eastern Uttar Pradesh were considered the 'area of high out-migration' (Mohan, 1982: 42). The migration from the countryside of this area has been projected as exemplifying 'push migration'. Hence, migration from this area of high out-migration is an integral part of analysis in this study, both the supervised analysis and the unsupervised analysis.

Hypotheses

Migrants are recruited to the urban labour market and not expelled from the countryside – this is the central hypothesis of the present study. This can be broken into three specific hypotheses:

First, relative deprivation is a necessary condition (a facilitating factor), but it is not a sufficient condition for people to migrate from rural areas.

Second, the demand for labour in the urban areas is the sufficient condition (determining factor) for migration and a lack of it for return migration.

Third, the channels of recruitment select people with appropriate education and skills to match the demand for labour in urban areas.

Choice of Delhi for the case study

In the theoretical background of the research problem of recruitment versus expulsion, in its empirical context and in the light of the hypotheses, the present section discusses why Delhi was the appropriate choice for a case study.

The migration data provided by the population census in India is inter-State. Delhi is the only case where a State is equal to a city. The key justification for the choice of Delhi for a case study, in contrast to other territories, is that virtually all migration into it is inter-State.

There were a few other advantages as well. To put the issue in the context of India, two-thirds of inter-State rural to urban male migrants for employment in Delhi were found to be from the highly out-migrating States of Bihar and Uttar Pradesh. A greater-than-average proportion of migrants from these two States said they came for employment (GOI, Census of India, 1981. *Migration Tables, Delhi*, Table D-3). The primary survey for this study also corroborates this. A significant proportion of the sample migrants came from Northern and Central Bihar and Eastern Uttar Pradesh, which Mohan (1982) characterised as an area of high out-migration of the 'push' variety – the details are discussed in Chapter 3. These reasons made Delhi an ideal case to test the hypothesis of recruitment versus expulsion in the Indian context.

Generalising nature of the present case study

The context developed through the foregoing discussion in this chapter throws up India and Delhi in the line of representative sampling. The next chapter goes on to further develop the sampling design. In all, the effort has been to have a multistage stratified sampling to choose migrants on the basis of which one can generalise on the question of recruitment versus expulsion in rural to urban migration of labour in India. Thus, it is not merely a study of Delhi as such. Similarly, although the first sample survey was carried out in 1992 and the follow-up survey in 2009, it is not a 'period study'. A lot of effort has gone into the research design, as well as the sampling design, to maximise the representativeness of the survey sample so that the insights from this study can be generalised not just to rural to urban migrants in India, but also to other developing countries. Hence, this longitudinal study is in the nature of a *generalising case study* because the focus is on testing the recruitment versus expulsion hypothesis in a developing country perspective.

Structure of the book

The book is based on a micro-study of rural migrants in Delhi with its focus on the examination of pre-migration socioeconomic strata of migrants, the way they joined the urban labour market, changes in their course and how some of them returned. It is divided into eight chapters.

Chapter 1 presents the research problem and hypotheses along with their theoretical background and also refers to the trends of inter-State migration in India as a context for the key concern of the book – migration to Delhi. It briefly brings in the assertion of 'spill-over' and 'push' made by the poverty theory of migration. Chapter 2 examines the methodological questions encountered in the planning and execution of the sample surveys. Chapter 3 analyses the pre-migration social and economic profile of the migrants. Chapter 4 examines the role of the channels of recruitment and identifies the mechanism of migration that connects the demand for labour in urban areas with the mass of potential migrants in the rural areas. Chapter 5 ascertains change in location as well as demographic and occupational profiles of the respondents two decades since the first sample survey was undertaken in 1992.

Using insights from these chapters, a data-reduction exercise involving the selection of variables and recoding of values was carried out. The resulting dataset, the details of which have been provided in Appendix G, has been used for clustering analysis in Chapter 6 and decision-tree analysis in Chapter 7. Chapter 6 discovers groups from amongst the migrant respondents with the help of k-means clustering and discusses the implications of the results. Chapter 7 analyses the determinants of return migration. Chapter 8 concludes with a summary of the main findings of this study and juxtaposes these findings amongst current academic and policy debates.

In order to keep the chapters precise and flowing, the explanatory and statistical details have been placed in the appendices to this book. These appendices are useful for the readers who may wish to go into detail regarding statistical background, methodological techniques and survey methods.

Appendix A delves deeper into historical debates regarding the expulsion argument set in India. Appendix B supplements Chapter 2 by providing the methodological details of the sample surveys and demographic profile of the criteria migrants. Migrants who fulfilled certain criteria for being selected for detailed interviewing are called *criteria migrants* throughout this book. For details of the criteria, please see Chapter 2. Appendix C, through its exclusive focus on the migrants who owned or leased-in land, complements the assessment of pre-migration economic status in the agricultural context that has been provided in Chapter 3. Appendix D disaggregates occupational mobility discussed in Chapter 5. Appendix E provides the more technical, methodological details relating to data-mining techniques applied in Chapter 6 and Chapter 7 of this book. Appendix F contains all the statistical tables that would have affected the ease of reading in various chapters and appendices of this book, and the prefix 'A' has been attached to each of these tables.[8] Appendix G supplements the results of the analysis reported in Chapters 6 and 7 in the sense that this appendix contains a list of variables in the reduced dataset, value labels of each variable and, more importantly, the categories that were merged in order to reduce the number of values for most of the variables in this dataset. Appendix H provides all questionnaires and other survey materials used for conducting the surveys and resurveys of migrants for this longitudinal study.

The non-English words in this book have been italicised and a glossary of non-English words has been provided to give an English translation of such words. A list of abbreviations has also been provided.

Notes

1 Several authors have concluded that some of the core concepts of development economics so vital for the analysis of the phenomenon of population transfer are extensions of the thoughts already expressed by the 'pioneers' of economic science. Martin (1991: 30) offers the example of how the concepts or the phenomena of rural underemployment, often referred to as 'disguised unemployment', is a rediscovery of the Marxian concept of latent surplus population in agriculture. Martin gives an example of Lewis (1954) using this concept without explicit acknowledgement. Also see, Williamson (1988a: 426). Gollin (2014: 71) also brings out Lewis's use of classical ideas on the issues of employment and labour transfer.
2 Lewis (1954) and later formalised by Fei and Ranis (1961). Revenstein (1885), although a pioneering effort, added little to what had already been established in economic theory.
3 As such, there is no consensus on what 'informal sector' should really mean. According to Gregory (1986: 12), "typically, the informal sector is viewed as having very limited capital resources and as suffering from low productivity and earnings". The inventor of the term 'informal sector' mainly meant petty trade and crafts encountered in the streets of Third World cities (Hart, 1973). Breman (2010: 175) observes that the term did not originate from among conventional researchers into labour, who were mainly interested in the formal sector employment.
4 Given modern-sector wages double that of rural wages, given some unemployment duration before the migrant secures the modern-sector job, and given some discount rate, how long a time horizon would a potential migrant have to have before present values were equated? Cole and Sanders have made the calculation where discount rates are allowed to vary between 5 and 15 per cent (Cole and Sanders, 1985: 485).
5 All table numbers with the prefix 'A', (e.g., Table A-1.1), are in Appendix F which contains statistical tables.

6 Table A-1.1 reveals considerable variation in the proportion of inter-State migrants in the male population among the States of India. Tables A-1.3 and A-1.4 show the broad magnitudes of inter-State out-migration for each major State of India.

7 Bihar, Uttar Pradesh and Rajasthan are most typical of such States. For a discussion providing background to this statement, see Appendix A and the supporting tables in Appendix F. A more detailed statistical analysis of these trends is available in Ratnoo (1987).

8 Although the prefix 'A' before each of the tables in this appendix indicates the location of the table being here, the numeral following the hyphen indicates the chapter number to which this particular table supplements, and the numeral after the decimal point indicates the table number in this appendix relating to that particular chapter. Thus, for illustration, the prefix 'A' in Table A-2.1 means it is related to Chapter 2 but has been located in Appendix F which contains statistical tables, rather than in Chapter 2 on methods in the sample survey or in Appendix B that contains methodological details of the sample surveys and demographic profiles of the criteria migrants.

References

Au, C.C. and Henderson, J.V. (2006). How migration restrictions limit agglomeration and productivity in China, *Journal of Development Economics*, 80(2): 350–388.

Bairoch, P. (1975). *The economic development of the third world since 1900*. Berkeley, CA: University of California Press.

Banerjee, B. (1986). *Rural to urban migration and the urban labour market: A case study of Delhi*. Delhi: Himalaya Publishing House.

Berry, A. and Sabot, R.H. (1984). Unemployment and economic development, *Economic Development and Cultural Change*, 33: 99–116.

Bhattacharya, P.C. (1993). Rural-urban migration in economic development, *Journal of Economic Surveys*, 7(3): 243–281.

Bhattacharya, P.C. (2015). *A model of optimal development*. Working Paper No. 2015–04. Edinburgh: Department of Economics, Heriot-Watt University.

Borjas, G. (1987). Self-selection and the earnings of immigrants, *American Economic Review*, 77: 531–553.

Breman, J. (1996). *Footloose labour: Working in India's informal economy*. Cambridge: Cambridge University Press.

Breman, J. (2010). *Outcast labour in Asia: Circulation and informalization of the work force at the bottom of the economy*. New Delhi: Oxford University Press.

Buchanan, D.H. (1966). *The development of capitalist enterprise in India*. London: Frank Cass & Co. Ltd.

Carrington, J., Detragiache, E. and Vishwanath, T. (1996). Migration with endogenous moving costs, *American Economic Review*, 86(4): 909–930.

Cole, W.E. and Sanders, R.D. (1985). Internal migration and urban employment in the third world, *American Economic Review*, 75: 481–494.

Contreras, D., Gillmore, R. and Puentes, E. (2015). Self-employment and queues for wage work: Evidence from Chile, *Journal of International Development*, DOI: 10.1002/jid.3074.

Crook, N. (1993). *India's industrial cities: Essays in economy and demography*. Delhi: Oxford University Press.

Dandekar, V.M. and Rath, N. (1971). *Poverty in India*. Bombay: Indian School of Political Economy.

de Haan, A. (1999). Livelihoods and poverty: The role of migration – A critical review of the migration literature, *Journal of Development Studies*, 36(2): 1–47.

de Haan, A. and Rogaly, B. (2002). Migrant workers and their role in rural change, *Journal of Development Studies*, 38(5): 1–14.

Duesenberry, J.S. (1949). *Income, savings and the theory of consumer behavior*. Cambridge, MA: Harvard University Press.

Dustman, C. (1997). Return migration, uncertainty, and precautionary savings, *Journal of Development Economics*, 52(2): 295–316.

Dyson, T. (2011). The Role of the demographic transition in the process of urbanization, *Population and Development Review*, 37(Supplement): 34–54.

Ellis, F. and Harris, N. (2004). *Development patterns, mobility and livelihood diversification*. Keynote paper for DFID Sustainable Development Retreat, University of Surrey, Guildford. Retrieved from http://www.researchgate.net/publication/255039830

Fallon, P.R. (1983). Education and the duration of job search and unemployment in urban India, *Journal of Development Economics*, 12: 327–340.

Fay, M. and Opal, C. (1999). *Urbanization without growth: A not-so-uncommon phenomenon*. World Bank Policy Research Working Paper No. 21412. Washington, DC: World Bank.

Fei, J.C.M. and Ranis, G. (1961). A theory of economic development, *American Economic Review*, September: 533–565.

Fields, G. (1975). Rural-urban migration, urban unemployment and underemployment and job-search activity in LDCs, *Journal of Development Economics*, 2: 165–187.

Fox, S. (2011). *Understanding the origins and pace of Africa's urban transition*. Crisis States Working Paper No. 89 (Series 2). London: Crisis States Research Centre, London School of Economics and Political Science.

Fox, S.R. (2013). *The political economy of urbanization and development in sub-Saharan Africa*. PhD thesis, London School of Economics and Political Science, London.

GOI, Census of India (1981). *Series-31, Delhi; Migration tables, Part V – A & B*. New Delhi: Registrar General and Census Commissioner, Government of India.

Gollin, D. (2014). The Lewis model: A 60-year retrospective, *Journal of Economic Perspectives*, 28(3): 71–88.

Gregory, P. (1986). *Myth of market failure: Employment and labour market in Mexico*. Baltimore: The Johns Hopkins University Press.

Harris, J.R. and Todaro, M.P. (1970). Migration, unemployment and development: A two sector analysis, *American Economic Review*, 60: 126–142.

Harris, N. (1992). *Cities in the 1990s: The challenge for developing countries*. London: UCL Press Limited.

Hart, K. (1973). Informal income opportunities and urban unemployment in Ghana, *Journal of Modern African Studies*, 11(1): 61–89.

Hoselitz, B.F. (1953). The role of cities in the economic growth of underdeveloped countries, *Journal of Political Economy*, 61: 195–208.

Hoselitz, B.F. (1955). Generative and parasitic cities, *Economic Development and Cultural Change*, 3: 278–294.

Hoselitz, B.F. (1957). Urbanization and economic growth in Asia, *Economic Development and Cultural Change*, 5: 42–54.

Hoselitz, B.F. (1962). The role of urbanisation in economic development: Some international comparisons. In Turner, R. (Ed.), *India's urban future* (pp. 157–181). Berkeley and Los Angeles: University of California Press.

Hume, D. (1955). On refinement of arts. In Rotwein, E. (Ed.), *David Hume: Writings on economics* (pp. 19–32). Edinburgh and London: Nelson.

Kannappan, S. (1985). Urban employment and the labour market in developing nations, *Economic Development and Cultural Change*, 33: 669–730.

Katz, E. and Stark, O. (1984). Migration and asymmetric information: Comment, *American Economic Review*, 74(3): 533–534.

Katz, E. and Stark, O. (1986). Labor mobility under asymmetric information with moving and signaling costs, *Economics Letters*, 21(1): 89–94.

Katz, E. and Stark, O. (1987). International migration under asymmetric information, *The Economic Journal*, 97(387): 718–726.

Kothari, U. (2003). Staying put and staying poor? *Journal of International Development*, 15(5): 645–657.

Lall, S.V., Selod, H. and Shalizi, Z. (2006). *Rural-urban migration in developing countries: A survey of theoretical predictions and empirical findings*. World Bank Policy Research Working Paper 3915. Washington, DC: The World Bank.

Lee, E.S. (1966). A theory of migration, *Demography*, 3(1): 47–57.

Lenin, V.I. (1956). *Development of capitalism in Russia: The process of formation of home market for large scale industry*. Moscow: Foreign Languages Publishing House.

Lewis, W.A. (1954). Economic development with unlimited supplies of labour, *The Manchester School of Economic and Social Studies*, 20: 139–192.

Lewis, W.A. (1988). Reflections on development. In Ranis, G. and Shultz, T.P. (Eds.), *The state of development economics: Progress and perspectives* (pp. 13–23). Oxford: Basil Blackwell.

Liebig, T. and Sousa-Poza, A. (2004). Migration, self-selection and income inequality: An international analysis, *Kyklos*, 57: 125–146.

Lucas, R. (1997). Internal migration in developing countries. In Rosenzweig, M.R. and Stark, O. (Eds.), *Handbook of population and family economics* (Volume 1B, Chapter 13, pp. 721–798). North Holland: Elsevier.

Mallick, S.K. (2012). *Disentangling the poverty effects of sectoral output, prices and policies in India*. New Delhi: Subregional Office for South and South-West Asia (SRO-SSWA), Economic and Social Commission for Asia and the Pacific (ESCAP).

Martin, K. (1991). *Strategies of economic development: Readings in the political economy of industrialization*. London: Macmillan Academic and Professional Limited.

Marx, K. (1954). The general law of capitalist accumulation. In Engels, F. (Ed.), *Capital: A critique of political economy*, Volume I, Book one, the process of production of capital (reproduction by Progress Publishers, Moscow of the text of the English edition of 1887, edited by Frederick Engels) (S. Moore and E. Aveling, Trans.) (pp. 574–666). Moscow: Progress.

Marx, K. (1965). *Pre-capitalist economic formations* (Translated by J. Cohen and introduced by E.J. Hobsbawm). London: Lawrence and Wishert.

Marx, K. (1976). *Wage-labour and capital & value, price and profit* [First paperback (combined) edition]. New York: International Publishers. Retrieved from https://www.marxists.org/archive/marx/works/1847/wage-labour/index.htm

Mazumdar, D. (1976). The urban informal sector, *World Development*, 4(8): 655–679.

Mitra, A. (1990). Duality, employment structure and poverty incidence: The slum perspective, *Indian Economic Review*, XXV(1): 57–73.

Mitra, A., Mukherji, S. and Bose, R. et al. (1980). *Indian cities: Their industrial structure, immigration and capital investment 1961–71*. New Delhi: Abhinav.

Mohan, R. (1982). *The morphology of urbanisation in India: Some results from the 1981 Census*. Paper presented in the seminar on Urbanisation and Planned Economic Development – Present and future perspectives, organised by the Centre for the Study of Regional Development, Jawaharlal Nehru University, New Delhi.

Montgomery, M. (1985). *The impacts of urban population growth on urban labour markets and the costs of urban service delivery: A review*. Princeton: Office of Population Research, Princeton University.

Oucho, J.O. and Gould, W.T.S. (1993). Internal migration, urbanization, and population distribution. In Foote, K.A., Hill, K.H. and Martin, L.G. (Eds.), *Demographic change in sub-Saharan Africa* (pp. 256–296). Washington, DC: National Academy Press.

Papola, T.S. (1981). *Urban informal sector in a developing economy.* New Delhi: Vikas Publishing House.

Papola, T.S. (2006). *Employment and poverty.* New Delhi: UNDP.

Preston, S.H. (1979). Urban growth in developing countries: A demographic reappraisal, *Population and Development Review*, 5(2): 195–215.

Rao, V.K.R.V. (1987). Growth and structural change in the Indian economy. In Brahmananda, P.R. (Ed.), *Development process of the Indian economy* (pp. 1–41). New Delhi: Himalaya Publishing House.

Ratnoo, H.S. (1987). *Migration, urbanisation and economic development: Rajasthan in the all India context (1961–81).* Unpublished MPhil dissertation, Jawaharlal Nehru University, New Delhi.

Revenstein, E.G. (1885). The laws of migration, *Journal of the Royal Statistical Society*, 48: 167–227.

Ricardo, D. (1951). On machinery. In Sraffa, P. and Dobb, M.H. (Eds.), *The works and correspondence of David Ricardo, Volume I: On the principles of political economy and taxation* (pp. 386–397). Cambridge: Cambridge University Press.

Smith, A. (1970). *The wealth of nations, books I–III.* Skinner, A. (Ed.). Harmondsworth, Middlesex: Penguin Books Ltd.

Stark, O. (1984). Rural to urban migration in LDCs: A relative deprivation approach, *Economic Development and Cultural Change*, 32: 475–486.

Stark, O. (1991). *The migration of labour.* Oxford: Basil Blackwell.

Stark, O. (2006). Inequality and migration: A behavioral link, *Economics Letters*, 91: 146–152.

Stark, O., Micevska, M. and Mycielski, J. (2009). Relative poverty as a determinant of migration: Evidence from Poland, *Economics Letters*, 103: 119–122.

Todaro, M.P. (1969). A model of labour migration and urban unemployment in less developed countries, *American Economic Review*, 59: 138–148.

Todaro, M.P. (1976). *Internal migration in developing countries.* Geneva: International Labour Office.

Todaro, M.P. (1980). Internal migration in developing countries: A survey. In Easterlin, R.A. (Ed.), *Population and economic change in developing countries* (pp. 361–402). Chicago: University of Chicago Press.

UN Economic and Social Council (1978). *Concise report on monitoring of population policies* (E/CN. 9/338), Population Commission, Twentieth Session. New York: UN Economic and Social Council.

United Nations (1984). *Fifth population enquiry among governments: Monitoring government perceptions and policies on demographic trends and levels in relation to development as of 1982.* New York: Population Division.

United Nations (2013). *World population policies 2013.* New York: United Nations. Retrieved from http://www.un.org/en/development/desa/population/publications/pdf/policy/WPP2013/wpp2013.pdf#zoom=100

Whalley, J. and Zhang, S. (2004). *Inequality change in china and (Hukou) labor mobility restrictions.* National Bureau of Economic Research Working Paper No. 10683. Cambridge, MA: National Bureau of Economic Research.

Williamson, J.G. (1988a). Migration and urbanisation. In Chenery, H. and Srinivasan, T.N. (Eds.), *Handbook of development economics* (Volume I, pp. 425–465). North Holland: Oxford.

Williamson, J.G. (1988b). Comments on 'Reflections on Development'. In Ranis, G. and Shultz, T.P. (Eds.), *The state of development economics: Progress and perspectives* (pp. 24–30). Oxford: Basil Blackwell.

Willis, R.J. (1980). Comment. In Easterlin, R.A. (Ed.), *Population and economic change in developing countries* (pp. 394–397). Chicago: University of Chicago Press.

Yap, L. (1976). Rural-urban migration and urban underemployment in Brazil, *Journal of Development Economics*, 3: 227–243.

Yap, L. (1977). The attraction of cities: A review of migration literature, *Journal of Development Economics*, 4(3): 239–264.

2 Method in the sample survey

Introduction

This chapter explains how the data were collected for the case study of Delhi. It describes the assumptions and choices made and describes the different stages of the sample survey of rural migrants in Delhi.

Why only the squatter settlements?

To test the null hypothesis that migrants are recruited (not expelled) from rural areas, the migrant was to be the ultimate sampling unit. Due to time and resource constraints, the sample size had to be small. A random sample from the entire population of Delhi would have given the results pertaining to a very heterogeneous population, on the basis of which we might not have been able to draw conclusions with confidence. Therefore, it was decided to restrict the survey to the areas whose populations were more likely to be on the poorer side of the curve of income distribution. The idea was that if the null hypothesis were true for the less well-off migrants, it would certainly be true for those who were better off.

In this context, two types of settlements were thought to be candidates for the survey: the resettlement colonies built during the 1960s and the 1970s to resettle the squatters (Misra and Gupta, 1981) and the squatter settlements. Misra and Gupta (1981: 42) and Suri (1991: 99) indicated that original residential allottees of the resettlement colonies had been selling off allotted plots and houses to the better-off buyers and, as a consequence, the residents of the resettlement colonies were expected to be better off compared with the residents of squatter settlements.

There were indicators to suggest that a relatively poor population inhabited squatter settlements. For example, according to the Delhi Development Authority (DDA, Socio-Economic Wing, 1983: 61), the majority of the workers in the squatter settlements (70 per cent) were labourers. Of this, 71 per cent were unskilled labourers. About 94 per cent of the respondents in this survey gave 'employment factor' (71 per cent) and 'economic factor' (23 per cent) as the reason for migration, indicating a higher percentage of economic migrants in the squatter settlements compared with those in Delhi in general (DDA, Socio-Economic Wing, 1983, p. 67). Likewise, the data on distance between residence and workplace indicate their relative poverty. It was found that 72 per cent of the workers lived within a 3-kilometre radius of their workplace (DDA, Socio-Economic Wing, 1983, p. 69). We took this and also the information from the DDA, Perspective Planning Wing (1986: 9) to mean that the areas with a high incidence of squatting were the areas of high demand for labour and the squatters were relatively poor.

A survey by the Institute for Socialist Education (1989: 6) found that the female-male ratio of 732:1,000 in the squatter population in Delhi was lower than the same for the general population of Delhi. The corresponding figure is 836 females per 1,000 males for Delhi Municipal Corporation (urban) and 809 for New Delhi Municipal Committee (GOI, Census of India 1991, 1991: 31). Because the census data had revealed that migration to Delhi for employment was gender selective, with more males than females migrating to Delhi, the higher proportion of males in the squatter population of Delhi was taken as an additional indicator that the proportion of migrants among squatter population in Delhi would be higher compared with the proportion of migrants among the population of Delhi in general.

Moreover, preparing an updated sampling frame was possible in the case of squatter settlements due to the existence of relatively detailed and updated information on them. A list of the squatter settlements and the estimates of the number of *jhuggies* for each of these prepared by the Slum Wing of the DDA became available just when the sampling scheme for this study was being devised (DDA, Slum Wing, n.d., C.1990). Availability of the latest baseline information from the Institute for Socialist Education (1989) was a great advantage in focusing on the squatter settlements of Delhi.

The process of sample selection

To make the best use of the information and to ensure a representative sample, a four-stage sampling scheme was devised.

Stage I: selecting a part of Delhi

To make the fieldwork more manageable, the sites had to be within a part of Delhi and not spread all over it. It was assumed that a part of Delhi with a high percentage of migrant households and a high percentage of the population living in squatter settlements would be more representative.

The only information on the proportion of migrant households was from a survey conducted in 1968–1969.[1] The proportion of the migrants according to this survey was highest in South Delhi. Any new calculations were not possible due to unavailability of data disaggregated by parts of Delhi.

The percentage of the squatter population for different parts of Delhi (Table A-2.1)[2] was estimated through adjustments of data from various organisations.[3] The South Delhi Zone was selected because the percentage of its population living in squatter settlements was found to be higher compared with other zones and also because, as per an earlier survey referred to by Banerjee (1986: 13), the proportion of migrant households was considered to be the highest in South Delhi compared with other parts of Delhi.[4]

Stage II: selecting squatter settlements in South Delhi

A socioeconomic baseline survey of 457 *jhuggie jhonpari* clusters (squatter settlements) in Delhi covering all parts of Delhi on the west of the Yamuna river was conducted during 1988–1989 (Institute for Socialist Education, 1989).[5] Using information from this survey, an 'index of poverty and recentness of migration' was calculated for the 159 clusters of South Delhi. This index was used to select ten settlements, as detailed in Appendix B.

Stage III: selecting census blocks

The census blocks[6] of the 1991 population census provided the latest sampling frame (GOI, Census of India 1991, 1992). A list was made of the 48 census blocks that cover the ten selected squatter settlements. Five census blocks were selected by probability-proportionate-to-size, with a random start. The details of the selected census blocks and the problem of locating them are described in Appendix B.

Stage IV: selecting the criteria migrants through a listing survey

A listing survey of all the heads of household in the selected census blocks was conducted. Following the UN definition of household (Casley and Lury, 1982: 162), during this survey, persons living in the same *jhuggie* but cooking separately or keeping a separate account of one's own share in the expenses in the common cooking were treated as separate households. The questionnaire is provided in Appendix H. At this stage the migrants meeting the following criteria were selected for detailed interviewing:

(a) The people who were born in or last resided in the rural areas outside the Delhi State boundary.
(b) The age at arrival in Delhi was 12 years or more. (The intention was to exclude non-decision-making migrants.)
(c) Those arriving in 1972 or after. (Due to the prominence of the National Emergency of 1975–1977 in the public memory, it was easy for the respondents to recall the dates near to this point of reference. Moreover, the memory of the migrants of more than 20 years would have been less reliable).
(d) Those arriving after securing employment or in search of employment (so that only the decision-making migrants were chosen and those who came on transfers or as dependents were excluded).

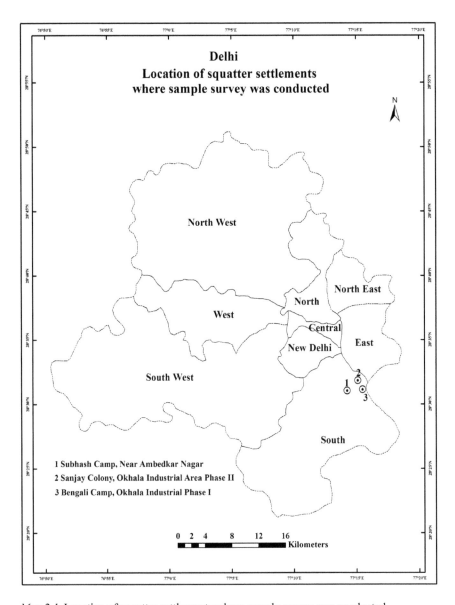

Map 2.1 Location of squatter settlements where sample survey was conducted

The migrants meeting the four criteria are called *criteria migrants* in this book. While planning the survey, a target of 150 criteria migrants was considered desirable and feasible, keeping in view the need for the minimum acceptable sample size and also the time and resource constraints. The percentage of criteria migrants among the heads of the household of the listing survey was 36 per cent, which was higher than the 17.5 per cent found in an earlier survey (Banerjee, 1986: 13). Out of the 506 heads of the household interviewed during the listing survey, of the first four of the selected five census blocks, 184 were the kind of migrants who meet the four conditions. Because the target number of 150 criteria migrants was exceeded, the listing of the fifth census block was not necessary.

Two of the census blocks where the listing survey was conducted were situated in a squatter settlement called Subhas Camp, located in the vicinity of a resettlement colony called Ambedkar Nagar in South Delhi. The third census block was in the locality of squatters called Sanjay Colony, which is located in the Okhla Industrial Area, Phase-II. The fourth census block of our sample survey was in a squatter settlement called Bengali Camp, which was situated in the Okhla Industrial Area, Phase-I. The locations of these three squatter settlements where fieldwork was conducted are marked on Map 2.1 by numbers 1 to 3 as follows:

1   Subhas Camp, near Ambedkar Nagar
2   Sanjay Colony, Okhla Industrial Area Phase-II
3   Bengali Camp, Okhla Industrial Area Phase-I

The survey

Given our hypothesis of recruitment versus expulsion, there were immediately some obvious relationships to test. For example, the pre-migration economic position and employment status were relevant to see if and how the migrants had been deprived in the areas of origin. The knowledge of urban jobs and the availability of channels of recruitment were important factors to explore to see if and how connectivity with the urban labour market determined migration. In this framework, the two questionnaires of the sample survey conducted in 1992 covered a range of variables.[7] These results are discussed in Chapters 3 and 4.

Retracing the criterion migrants after 17 years for a resurvey in 2009

In 2009, after a gap of 17 years since the migrant survey in 1992, efforts were made to ascertain the whereabouts of the 184 criteria migrants.[8] Interviews were conducted with the migrants who could be reached again in Delhi to find out what changes had taken place in their education, skill and jobs and to ask them how they look back and assess, on balance, why they had migrated to Delhi.[9] These results are reported in Chapter 5.

Notes

1   The survey was carried out by the Demographic Research Centre of the Institute of Economic Growth, New Delhi. The focus of the survey was on fertility and family planning (Banerjee, 1986: 12).
2   All table numbers with a prefix 'A' (e.g., Table A-2.1) are in Appendix F which contains statistical tables.

3 For details of the method of estimation, see Appendix B.
4 The popular perception that squatter population by area unit (density) is a more appropriate indicator for the purpose of getting to the poor migrant did not stand up to scrutiny. For details see Appendix B.
5 Incidentally, this baseline information was not available for East Delhi, which falls to the east of the Yamuna river.
6 The unit of area with defined boundaries which normally one enumerator covers during a population census is called a *census block*. It normally has between 100 and 200 households. For details of the concept of the census block in the Indian Census, see GOI, Census of India 1991 (1991) *Delhi: provisional population totals*.
7 Questionnaires are given in Appendix H. For the report on pre-testing as well as for information on data collection and the demographic profile of the criteria migrants, see Appendix B.
8 For a detailed discussion on the methods for ascertaining the whereabouts of the criterion migrants in 2009 and the outcome, see Appendix B.
9 The questionnaire is given in Appendix H.

References

Banerjee, B. (1986). *Rural to urban migration and the urban labour market: A case study of Delhi*. Delhi: Himalaya Publishing House.
Casley, D.J. and Lury, D.A. (1982). *Data collection in developing countries*. Oxford: Clarendon.
Delhi Development Authority, Perspective Planning Wing (1983). *Higher educational facilities: Development plan for Delhi 2001* (Unpublished).
Delhi Development Authority, Perspective Planning Wing (1986). *Transportation for Delhi* (Unpublished).
Delhi Development Authority, Slum Wing (n.d., C. 1990). *List of identified jhuggie clusters in Delhi* (Unpublished).
Delhi Development Authority, Socio-Economic Wing (1983). *Dimensions of squatter settlements in a super metropolitan city - Delhi* (Unpublished).
GOI, Census of India 1991 (1991). *Series-31, Delhi- provisional population totals, paper 1 of 1991*. Delhi: Director of Census Operations, Delhi, Government of India.
GOI, Census of India 1991 (1992). *Delhi, series-31, Occasional paper no. 1 of 1992, provisional total population and scheduled caste population*. Delhi: Director of Census Operations, Delhi, Government of India.
Institute for Socialist Education, New Delhi (1989). *Socio-economic baseline survey of 457 J.J. clusters in Delhi* (Unpublished).
Misra, G.K. and Gupta, R. (1981). *Resettlement policies in Delhi*. New Delhi: Centre for Urban Studies, Indian Institute of Public Administration.
Suri, P. (1991). *Housing for the urban poor: People's needs, priorities and government response – Case study of Delhi*. Unpublished doctoral thesis, School of Planning and Architecture, New Delhi.

3 Socioeconomic status of migrants before migration

Introduction

This chapter presents evidence concerning the pre-migration socioeconomic status of the criteria migrant[1] respondents, with the objective of examining the role of deprivation in rural to urban migration of labour. It tests the prevalent argument of migration being determined by area of origin via comparing migrants from a region of high out-migration with those from other regions of India. It examines diverse aspects of the pre-migration social and economic profile of the migrants' occupational status and employment; their economic position in the agricultural context; other socioeconomic, cultural and educational indicators of status; and their economic and social position relative to the village social structure. The qualitative analysis of the socioeconomic position of the migrants is carried out on the basis of their descriptive responses to direct questions demanding categorical answers, their verbal accounts in response to open-ended questions and some of their extra comments. The significance level of 5 per cent has been used for all the statistical results discussed in this chapter and Chapter 4, unless otherwise stated.

The poverty hypothesis that takes area as the basis of studying migration assumes pre-migration socioeconomic status by the area of origin. Rural to urban migration in developing countries is often interpreted through this hypothesis. In the case of India, for example, an area consisting of North and Central Bihar and Eastern Uttar Pradesh has been identified as a highly out-migrating area that sends migrants from its rural areas due to its being poor, and hence it is considered a case of poor migrants being 'pushed off' this area into different cities and towns of India (Mohan 1982: 42). This assumption is examined in the next section by comparing the migrants from this highly out-migrating region with those from the rest of India.

Diverse aspects of the pre-migration social and economic profiles of the migrants are examined in the next five sections. Occupational status and employment are discussed in the third section. The migrants who were agriculturists, whether through ownership or leasing-in of land, are considered in the fourth section. Certain socioeconomic indicators are taken up in the fifth section. This section also considers some of the extra comments by respondents, which throw light on their socioeconomic status.

The sixth and seventh sections are complementary to each other in ascertaining the economic and social positions of the migrants vis-a-vis the village social structure. However, the nature of information examined in these two sections is different from each other. The sixth section is based on direct questions demanding categorical answers, whereas the seventh section depends on verbal accounts in response to open-ended questions. The eighth section summarises the conclusions of the chapter.

A test on the area explanation of migration

As mentioned in Chapter 1 and described in Appendix A, Mohan (1982: 42) identified a contiguous area covering North and Central Bihar and Eastern Uttar Pradesh. Map 3.1 indicates the location of this area.

Put in the context of the State-level trends, this area is believed to be one of the most out-migrating regions of the push variety in India. If causation implied in the area argument of migration were true, the greater proportion of the migrants from this region would be from poorer sections of the area of their origin compared with the proportion among those coming from other areas. This section examines the proposition through the use of the present survey results.

Two-fifths of the respondents of the sample survey were from the districts belonging to the previously mentioned region. It is possible to compare the group of migrants who came from this area with the rest of the sample migrants to find out if any significant difference exists between the two groups regarding their pre-migration economic status. Figure 3.1 presents the percentage distribution of the migrants by economic status and by area of origin.

This three-category classification is based on responses to a categorical question. The detailed discussion of the variable is given in a later section. The results of chi-square testing indicate that there were a larger number of average and fewer below average than expected among the migrants from this particular area compared with those from other parts of India.[2] The survey results also show that migrants from this area of Bihar and Uttar Pradesh were more likely to be owners of land or animals compared with the rest. They were also more likely to be peasants than wage earners or artisans and traders. However, a significantly larger number of the peasant migrants from this area, compared with those from the rest of India, also reported that their families had to borrow due to being unable to fulfil their year-round food requirements from their own agricultural produce. It is a sign both of relative deprivation and credit worthiness in the rural socioeconomic context that goes pretty well with their high potential for mobility for work.

The results of the clustering exercise reported in Chapter 6 very clearly and amply portray the *poorvee* (Eastern) migrants as better off compared with the *non-poorvee* (non-Eastern) migrants and hence support the aforementioned conclusions.

The evidence from the sample survey suggests that the proportion of poor among the migrants from this particular area of high out-migration was lower than that among migrants from the rest of India. It contradicts the causation implied in the area argument of migration referred in Chapter 1, which expected

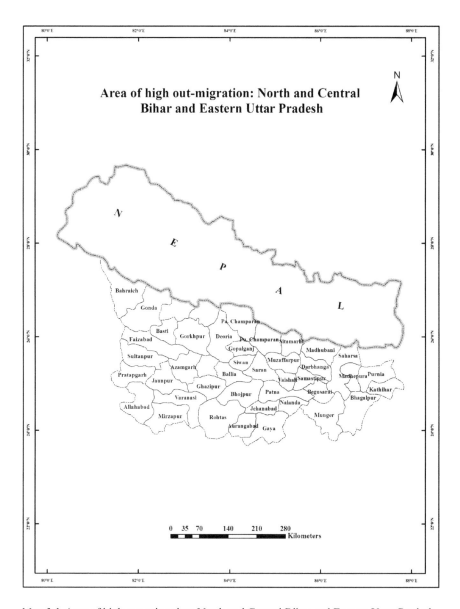

Map 3.1 Area of high out-migration: North and Central Bihar and Eastern Uttar Pradesh

this proportion to be higher. As argued in Chapter 4, it is more to do with relative deprivation and demand for labour at the destination communicated to the
potential migrants back in the area of origin through channels of information that
is decisive in the potential migrants' decision to migrate rather than merely any
misery in the area of origin.

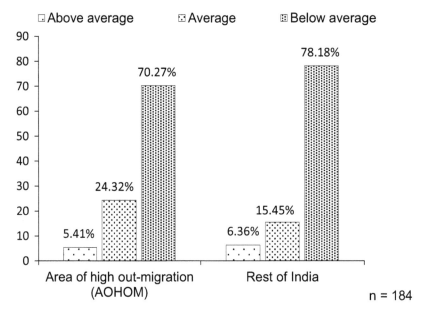

Figure 3.1 Percentage distribution of the migrants by economic status and by area of origin

Occupational status and employment

This section considers the main and subsidiary occupations that the migrants had before migration, the basis of employment in the main occupation and the reason for quitting. All those who had some kind of job before migration were asked if and for how long they were unemployed during their last year in the village and a complementary question on the months of employment during that year. The results are discussed later in the section where we considers the group consisting of nonworkers in the year before migration, most of whom were young school boys in their village and started their working life in the city. They were 15 per cent of the sample.

Main jobs before migration

Eighty-five per cent of the criteria migrants had worked before they came to Delhi. Their occupational history is discussed here. Table 3.1 shows that the sector-wise distribution of pre-migration employment of the respondents was 69 per cent agriculture, 20 per cent secondary and 11 per cent tertiary. It was similar to the then-prevailing occupational distribution for India as a whole, and, in fact, the migrants' rural jobs can be said to be more nonagricultural than the all-India norms.

The categorisation of the main occupations of the migrants has been shown in Table 3.1. The description of his pre-migration occupation by the respondent

Table 3.1 Main job of the criteria migrants before migration

Code	Main job	Valid per cent	Cumulative per cent
1	Agriculture	30.6	30.6
2	Animal husbandry	2.5	33.1
3	Grazing /Cow keeping	8.9	42.0
4	Sharecropper	3.2	45.2
5	Agricultural worker	24.2	69.4
6	Unskilled construction worker (*beldar*)	3.2	72.6
7	Other unskilled construction-sector worker	2.5	75.2
8	Factory and mill worker	3.2	78.3
9	Tailor	5.1	83.4
10	Other artisan and craft person	5.7	89.2
11	Shopkeeper/vendor	3.8	93.0
12	Service worker	5.1	98.1
13	Others	1.9	100.0
		100.0	

(n = 157)

was used while constructing this classification. It was possible to reduce these 13 occupational categories to three classes. Figure 3.2 shows the distribution.

It was found that about 33 per cent were engaged in what may broadly be termed peasant occupations (self-cultivation and animal husbandry) based on their own property. The categories 3, 4 and 5 may broadly be termed agricultural workers who worked on the means of production owned by others – they were 36 per cent of the sample. About 6 per cent were engaged as construction workers and 3 per cent in factories and mills. These 9 per cent of the respondents could be termed nonagricultural workers who were working for others. The category of service workers included a few domestic servants, sweepers, one bullock cart driver and one teashop worker. So, 50 per cent could be broadly termed the workers who were mostly employed by others for wages (except share-croppers, who received a share in the produce). The category 'others' included a labour supervisor and a homeopathic practitioner. The 17 per cent who came under categories 9, 10, 11 and 13 were artisans, shopkeepers and others – the common element among them, which differentiates them from workers, was their entrepreneurship. This category could be called artisans, traders, etc. This rather broad classification would be judged in the light of other relevant variables later in this chapter.

Forty per cent of these migrants who were engaged in some work before migration had one or more subsidiary jobs. The distribution of subsidiary occupations confirmed the occupational classification discussed in the preceding paragraphs. Moreover, cross-tabulation shows that even the peasants or the self-employed landowners often had subsidiary occupations as wage workers and vice-versa. Our analysis leads us to conclude that the migrants were more of the type that earned part of their living from the labour market rather than them being the independent, self-employed and propertied type.

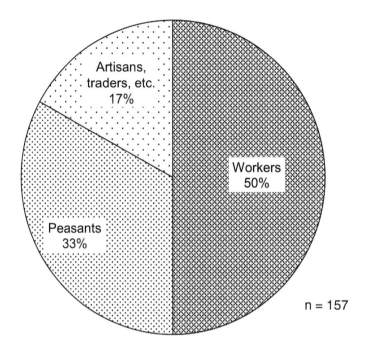

Figure 3.2 Classes by occupation

Nature of employment

This sub-section considers security of employment. It does so separately for those who were hired and those for whom it was a family business. Forty-seven per cent of the respondents were hired workers before migration. Figure 3.3 provides the details of the basis of employment for these workers.

Out of those who were hired, about two-thirds were hired on a daily basis. The verbal description of the nature of their jobs by the respondents during the interviews indicates that employment on a daily basis entailed uncertainties and insecurities. Sixteen per cent were hired by the month and 11 per cent by the year. A very tiny minority reported payment by harvest and season. About 3 per cent were paid by piece-meal rate.

Regarding the category of those who were not working for others prior to migrating (i.e., who were not hired and hence were perhaps self-employed or participated in a family occupation), it emerged that a very small proportion (4 per cent) were replaced by someone on their leaving work in the village. In 96 per cent of the cases there was no replacement for their village jobs when they migrated. This indicates that almost all of these migrants were apparently work-ing, but were, in fact, not needed in their pre-migration work, that is, they were in disguised unemployment before they migrated. This shows the high extent of rural disguised unemployment and underemployment among those who were self-employed before migration.

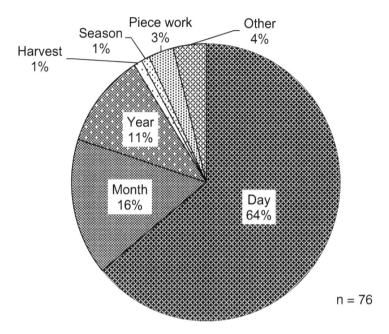

Figure 3.3 Hiring basis in the pre-migration job

Reasons for leaving the main job

The preceding sub-section gave a general picture regarding the nature of employment. This sub-section considers the details why the migrants left their pre-migration jobs. Table 3.2 presents the reasons for leaving the main occupation before migration.

About two-thirds of the respondents seem to have left due to low income and associated reasons like lack or insufficiency of land and indebtedness (Reason codes 2 to 6 in Table 3.2). The chi-square test result shows that the complaint of low income (Reason 4) was from all quarters. This is an indication of the overwhelming majority of migrants being deprived, at least relatively so. There was no significant difference between the peasants, the wage earners or the artisans, traders, etc. As expected, the reason 'no land' was mentioned by the people describing animal husbandry and agricultural wage work as their main occupation, and the reason 'insufficiency of land' was given by those whose main job was agriculture.

Sixteen per cent said they left due to unemployment or underemployment (Reason code 7 in Table 3.2). These were mainly wage workers and about half of them were agricultural workers. The common complaint of the tailors was that the availability of work in the village was only seasonal (i.e., tailoring work in the rural areas was available only during marriage and festival seasons) and that it was therefore an irregular source of income. This description by the tailor migrants

Table 3.2 Reasons for leaving the pre-migration job

Code	Reason	Percentage of respondents mentioning the reason*
1	Have not stopped (go during the season)	0.6
2	No land	1.3
3	Insufficiency of land	4.5
4	Low income	58.6
5	Paid off debt	00.0
6	To repay debt/was indebted	4.5
7	Unemployment /underemployment	15.9
8	Skill not in demand there	1.3
9	Irregularity/unpunctuality of payment	4.5
10	Trouble with the employer	1.3
11	Poor working conditions	4.5
12	To take another job	0.6
13	Apprenticeship/training over	0.6
14	To learn skill/join training	1.9
15	To set up business	1.3
16	Laid off, no work	1.3
17	Laid off, other reasons	00.0
18	Job completed	00.0
19	Could not continue study	1.9
20	To get married	00.0
21	Got married	0.6
22	Pregnant	00.0
23	Ill health/disability	1.3
24	Others lived here/were coming here	5.7
25	Wanted to move to another area	3.8
26	Family strategy	8.9
27	Family size large	3.8
28	Family social feud	2.5
29	Tragedy/illness in the family	1.9
30	Caste/social oppression/violence	1.9
31	Natural disasters	7.6
32	Other reasons	3.8

(n = 157)

* *Sum does not add up to 100*

was construed as underemployment during the year before they migrated and hence, they were included in this figure.

About the same proportion gave reasons which relate to specific aspects and the type of job (Reason codes 8 to 15 in Table 3.2). So, wage earners, agricultural workers and nonagricultural workers mentioned the irregularity of payment and poor working conditions. Apart from low wages and irregular employment, such reasons also motivated the respondents to move to a job where at least the timely payment of wages was assured. Tailors mentioned the completion of training or an apprenticeship. The peasants among whom the incidence of literacy and education was higher compared with workers mentioned reasons such as an urge to learn a skill or join a training programme or to set up their own business. This group of reasons seems to reflect in various ways the importance of specific aspects of jobs, such as the development of a particular skill and the knowledge that would be in demand in the urban labour market. This amounts to an inducement to leave for a more promising labour market in urban areas.

The next important group of reasons related to the family, indicating the importance of family in decisions (Reason codes 26 to 29 in Table 3.2). The family strategy (Reason 26) was particularly associated with peasants. The family strategy behind migration can be gleaned from the respondents' mention of the need to supplement family earnings and diversify its earnings base, find a solution to the problems of debt or economic difficulties or to strengthen the position of the family. Caste oppression as a reason for quitting the job was mentioned by only three respondents, all of whom were working in the agricultural sector (one land owner, one sharecropper and an agricultural worker).

The presence or arrival of known people in the city and the desire of the respondents to move to the city were mentioned by one in ten (Reason codes 24 and 25 in Table 3.2). This indicates the importance of the channels of recruitment in moving out of earlier jobs. Natural disasters were mentioned by about one in fifteen. As expected, people who mentioned this reason were peasants (two-thirds) or agricultural labourers (one-third).

It emerges that the main reasons for leaving the pre-migration jobs were low income, lack of regular employment, incompatibility of skills and jobs in the rural setup and family reasons.

An exercise was carried out to ascertain the first and foremost reason for leaving the pre-migration job and then recompute the reasons into groups in such a manner that the overlapping ends. The categories in Table 3.2 were specified against the new classes in the reduced dataset that are mentioned at serial number 11 in Table G1 of Appendix G. The results by group of reasons as specified in reduced dataset are shown in Figure 3.4. These results, although matching the description in the foregoing paragraphs, present the situation more succinctly.

Level of employment and unemployment

Lack of employment has been considered an important factor in almost all migration models. The present sub-section discusses the situation faced by the sample migrants in this regard.

Figure 3.5 shows that three out of every four respondents said they were unemployed or underemployed for some time in the year before migration. Sixty-eight per cent said that they were unemployed, and 6 per cent said they were underemployed for some time during the 12 months before migration.

The period of unemployment varied a lot. It ranged between 3 days (the shortest) and 11 months (the greatest) in the year. The median was 90 days, and the third quarter was unemployed for period between 90 and 180 days. The mode was 6 months. As for those describing themselves as underemployed before migration, the typical period of underemployment was one year. The duration

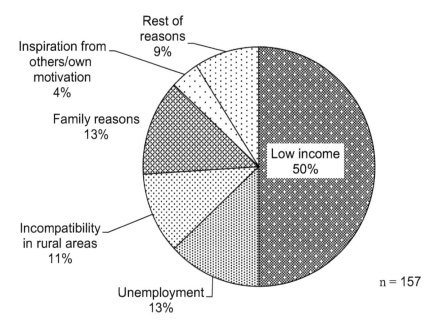

Figure 3.4 First main 'reason group' for stopping the pre-migration job

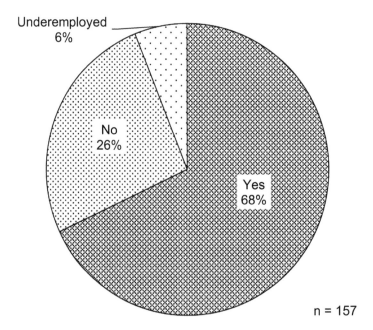

Figure 3.5 Unemployed for any time before migration

of unemployment can be considered together for all those without work before migration (i.e., the unemployed as well as underemployed). The resultant distribution based on this reclassification, the details of which can be found in Table G1 of Appendix G, is shown in Figure 3.6.

On average, the respondents had 6 months of employment during the period of 12 months before migration. The arithmetic mean was 6.7 months (standard deviation = 3.2) and the median was 6 months. In fact a quarter of the respondents had fewer than 4 months of employment in the year.

Official statistical data indicate that men belonging to rural labour households got an average of 242, 283 and 193 days of annual employment during 1974–1975, 1977–1978 and 1983, respectively (GOI, Ministry of Labour and Employment, 1991: 199). Almost all of our respondents were males who came between 1972 and 1992. We found that with 6 months of employment in a year, our respondents had less employment than the all-India norm.

The distribution in Table 3.3 is positively skewed. It is clear from this table and Figure 3.7 that only three in ten had employment for more than 8 months.

The data quality is satisfactory because the information on periods of unemployment and employment compliments each other. It was not possible to test the significance of the difference of the period of employment by each individual job. However, it was possible to carry out the chi-square test for both the period of employment and period of unemployment with main occupation before migration, using a three-category classification for each of these three

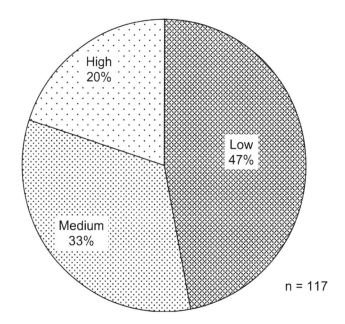

Figure 3.6 Duration of unemployment

Table 3.3 Months of employment in the year before migration

Months of employment	Valid per cent	Cumulative frequency
Up to 2.00	7.5	7.5
2.01 to 4.00	20.3	27.8
4.01 to 6.00	30.1	57.9
6.01 to 8.00	14.3	72.2
8.01 to 10.00	12.0	84.2
10.01 to 12.00	15.8	100.0
	100.0	

Valid cases 133   Missing cases 24

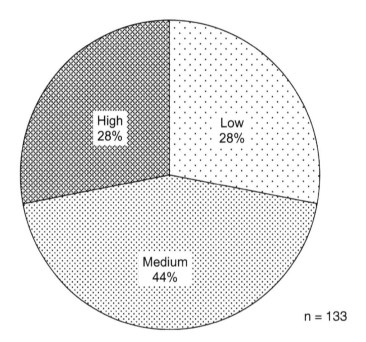

Figure 3.7 Levels of employment

Period of employment could not be ascertained for 24 respondents; No. of valid cases = 133. Low: Up to 4 months; Medium: 4.01 to 8 months; High: 8.01 to 12 months

variables. The results show there was no significant difference in the period of employment (or unemployment) among the peasants, the wage earners and the artisans and the craftsman (Figure 3.7).

Nonworkers during the year before migration

As mentioned in the introduction to this section, 15 per cent of the respondents in the sample did not work in the year before migration. The t-test results indicate that those not working before migration were, on average, significantly younger and better educated compared with those who were working before migration. This makes sense, given the fact that those not working before migration were mostly attending school, and four-fifths of these twenty migrants were people who had never worked (i.e., they were new entrants to the workforce). Because the details of income from various sources were recorded only for those from agricultural families, it can be said that from among the agriculturists, the non-workers tended to have, on average, a higher proportion of their income from *nau-kari* (service) – a regular income by some member of the family. The conclusion from these facts is that these were the better-off villagers.

Four of these twenty respondents were nonworkers in the year before migration but had worked earlier on and, that way, they were old entrants in the workforce. Their period of unemployment was 12 months on average. Looking at the nature of the jobs of these old entrants, it can be said that their jobs involved what could broadly be called nonagricultural skills. This suggested perhaps a higher level of skill compared with their village's social structure where agricultural occupations generally dominated. All four were pursuing different occupations – one was a grocer, one a sweeper, one was an apprentice working in electricity line erection and one was in the Central Industrial Security Force.

Assessment of economic position in the agricultural context

This section evaluates the economic position of the migrants who were involved in agriculture in the countryside in the year before they migrated. The first sub-section analyses the size of land holdings and tenurial status in terms of operational holdings. The next sub-section tries to draw inferences about the livelihoods of the agriculturists by analysing the number of crops they grew, the marketable surplus from agricultural output, the number of months of food supply for the household they manage to have from their own harvests and the assessment of difficulties of those who did not have enough food output to last throughout the year. The third sub-section assesses the diversity of the sources of the income of those involved in agriculture.

Operational holdings

The object of this sub-section is to compare the operational holdings of our respond-ents with data from the all-India agricultural census conducted during 1980–1981, the year closest to their year of migration. Because the Agricultural Census of India provides data by operational holdings, the information on ownership hold-ings and leasing-in for the sample migrants was used to compute operational hold-ings. A discussion on ownership distribution can be found in Appendix C.

Table 3.4 and Figures 3.8 and 3.9 show the percentage distribution of opera-tional landholding by size groups and by tenurial status. It shows that most of our respondents came from households which were marginal, small or semi-medium land operators. However, this proportion of marginal holdings was lower and the proportion of small holdings and semi-medium holdings higher compared with the norm (the weighted average was based on the 1980–1981 Agricultural

Table 3.4 Percentage distribution of operational holdings by tenurial status and size groups

Category of holdings and size group (in acres)	All holdings		Wholly owned and self-operated		Partly owned and partly leased-in		Wholly leased-in	
	AIRAC	SS	AIRAC	SS	AIRAC	SS	AIRAC	SS
Marginal (up to 2.47)	67.3	54.2	56.4	65.4	50.8	36.4	65.4	54.5
Small (2.48 to 4.94)	15.5	25.2	18.0	21.2	22.6	24.2	18.1	36.4
Semi-medium (4.95 to 9.88)	10.2	16.8	14.0	9.6	14.9	33.0	10.9	9.1
Medium (9.89 to 24.70) and large (24.71 and over)	6.9	3.7	11.5	3.8	11.3	6.1	5.6	–

Source:
1) GOI, Ministry of Agriculture (1987). *All India report on agricultural census 1980–81*. New Delhi: Ministry of Agriculture, Government of India. *All India Report on Agricultural Census 1980–81*: for all holdings, the weights assigned to the States in proportion to the migrants from them.
2) GOI, Ministry of Agriculture (1987: 23). *All India Report on Agricultural Census 1980–81*: for the rest – for data by tenurial status.
3) The sample survey.

Note:
1) The number of all operational holdings in the sample survey was 107.
[The disaggregation by tenurial status is follows: wholly owned and self-operated (52), partly owned and partly leased-in (33) and wholly leased-in (22)].
2) AIRAC: All India Report on Agricultural Census; SS: Sample survey.

Census). Thus, it appears that the propensity to migrate was greater not among the lowest stratum (marginal holdings), but the strata just above the lowest (small and semi-medium holdings). People from small landholdings as well as those from semi-medium landholdings were approximately twice as likely to migrate as those from marginal holdings.

Considering tenurial status, some additional observations can be made. Landholdings of the marginal group were more of the wholly owned and self-operated type than the norm. Those from the small group were particularly the wholly leased-in type and those from the semi-medium group more the partly owned and partly leased-in type. So, our typical agriculturist respondent came from a household with small operational holdings who had a part of it leased-in from others.

Income levels of the agriculturists

One of the ways to have a broad idea of the livelihood of people engaged in agriculture is through the number of crops they grow and the marketable surplus from their agricultural output. The first part of this sub-section discusses the livelihood of the respondents from these two angles. It is very common among agricultural

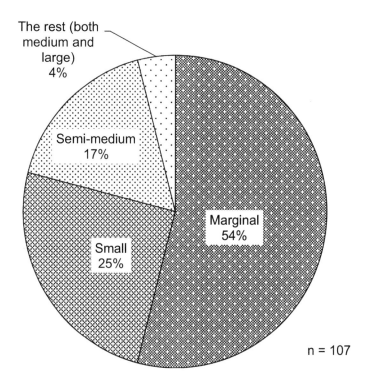

The rest (both medium and large) 4%

Semi-medium 17%

Marginal 54%

Small 25%

n = 107

Figure 3.8 Operational holdings by size groups

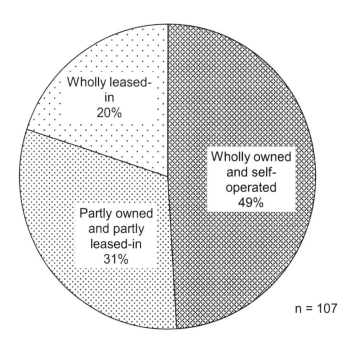

Wholly leased-in 20%

Wholly owned and self-operated 49%

Partly owned and partly leased-in 31%

n = 107

Figure 3.9 Operational holdings by tenurial status

communities to measure the well-being of families by the months of food supply for the household, which they manage to retain from their own harvests. The
present study found that this measure has a good association with other indicators
of socioeconomic status. The second part of the sub-section discusses the results
according to this measure and tries to assess the difficulties of those who did not
have food output enough to last year-round.

Number of crops and marketable surplus

Figure 3.10 shows the distribution of agriculturists (i.e., the respondents who
owned land or leased-in land) by the number of harvests taken in the year before
migration. The majority (two in three) of such respondents reaped two harvests in
the year before migration; 23 per cent took one harvest, 8 per cent had three and
3 per cent had none.

The survey results show that most of the people involved in agriculture did not
produce for the market. Only 16.8 per cent of them sold any agricultural produce
in the year before migration. Figure 3.11 shows the distribution of migrants by the
proportion of agricultural output sold. It was found that out of the tiny minority of
agriculturists who sold any agricultural output during the year before migration,
65 per cent sold less than half of their agricultural output. Only one respondent
sold more than half of his agricultural produce.

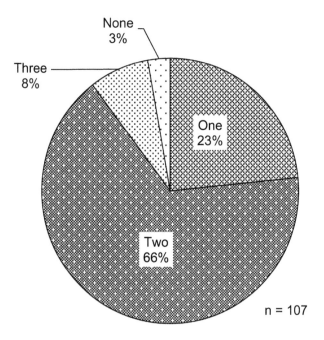

Figure 3.10 Number of harvests in the year before migration

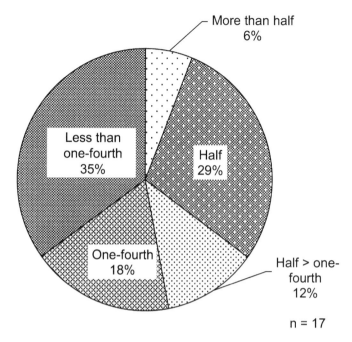

More than half
6%

Less than
one-fourth
35%

Half
29%

One-fourth
18%

Half > one-
fourth
12%

n = 17

Figure 3.11 Proportion of agricultural output sold

Food output and requirement

The question of how many months the harvest lasted for a family's food requirements was asked of all those who cultivated any land, regardless if it were their
own land or they leased it in. Table 3.5 summarises the distribution of responses.
It shows that two-thirds of the respondents involved in agriculture had enough
grain from their own harvest to last for up to 6 months only. For one-third of them,
it was between 6 months and 12 months. Hardly anyone had enough grain from
their own harvest to last more than 12 months.

It turned out that four in five found it difficult to meet annual food requirements. Actually, two-thirds found it very difficult. The survey also tried to find
out how many of those reporting difficulty in fulfilling food requirements had to
borrow as a result. The results indicate that most of them (94 per cent) had to borrow because of such difficulties.

For 77 per cent of the respondents, the food from their own harvest lasted for
less than 12 months. Each of the migrants reporting less than 12 months was
asked how difficult it was to meet his or her family's food requirements in the off-
season. The results are given in Figure 3.12.

The overall conclusion on the basis of an assessment of food production and
requirement is that of the 107 cultivators, for 77 per cent, their harvest did not last year

Table 3.5 Months of food from own harvest

Months	Valid per cent	Cumulative per cent
0.00 to 3.00	18.7	18.7
3.01 to 6.00	46.7	65.4
6.01 to 9.00	8.4	73.8
9.01 to 12.00	25.2	99.1
12.01 to 18.00	.9	100.0

Valid cases 107   Missing cases 0

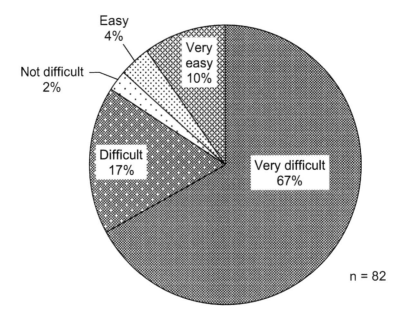

Figure 3.12 Fulfilling food requirements in the off-season

round, 64 per cent had difficulty in meeting their food requirements and 62 per cent borrowed as a result. The official Rural Labour Inquiry data showed that roughly 51.5 per cent of rural labour households were in debt at three different points during the period 1974–1975 and 1987–1988 (i.e., the average for years 1974–1975, 1977–1978 and 1987–1988), the points relevant for comparison with rural migrant respondents in Delhi who were surveyed for this study because most of them moved to Delhi between and around these points of time (GOI, Ministry of Labour and Employment, 1991: 200). Our respondents were more indebted than the norm for rural labour.

Diversity of the sources of income of the agriculturists

The traditional description of rural as being synonymous with agriculture needs re-examination. The survey results reveal that not all rural migrants were involved in agriculture before they left the countryside – 'only' 61 per cent (112 of the

184) of the migrants were involved in agriculture either as ownership holders or operational holders of land when they were in the countryside before migration to Delhi. But to what extent were these migrants dependent on agriculture for their income? Table 3.6 investigates the distribution of such respondents by the percentage of income from different sources.

Only 15 per cent of the respondents involved in agriculture in the year prior to migration depended wholly on income from land. For about a quarter of respondents involved in agriculture prior to migration, leasing-in contributed from a quarter up to a half of their income during the year before their migration to Delhi. The situation was similar with regard to income from work as a labourer. Eight per cent of the respondents mentioned loans as a means of meeting the expenditure in the year before migration. Table 3.6 gives an idea of how diverse the sources of income were for those who apparently depended on agriculture.

Some of the sources of income were marked by exclusiveness. The higher the income from these sources, the less was the involvement in other sources of income. This tendency of exclusiveness was reflected in the negativity of correlation of sources with each other. In fact, three sources tended to be more exclusive than others. The share of income from cultivation of own land, animal husbandry and tailoring each tended to have a negative relation with all sources of income individually. This means that the more stake any person had in any one of these sources, the more he tended to be dependent on that source and have less to do with any other source of income. Only leasing-out and shopkeeping/vending had a significant positive correlation with each other. This corroborates the related discussion in Appendix C. The shopkeepers also tended to have income from mortgage or sale of property, apart from the significant relationship of their income with leasing-out. This means that the income of shopkeepers was most diverse.

Table 3.6 Percentage distribution of respondents by the percentage of income from different sources

	% of income →↓ Sources of income	0	1–30	31–60	61–90	91–100	Total
1	Cultivation of own land	21.6	14.4	28.8	19.8	15.3	100
2	Leasing-out	92.8	2.7	4.5	0.0	0.0	100
3	Leasing-in	60.4	17.1	18.9	1.8	1.8	100
4	Animal husbandry	93.7	3.6	0.0	2.7	0.0	100
5	Grazing /cow-keeping	97.3	0.9	1.8	0.0	0.0	100
6	Work as labourer	60.9	10.9	24.5	2.7	0.9	100
7	Tailoring	96.4	1.8	0.9	0.9	0.0	100
8	Other artisanship/ craftsmanship	95.5	0.0	2.7	1.8	0.0	100
9	Shopkeeping/vending	92.8	4.5	0.9	0.9	0.9	100
10	Service (*naukari*)	94.6	1.8	2.7	0.9	0.0	100
11	Mortgaged/sold property	97.3	0.9	0.9	0.9	0.0	100
12	Loans	91.0	1.8	5.4	1.8	0.0	100
13	Other source (s)	94.6	2.7	1.8	0.9	0.0	100

Valid cases 111 Missing cases 1

The share of income from the cultivation of one's own land had a significant negative correlation with the share of income from leasing-in and the work as labourers separately. This means those with less income from their own land tended to get involved in leasing-in and work as labourers. As already discussed in an earlier section of this chapter, the incidence of leasing-in was high. The share of income from leasing-in had a significant negative correlation with the share of income from the cultivation of one's own land and a nonsignificant but positive relation with the share of income from grazing/cow-keeping and work as labourer. This means those who leased in any amount of land were either landless or owned a smaller amount of land and tended to work as keepers of others' cattle or as labourers.

Thus, it emerged that those who were apparently agriculturists, in fact, tended to have a diversity of sources from which they earned their livelihood. The correlation results indicate that exclusiveness developed as a higher share of income came from sources like cultivation of one's own land, animal husbandry and tailoring. But because the labour migrants were not big operators of land, their income was quite diverse. The image of rural as being synonymous with agricultural occupations is based on the observation of substantial operators of land. In reality, most of our respondents were not like that and they earned their livelihood from different sources. These results corroborate the profile of our respondents with agriculturist background that was discussed earlier in this chapter.

Socioeconomic indicators of status

This section tries to assess the pre-migration status of the migrants in terms of some commonly used indicators of socioeconomic status in villages.

Ownership of livestock

The survey results showed that more than two-thirds of the respondents owned animals. Table 3.7 provides the percentage distribution of respondents by the number of large animals and small animals separately.

On average, the respondents had two large animals. Fifty-eight per cent had no small animals. There was a high variation among those who had any animals

Table 3.7 Percentage distribution of respondents by number of animals owned

Number of animals	Large animals	Small animals
No animals	13.6	58.3
1 to 2	39.4	11.4
3 to 4	34.1	13.6
5 to 6	8.3	4.5
7 to 8	3.0	3.8
9 to 10	–	3.0
11 and more	1.5	5.3
	100.0	100.0

Valid cases 132   Missing cases 0

at all. The animals put in the category of large animals were cows, bullocks, buffalos and horses. The animals put in the category of small animals were sheep, goats and pigs. About 12 per cent of the respondents owned young offspring of the large animals. One out of ten had some sort of milch animal. One in thirteen respondents had one or more birds.

Two-fifths of the owners of livestock sold some livestock or their products in that year. Unfortunately, the comparison of the livestock figures with the Livestock Census data was not possible due to differences in coverage and the wide variation by area in species and types of animals.

The use of electricity as an indicator

Three-fifths of the respondents came from places where an electricity connection was not available and hence the question was inapplicable. Amongst the respondents whose villages had electricity and to whom the question was applicable (two-fifths of all respondents), only one in eight had an electricity connection. Hence, the question of whether they had any electric gadgets applied only to those who had an electricity connection (ten respondents). The results indicate that the ownership of electric gadgets was very low. Three people owned one fan each, and one person each owned two fans, one television and a water heater.

Ownership of durable items

A list of durable items was read out to the respondents, and they were asked to say if they had any of these items. If the response was affirmative for any particular item, then they were asked to state the numbers of that item. We report the results in Table 3.8. More people owned a pair of bullocks and a bicycle compared with other items. Two-fifths of the respondents possessed a pair of bullocks. The same proportion owned a bicycle. Wells and bullock carts were the next important assets. None of the respondents had items like tractors, scooters, motorcycles or three-wheelers.

The correlation results indicate that the number of bullocks or those of bicycles owned turned out to be the best indicators of status compared with other items.

People with these items did significantly better with respect to other variables of socioeconomic status. For example, they had more years of schooling, tended to come to Delhi at a higher age and lived in Delhi for shorter periods compared with those without these items.

The conclusion from the exercise is that about two in five who had these assets were a better-off group compared with the rest of the sample migrants. The latter group had a greater tendency to come to Delhi at a lower age and stay longer in the city.

Sociocultural and educational indicators

This sub-section considers two variables: elements of literacy in the family and whether the respondents sent their children to school. According to the chi-square

Table 3.8 Percentage distribution of the respondents by ownership of certain durable items

Number → Item ↓	0	1	2	3 and more	Total per cent
Water engine	91.8	7.8	0.5	0.0	100
Well	81.0	13.6	4.9	0.5	100
Drinking-water well	97.8	2.2	0.0	0.0	100
Horse	97.3	2.7	0.0	0.0	100
Bullock	58.7	6.5	31.5	3.2	100
Bullock cart	87.0	12.5	0.5	0.0	100
Bicycle	58.7	38.0	1.6	1.6	100
Radio	82.6	16.3	1.1	0.0	100

(n = 184)

test results, these two variables were found to have significant association with membership of a representative body like the *panchayat*, one of the most important indicators of social status. In addition, this sub-section considers some extra information received during the question on child education.

About 56 per cent of our respondents were literate. This was higher than the relevant norm of 50 per cent among the rural male population at that time (GOI, National Institute of Adult Education, 1992: 5). Two-thirds of all migrants reported at least one literate person in their respective families. Of the 122 families with at least one literate member, only 3 families received a daily newspaper and only 7 families received a magazine.

Of the respondents who had a child of school-going age in their family, two-thirds were sending their children to school. About 88 per cent of the respondents said the children had books.

To questions on their children's education, some of the respondents made additional comments explaining why their children did not go to school. About three-fourths of these extra comments indicated a poor economic position [Poor economic condition (ten respondents); children had to work due to economic problems (five respondents)] as the reason for not sending their children to school. Other reasons mentioned were the practice of untouchability – the children belonging to the depressed castes were made to sit at a distance so as not to touch children belonging to 'higher castes' and made to feel discriminated (three persons), lack of motivation in the children (three persons) and female children were not sent to school (one person).

Migrants' economic and social position

The goal of this section is to examine the economic and social position of the migrants' families in the countryside before they came to Delhi relative to the village social structure. It does so through a discussion around the following three categorical variables: being in debt or not, livelihood compared with other families in the village and membership of a representative body.

Livelihood categories

In the sample survey three in five migrants said their families were in debt. As mentioned earlier, the Rural Labour Inquiry average for rural labour is 52 per cent. Of those who were not in debt, only one in ten lent money. Others neither borrowed nor lent.

The respondents were asked to rate their family's economic position in relation to other families in the village. Figure 3.13 presents the results. Only a quarter ranked the livelihood of their families as average or higher compared with other families in the village. Most of them (75 per cent) called themselves below average. However, the majority did not belong to the lowest stratum.

The chi-square test results reveal that this variable had significant association with important indicators of economic and social position, such as membership in an elected body like a *panchayat*, indebted or not, ownership of land and grain from harvest year round. So, this can be taken as a more reliable indicator of the economic position of the migrants' families before migration. A discussion of some important results of the chi-square of this variable with others can be useful.

It was found that, by and large, the ability to read, the ability to write, whether he or she went to school or not and the ownership of animals were not significantly different for the three-category classification of the families' economic position

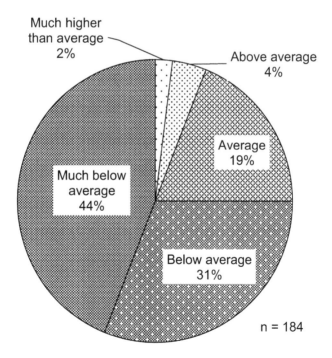

Figure 3.13 Livelihood compared with others

(above average, average, below average). However, the ownership of land had a significant association with families' economic status. The landless were more likely to describe their families' economic status as below average.

The results, though not significant, indicate that relatively speaking, workers were more likely to be below average and peasants more likely to be average or above average compared with other families in the village.

Regarding those who were agriculturists – whether through ownership or leasing-in of land – the fact whether a family had food from its own harvest to last the year round or not turned out to be significantly associated with the status of the families. Moreover, below-average-status families were less likely to employ any labour in their agriculture.

The cross-tabulation enables a discussion of some important trends. Migrants from below-average families were more likely to have their first jobs at the urban destination in construction and service sectors, those from average families were more likely to be in the garment factories and those from above-average families were more likely to be in the nongarment factories. The migrants coming from average and above-average families were less likely to prefer living in the village for the same income or prefer doing in a village a job similar to their first urban job.

Status categories

One in five respondents reported that someone from the family was a member of a representative body like a village *panchayat*.

This indicator of social position turned out to be very important. According to the chi-square results, the families with a member in a representative body were more likely to be economically better off and have a literate person in the family, and the migrants from such families were more likely to be educated. Taking membership in an elected body as an indicator of the social status of the family in the village, it can be said that the peasants were likely to command greater status in the village life than those working for wages.

The chi-square test results indicate that this variable did not have any significant difference on the migrant's first job in Delhi or the preference to work for the same income or do a similar job in the village. In this regard, economic condition (as discussed in terms of the livelihood categories in the previous sub-section) seemed to matter more than social status.

Qualitative analysis of the socioeconomic position

The chapter has so far considered information that was quantifiable. This section turns now to the gist of information from the open-ended questions relevant to the study of the socioeconomic position of the migrants before migration. The first and second sub-sections are based on the verbal accounts of the migrants in response to the open-ended questions on their family's economic position and their father's status in the village, respectively.

Description of the economic position of the family

The respondents were asked to describe the pre-migration economic position of their families. One key adjective or phrase from each migrant's description was identified. Economic position of the families was classified in five groups according to these key phrases.[3] The distribution is presented in Figure 3.14.

It appears that nearly 75 per cent of the respondents described the economic position of their family in negative terms equating to bad or worse economic conditions. The distribution according to this classification matches the classification based on livelihood categories, which was discussed in the previous section, where exactly the same proportion of the respondents of this study (i.e.,75 per cent) identified themselves as 'below average' compared with other families in their respective villages. This suggests that our respondents were from relatively deprived backgrounds. Hence, the socioeconomic position of the migrants as reflected by the quantitative information presented earlier in this chapter is corroborated by the details that emerge through a complementary classification in this sub-section.

Father's status

The question "Did people turn to your father for advice?" was asked of all the migrant respondents of this case study. Due to the open-ended nature of

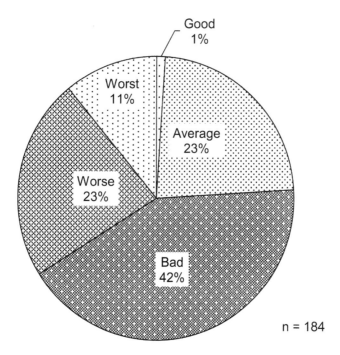

Figure 3.14 Classification of families by economic position

the question, the responses tended to take a very broad form. Moreover, the equivalent word for advice in Hindi – the main language of interviewing in the present sample survey – was vague in its scope. The Hindi word *ray*a can mean both advice and opinion. Hence, some of the people giving affirmative responses may have meant people took their fathers' opinion. This was a limitation on the use of this question as an indicator of pre-migration socioeconomic position.

Nevertheless, it is possible to make a few observations. First, one in nine respondents reported that their father died too early for them to remember or say much about him. Leaving such cases aside, along with those who said they 'did not know', broadly the number of affirmative responses to this question turned out to be almost equal to the number of negative responses (82 and 80, respectively). However, the figure of positive responses is probably an overestimate, partly due to the cultural-linguistic context of the fieldwork and status consciousness ('the ego factor'), but also to a large extent due to the fact that the group with a high mortality of fathers was excluded. This group was more likely to be similar to those who gave negative responses, on the premise that mortality and poverty statistically have a positive relation.

The reasons given by the respondents for people consulting their fathers were related to agricultural work, social relations, economic problems and official (i.e., governmental) matters. There was also the mention of the importance of skills and the knowledge of the urban labour market. A few respondents said people respected and listened to their fathers, either because they were artisans of woodwork or barbers or because their fathers knew about the urban labour market – for example, through the latter's stay in cities such as Delhi or Bangalore.

For those who said others did not consult their fathers, the main reasons mentioned were poverty, weak economic position, landlessness, old age or being junior in age and the arrogance of the better off.

A substantial number of those who said their fathers died early can be added to this low-status group. Moreover, because one does not expect people to be very talkative about a downgraded position in society, it is reasonable to conclude that the number in the group with a low status by this indicator would be greater than in the group with a high status.

Conclusion

The evidence examined in this chapter shows that the majority of our respondents were of below average (but not of the lowest) economic and social status in the countryside before migration to Delhi.

In occupational terms, the majority of them were labourers. Most of those hired for wages were hired on a daily basis. The main reasons for leaving the pre-migration jobs were low income, lack of regular employment, incompatibility of skills and jobs in the rural setup and family reasons. The days of employment in the year before migration were below the norm. The literacy amongst our respondents was higher than the rural norm.

Of our respondents who were involved in agriculture, the proportion of marginal holdings was lower and the proportion of small holdings and semi-medium holdings higher compared with the norm. From this, it appears that the propensity to migrate was greatest not among the lowest stratum (marginal holdings), but among the strata just above the lowest (small and semi-medium holdings). Our typical agriculturist respondent came from household with small holdings and had a part of it leased in from others. A slightly higher proportion of the respondents were in debt than the rural norm.

The qualitative analysis also corroborates that the majority of our respondents were not from the lowest, but from just below average or the average strata.

The correlation results also corroborate the previous point in relation to status. The better off tended to be more educated and have fewer children. It also appears that people with a means of production, like bullocks and wells, tended to get employment in the village before migration.

Despite some evidence that relative deprivation in the areas of origin makes people ready to leave, what needs to be explained is why a much larger number of people of similar status and circumstances in rural areas do not leave. Deprivation is a necessary but not a sufficient condition for migration to take place. The presence in rural areas of a labour mass in poor conditions that can expect higher earnings in urban areas through their skills is no guarantee that migration would take place. Nor is the demand for labour a guarantee in itself. The demand for labour gets communicated to the sending areas through the 'culture of migration' – the channels of recruitment that bring labour to cities.

Thus, although presenting evidence that relative deprivation in the areas of origin makes people ready to leave, the next chapter analyses why a much larger number of people of similar status and circumstances in rural areas do not leave. Thus, this chapter sets the stage for exploring how a specific group of migrants get into particular jobs, which is the subject matter of the next chapter.

Notes

1 The respondents were requested to refer to a period of one year before migration while answering questions regarding their socioeconomic status. The migrants who met the criteria of selection are referred as criteria migrants throughout this book. For details of the criteria of selection, please see Chapter 2. The demographic and mobility profiles of the criteria migrants have been provided in Appendix B.

2 The significance level was 14 per cent. A comparison was made on the basis of two categories only: 'average' and 'below average'. The category 'above average' was excluded from the analysis because this was not a notable and reliable category and also because this was not at all differentiating the two groups.

3 Whereas the category 'Good economic position' was made on the basis of descriptions of economic position of the family as good, quite good, the category of 'average economic position' was made on the basis of the following descriptions: just alright, alright, all right, not very good, not particularly good, so-so, average, normal, keeping the pot boiling, just able to subsist. The category 'bad economic position' included the following descriptions: poor, poverty, difficult\difficulty, bad, bad and useless, weak, quite weak, not alright, miserable, miserable only, down-graded, downgrade, bit low,

not good, not so good, trouble, bit deteriorated, deteriorated, in a lot of mess, bit spoilt, spoilt, were not able to subsist. The category 'worse economic position' covered the following descriptions of a family's economic position: very poor, a lot of poverty, very bad, utterly bad, extremely bad, critical, very weak, very miserable, very downgrade, serious, very defeating, a lot of trouble, great trouble, pitiable, distressed, distressful, ragged, shattered, indebted. The category 'worst economic position' covered the following descriptions of the family's economic position: utter poverty, extreme poverty, worst, very critical, very much critical, helplessness, great helplessness, extremely miserable, completely miserable, absolutely miserable, very serious, very distressful, very ragged, very depressed.

References

GOI, Ministry of Labour and Employment (1991). *Indian labour year book.* New Delhi: India, Ministry of Labour and Employment, Government of India.

GOI, National Institute of Adult Education (1992). *Statistical database for literacy, Volume 1.* New Delhi: National Institute of Adult Education, Government of India.

Mohan, R. (1982). *The morphology of urbanisation in India: Some results from the 1981 census.* Paper presented in the seminar on Urbanisation and Planned Economic Development – Present and future perspectives, organised by the Centre for the Study of Regional Development, Jawaharlal Nehru University, New Delhi.

4 Channels of information, job expectation and the process of migration

Introduction

It was suggested in Chapter 3 that the existence of a mass of people in the countryside who are objectively ready to move out (the necessary condition of migration) is met by the demand for labour in urban areas (the sufficient condition of migration).

In this context, this chapter aims to examine the role of the channels of recruitment and to dig deeper into the mechanisms of migration in order to understand how a mass of people in the countryside who are objectively ready to move out is met by the demand for labour in urban areas. For this, it considers the pre-migration contacts of the migrants with the urban labour market through visits, acquaintances and the flow of information and advice from them; discusses whether migrants knew of job vacancies before migration and their assessment of the chances to get work in Delhi; examines the role of the family in the migration decision; considers how the migrant survived during the waiting period; provides information on all jobs that migrants did in Delhi, with special emphasis on various aspects of the first job; explores the noneconomic factors in migration; and considers some additional observations on rural to urban migration.

The chapter is divided into nine sections. The second section provides details of the pre-migration contacts of the migrants with the urban labour market through visits, acquaintances and the flow of information and advice from them. The third section discusses whether migrants knew of job vacancies before migration and their assessment of their chances to get work in Delhi. The fourth section examines the role of the family in the migration decision. The fifth section considers how the migrant survived during the waiting period. The sixth section provides information on all jobs that migrants did in Delhi, with special emphasis on various aspects of the first job. The seventh section explores the noneconomic factors in migration. The eighth section considers some additional observations on rural to urban migration. The ninth section concludes the discussion of this chapter.

Pre-migration urban visits, contacts, information and advice

This section examines how far the migrants had links with the urban area before they migrated. The first sub-section considers details of their pre-migration visits to Delhi. The second sub-section explores how many migrants had acquaintances in Delhi before they migrated to the city. The third sub-section tells whether the acquaintances gave any information or advice to the potential migrants and explores the patterns of information flow.

Visits

It was found that nearly one-third of the migrants had visited Delhi before they came to settle there. As Figure 4.1 shows, most of these had visited more than once.

   The migrant respondents who had visited more than once before they moved to Delhi were asked why they visited so often. The responses are summarised in Figure 4.2.

   It appears that three in five of the frequent visitors gave reasons related to the presence of their relatives in the city. The rest (two in five) gave reasons related to work. Among the former class of reasons, visiting the relatives was most promi-nent (47 per cent), followed by attendance at marriage (8 per cent) and staying with relatives (6 per cent). From among the latter class of reasons, 28 per cent of the frequent visitors had actually come to work earlier, 8 per cent came in search of work and 3 per cent to learn work.

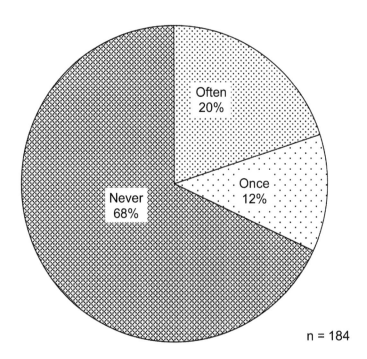

n = 184

Figure 4.1 Distribution of migrants by pre-migration visits to Delhi

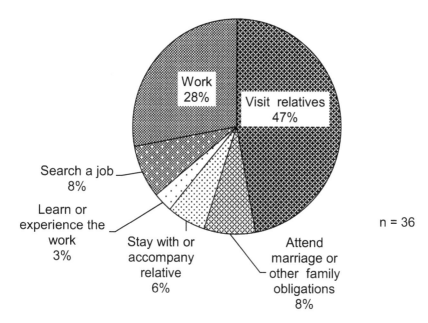

Figure 4.2 Reasons for visiting often

Information on the calendar month and year of visit, the purpose of the trip and the duration of stay were sought for those who had visited Delhi only once before migration.

Only about 55 per cent of them could recall the calendar month of their pre-migration visit. The distribution is given in Table A-4.1. Of those who could recall, there was strong evidence of summer and winter off-seasons in agriculture being the time when they did so. Of these two off-seasons, summer time was more prominent.

Table A-4.2 provides the distribution of respondents who visited Delhi only once before migration by the year of visit. It was discovered that the visits were highly concentrated in periods just before and after the 'Emergency' (1975–1977). This pattern seems to have an association with the pattern of migration as described in Appendix B.

Figure 4.3 presents the distribution of one-time visitors by the purpose of their visit. To visit and to stay with relatives were mentioned by only 15 per cent of these respondents. This is contrary to the case of those with multiple pre-migration visits for whom these were very dominant reasons.

These people were keen and explicit job searchers. Nine per cent said they had come to see Delhi in order to assess their chances of finding work. Five per cent came to learn/experience work and 27 per cent to search for a job.

'For pleasure trip' or to 'move around' were found to be euphemisms for a job search. Respondents giving these reasons were found suddenly saying: "Then, I saw a job opportunity and I took it!" With this, about 50 per cent of the one-time

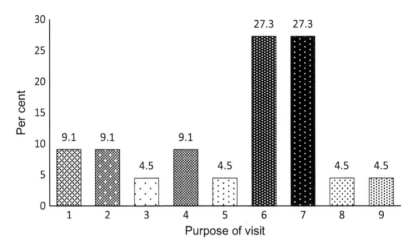

Figure 4.3 Purpose of pre-migration visit: percentage distribution of the one-time visitors

1: For pleasure trip/to move around   2: To visit (the relatives)
3: To stay with the relatives   4: To see Delhi (from work angle)
5: To learn work/experience   6: To search for a job
7: To work   8: To settle here   9: Other

visitors can be said to have come to search for a job. About 27 per cent said they had been to Delhi earlier as well in order to work there. That means that 77 per cent of those with one pre-migration visit knew something about the job market before they came to settle in Delhi.

About a quarter stayed up to a week, about half up to one month and most of them less than 6 months. On an average, the one-time pre-migration visitors to Delhi stayed for about a month (median) during the visit. The positive skewness of the distribution in Table A-4.3 indicates that the tendency was towards shorter-than-average trips.

In this sub-section, some differences between frequent and one-time visitors regarding the reasons for visiting were considered. It appears that the latter group were made up of more explicit job seekers. The one-time visitors often came to Delhi during off-seasons, mostly in the years around the 1975–1977 'Emergency' and stayed for a month on average.

Urban contacts

Most of the migrants in the present sample (95 per cent) knew somebody in Delhi before they moved there. Contrary to the simplicity and randomness of migration implied in many economic models, potential migrants were highly connected to the urban area. To explore this theme a little further, all the migrants who mentioned the presence of any urban contact were asked details about whom they knew and what work their acquaintances did. This information was noted for up to three contacts.

The most popular contact mentioned in the first place was a co-villager. However, family members and relatives together held the overall majority. The overwhelming dominance of what sociologists and anthropologists call *primary relations* (those based on kinship or due to belonging to the same village) is clear. *Secondary relations* (a friend or acquaintance not from the same village) accounted for only 5 per cent of the pre-migration acquaintance mentioned in the first place. Six per cent mentioned multiple contacts in the first instance during their response to the question.

Thirty per cent of respondents mentioned that they had a second acquaintance, and 10 per cent a third. The contacts mentioned in second and third places tended to be more relations of kith and kin and fewer co-villagers. One important thing is the more frequent mention of multiple acquaintances in the second and third instances.

A cross-tabulation shows that the migrants' first jobs were more likely to be similar to those of their pre-migration acquaintances. This holds true with respect to the acquaintances mentioned in the first and second place in the order of the up to three contacts noted by the researcher and not with respect to the ones mentioned in third place. Thus, it means the migrants tended to get their first jobs in the sectors in which their urban contacts were working.

This finding leads to the conclusion that not only did most of the migrants have at least one urban connection, but that they also tended to get jobs in the city in the sectors where their acquaintances were employed. It indicates the possibility of mechanisms carrying information about the demand for labour of particular skills and types to the workers who might be ready and able to do these jobs.

Information or advice from urban contacts

The respondents were asked whether they received any information or advice from their urban contacts. Three-fifths of the respondents received information or advice from the acquaintance who they named first. With regard to the acquaintance named in the second and third places, one-fifth of the respondents were in receipt of information or advice. The fact that such a large proportion of migrants received information and advice points to the fact that the connection with urban areas before migration was quite active.

The overall picture suggests that with rare exceptions of advice against migration, most of the information and advice flowing from the urban contacts was positive, informative, useful and assuring. In many cases (roughly one in ten), the respondents reported they were either brought along or called through a message by their urban contacts. For about one in six there was assurance from the urban contact that work would be found. A few (one in thirty) migrants, in fact, said that urban contacts had arranged jobs for them beforehand.

Apart from the generally positive advice for migration and the assurances of jobs, the most important thing to note is the information on the urban labour market. The kind of information that was being communicated included many aspects of life and work in the city. The essence of the information was that work of all sorts was available in Delhi, it was regular and better paid compared with rural areas, payment was made in cash, it was more formalised ("duty by duty", as one migrant put it) as opposed to the drudgery in the village (for example, in the work of a sweeper) and that the workers could earn more money in urban areas. Moreover, the information on the particular sectors travelled to the appropriate prospective migrants. For example, workers in different sectors, particularly those in the garment export sector, cleaning and construction described how they received the details of the kind of work, the rates and the basis of payment, as well as the situation regarding availability of jobs (i.e., if the work was flourishing or not).

One other thing observed was the importance of skills and education. There were numerous cases where the advice was that migrants must acquire a particular skill if he or she wanted to be successful. In fact, there were cases where the old-time migrants, who had moved to Delhi earlier than the respondents moved, offered to train the newly arrived migrants. It was particularly so in tailoring and sweeping. This was done through informal training at home or at the workplace. There were instances where the respondents received work trials by their urban contacts who had already been working as employees in Delhi.

Thus, it is reasonable to conclude that the migrants were well connected, well informed, well assured and often had their moves well planned.

Pre-migration knowledge of vacancies and chances to get work in Delhi

About 9 per cent of the respondents were offered jobs before they came to Delhi. How did the group that was offered jobs before coming to Delhi differ from those who did not? The t-test results show that the former had a significantly higher number of bullocks, horses or water-pump engines and animals. There is some evidence that among those working before migration, the duration of employment in the year before migration was higher in the case of the group who had arranged their jobs in Delhi before coming compared with the other group. These are the indications that the group was better off.

Questions regarding knowledge of the Delhi urban labour market were asked of those who did not have job offers before coming to Delhi (91 per cent of our sample). This section tries to assess it in two complementary ways. The first subsection is based on categorical questions to migrants about knowledge of job vacancies. The second sub-section provides an assessment of verbal accounts in response to an open-ended question.

Vacancies

The results indicate that of those who did not have a job offer, only a small proportion (one in twenty) knew about job vacancies before they came to Delhi.

All of those who said they knew about job vacancies before migration (nine respondents) were asked if they knew about any specific job vacancy. Two-thirds (six respondents) said they did. These migrants were asked what that particular job vacancy was.

Of six cases who knew about a particular job vacancy, three said it was a vacancy for a sweeper, and one each mentioned shopkeeping, peon and teacher in a 'spiritual school'. The channels seemed to be most active in the case of cleaning jobs. This was confirmed by the verbal account of the respondents in this occupation.

The news about a job vacancy came from close relatives – father, brother-in-law or first cousin – in the case of four respondents and from the co-villagers for the remaining two.

Chances to get work in Delhi

The previous half of the present section was based on straight questions about the migrants' knowledge of job vacancies. This part discusses the matter in more general terms. It is based on the narration of migrants who did not have a job offer before coming to Delhi in response to an open-ended question.

The respondents appeared quite realistic and methodical about the chances of getting work. Mostly the migrants were hopeful of getting work. This was reflected in the perception that other people were earning and hence they could also hope to. They were flexible – "ready to do whatever would be offered" as one of the migrants put succinctly. They had a definite idea of the kind of work they might get, usually based on the type and level of skill they possessed. This reflected a definite skill-led search. They had an idea of the skill in demand. One of the migrants summarised such an assessment: "[H]ouses are built everyday and a day worker is employed daily". They often had some idea of how they were going to get work (i.e., had the channels in mind). Even if they did not know the urban terminology before they migrated to Delhi, they had a feel and sense for it – for example, one migrant did not know what *beldari* (unskilled construction work) was, but he roughly knew that his skills were suited for this job. Migrants with education were realistic about its value. For example, one migrant with formal education but who was less confident of its use in getting a job said: "And what was there in Bihar education?" – meaning it was not of much value. Migrants realised that learning skills was more important in the urban labour market. Some of the migrants thought they 'would learn and then earn good money'. There is evidence that the migrants had definite plans in mind – the minimum was defined, had a particular job in mind – and had alternative plans in case the main plan failed. There were very few who did not have any idea. There was also evidence that the respondents had an idea about the length of the waiting period.

Attitudinal patterns of families towards migration to Delhi: an evidence of family strategy

Figure 4.4 presents the distribution of the migrants by the attitudes of their families towards migration.

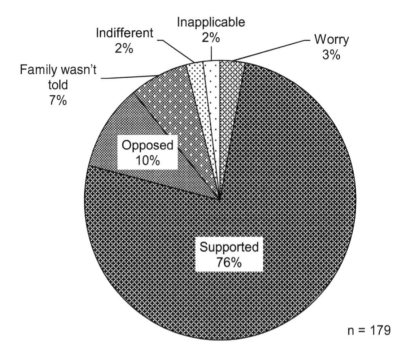

Figure 4.4 Family attitude to migration

In three-fourths of the cases, the family supported the move. One out of ten families was opposed.[1] About 7 per cent of respondents left without telling their families. Presuming that these were also the cases where families opposed the move and hence they had to leave, lack of family support can be inferred in 17 per cent of the cases. About 3 per cent of the families were worried and about 2 per cent were indifferent.

Despite diversity, the modes of help were quite simple. The migrants were given moral support as well as advice and ideas. The advice often reflected the need for them to migrate. The examples of particular patterns were the need to supplement earnings, diversify the earnings base of the family, find a solution to the problems of debt or economic difficulties or to strengthen the position, worry about the future of the family, etc. The forms of help were usually to provide uncooked food for a few days or weeks, cooked food for the journey and for the initial phase and money for fares and initial expenditures in the urban areas. The families sometimes borrowed money and even sold some asset – for example, a cow or a goat – to give money to the migrant. Support from the family was accompanied by the hope of remittances, respect and prestige associated with migration of a family member, the likelihood of repayment of the family debt and the hope that the migrant would share the responsibilities of the family. The patterns of advice in the cases of support indicate that the family strategy and view often governed the attitude towards migration. For example, observations such as "we will be well here and you go and exert yourself in Delhi" or the advice to be "careful with the mouth" (i.e., eat less and save more) are graphic examples of how the families advised the migrant and why they supported the move.

Because the cases of outright opposition are few, it would be sufficient here to state that the families with initial reservations about migration were usually worried about the security and safety of their members migrating to the city or about the level of help the family would subsequently receive from the migrant and the fear of losing his or her material or psychological support.

The survey results showed that three-fourths of the migrants were from parental families. Approximately 12.5 per cent came from extended families and 11 per cent from nuclear families. The fact that most of the families (nine of ten) were parental or extended suggests that the family strategy must have been an important factor in the sense of diversification of sources of income and risk aversion. The verbal accounts corroborate this observation.

If the migrant had children, there was a significant correlation between his age at migration and the age at which the respondent's first child was born. This corroborated the observations by respondents that the birth of a child induced them to move to increase their earnings. Another important point is that the people with more male children tended to stay longer in Delhi, leaving their children in the village. Presumably the male children of the respondents were considered more able to take up agricultural operations and other social responsibilities, leaving the adult males free to migrate – one of the ways in which the expansion of the family can be seen as leading to migration.

Evidence presented in this section strongly indicates the importance of family strategies in the process of rural to urban migration.

Patterns of job search, waiting and support in the urban labour market

It was noted earlier that 91 per cent of the respondents did not have any job offer before they came to Delhi. The present section looks at the patterns of job search, waiting and support for this group in order to discover the channels of recruitment associated with the process of migration.

The first sub-section considers the activities of migrants who started looking for jobs some time after arrival. The second sub-section looks at the waiting time for the first job. The third sub-section describes the survival strategies during the waiting period. The fourth sub-section examines the channels of recruitment in the first job. The fifth sub-section discusses the effectiveness of the various channels of recruitment in getting the first job in Delhi.

Beginnings on arrival

Figure 4.5 shows the distribution of migrants by the period they spent in Delhi before they started looking for a job.

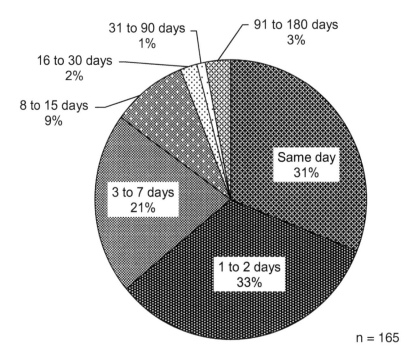

Figure 4.5 Job search start time
*Number of valid cases used = 165; missing cases excluded = 2

Four in five started looking for a job within one week of arrival and most within a fortnight. The migrants who did not start looking for a job on the day of their arrival in Delhi were asked what they did until they started the job search. Their replies are briefly reviewed in the following paragraphs.

A few of them reported they were tired and hence rested. The first reaction of most of the migrants was that they stayed idle (mostly at the places of relatives or other urban contacts) and went around to become familiar with the lifestyles and types or work there. But some of the detailed description of the activities of this 'idle period' reflected introspection, exploration and adjustment. It appears that many of the migrants (particularly those who had not had a pre-migration visit to Delhi) did not know what they described as "practices", "manners", "ways" and "place" and did not know "how to cross roads". They reported that they used to walk, wander and "see the place around". Apart from making these obvious but interesting observations, the migrants said that they used to visit fellow villagers or neighbours and express their desire to search for work. There were a few who helped their urban contacts with the jobs that the latter did or in household work like cooking food.

The conclusion is that not only did the migrants start looking for jobs soon after arrival, but also that even the time between arrival and job search was a period of moving towards the eventual job.

Waiting time

Figure 4.6 shows the distribution of those who had to wait for the first job in Delhi. Hence, it does not include the three respondents who got a job on the day of arrival.

The average waiting time was low. However, the dispersion was quite large. So, the arithmetic mean of 24.63 days (with a standard deviation of 48.04 and high positive skewness) was an overestimate of the average. Over half of the migrants got a job within a week of their arrival in Delhi, about three-quarters within a fortnight and 86 per cent got a job within a month. The results of our survey lend support to results from earlier studies of migrants in Delhi (Banerjee, 1986: 118–119; Suri, 1991: 250).

The cross-tabulation suggests that those who got their first job in the service sector had to wait longer compared with those in construction, garment factories and as artisans and craftspersons.

Survival strategies during the waiting period

Table 4.1 gives some idea of how migrants supported themselves during the waiting period and the percentages of respondents who mentioned different ways in which they sustained themselves. Some of the respondents mentioned more than one method and hence it does not add to 100.

There is strong evidence that about half of them received help from their families and relatives. They received support from the remaining family members in

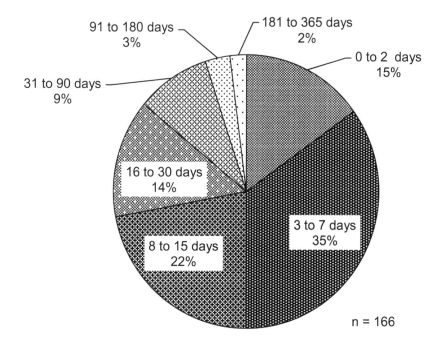

Figure 4.6 Waiting time

*Number of valid cases used = 166; one missing case excluded

Table 4.1 The method of support during the waiting period in Delhi*

	Method of support	Percentage of respondents mentioning the method
1	Past savings	3.9
2	Sold cattle/property in the village	1.9
3	Loan	20.0
4	Support from family in village	7.1
5	Brought food from the village	9.0
6	Family members' support in the city	11.0
7	Co-villager(s)' support in Delhi	15.5
8	Relatives' support in Delhi	34.2
9	Friends' support in Delhi	3.9
10	Help with domestic work of urban contact	4.5
11	Contractor arranged it	1.9
12	Other source	2.6

Valid cases 155   Missing cases 8

* *The sum does not add to 100 because of overlapping*

the countryside (7 per cent), from family members in the city (11 per cent) and from relatives in Delhi (34 per cent). Other more significant methods of support during the waiting period were the co-villagers' support in Delhi (16 per cent) and loans (20 per cent). Four per cent received friends' support in Delhi. Some helped their urban acquaintances with domestic work during the waiting period. About 4 per cent mentioned past savings, and 2 per cent sold their cattle and/or property in the village to meet their expenditures for migration.

An exercise was carried out to end the overlapping involved in Table 4.1 by assessing the order of importance of methods in the cases of respondents who had more than one method of support during the waiting period in Delhi. Through recoding, the twelve methods of support were reduced into four groups. The results are presented in Figure 4.7.

Methods of job search

Table 4.2 gives an idea of the methods that were tried. Usually more than one method was used while searching for the first job in Delhi. The search efforts of the urban contacts and approaching factories, work sites, etc., were the most prominent methods, being mentioned by 60 per cent and 54 per cent of the respondents, respectively.

The next most important methods used were jobbers (or subcontractors; 26 per cent) and presenting themselves at the *chowk* (market square) (15 per cent). The institutionalised methods like employment exchanges and newspapers were relatively less important, being tried by 7 per cent and 4 per cent of the respondents, respectively.

'Other methods' were mentioned by about 4 per cent. These were mixed and deserve mention. Out of six such cases two said it was sheer luck (*God's grace*)

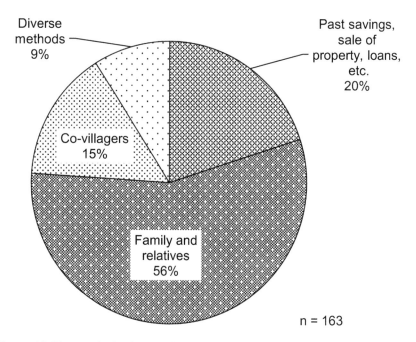

Figure 4.7 First 'methods of support' group during the waiting period

Table 4.2 The methods used for searching for the first job in Delhi

	Method	Frequency	Percentage of respondents mentioning the method
1	Jobbers	44	26.3
2	Private employment agency	0	0.0
3	Referrals	2	1.2
4	Information about 'impending recruitment'	1	0.6
5	Radio/television	1	0.6
6	Newspapers	6	3.6
7	Employment exchange	12	7.2
8	Search efforts of urban contacts	95	56.9
9	Approaching factories, worksites, etc.	90	53.4
10	*Chowk* (market square)	25	15.0
11	Tried to set up business	9	5.4
12	Other methods	6	3.6

(n = 167)

that they got in touch with the employers; one was invited by a "God-man" for recruitment as a "Brahman teacher". One of the female respondents said that she was squatting near a rich residential area and a "bungalow resident" (*kothiwala*) came to recruit her for household work. One of the others mentioned that he used to go with his brother to a dyeing factory where the latter worked and the brother told him how the work was to be done. And the last respondent said he simply rented a bicycle and started the rounds to buy scrap, which implies a considerable prior knowledge of the occupation as well as the area.

In order to remove the overlapping evident in Tables 4.3 and 4.4, an exercise was carried out to determine the order of importance of the channels in the cases of respondents who used more than one channel. The twelve categories of Table 4.3 were collapsed into five and the results are given in Figure 4.8

Table 4.3 The channels of recruitment for the first job in Delhi

	Channel	*Frequency*	*Per cent*
1	Jobbers	37	20.1
2	Private employment agency	0	0.0
3	Referrals	2	1.1
4	Information about 'impending recruitment'	0	0.0
5	Radio/television	0	0.0
6	Newspapers	1	0.5
7	Employment exchange	2	1.1
8	Search efforts of urban contacts	124	67.4
9	Approaching factories, worksites, etc.	22	11.9
10	*Chowk* (market square)	16	8.7
11	Tried to set up business	3	1.6
12	Other channels	3	1.6

(n = 184)

Note: Some of the respondents used more than one channel. The respondents who were offered jobs before coming Delhi are included in this table.

Table 4.4 The index of effectiveness* of the various channels of recruitment in getting the first job in Delhi

	Channel	*Found useful by*	*Tried by*	*Index*
1	Jobbers	36	44	88.82
2	Private employment agency	0	0	–
3	Referrals/recommendations from references	2	2	100.00
4	Information about 'impending recruitment'	0	1	0.00
5	Radio/television	0	1	0.00
6	Newspapers	1	6	16.67
7	Employment exchange	2	12	16.67
8	Search efforts of urban contacts	108	95	113.68**
9	Approaching factories, worksites, etc.	21	90	23.33
10	*Chowk* (market square)	16	25	64.00
11	Tried to set up business	3	9	33.33
12	Other channels	3	6	33.33

(n = 167)

Note: Some of the respondents used more than one channel. The respondents who were offered jobs before coming to Delhi are excluded.

* *Percentage ratio of the number who found a particular method useful by the number who had tried it.*
** *It seems the respondents did not realise they tried this method. It came 'automatically'!*

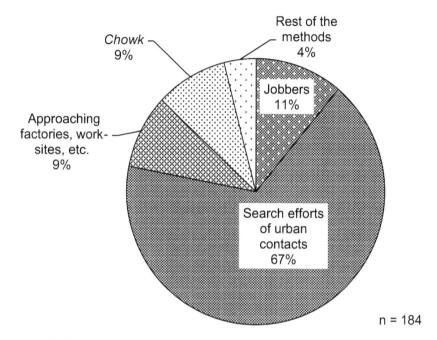

Figure 4.8 First 'channel of recruitment' (grouped) to the first job in Delhi

How useful were the different methods of job searching?

A look at Tables 4.2 and 4.3 gives only a partial idea of the difference in the effectiveness of various methods. This is crude judgement because these two tables are not comparable. The reason is that whereas the former is restricted to the 167 migrants who did not have a job offer before coming to Delhi, the latter includes those migrants who had their jobs arranged before migration. For the first group who came after finding a job, the role of urban contacts' search efforts and jobbers seems to be more important. This is clear from a comparison of the absolute figures for these methods in Tables 4.3 and 4.4.

As for the second group, Table 4.4 and Figure 4.9 present an index of effectiveness for each of the methods, which a comparison of the different methods.

The most used of all the methods was the search efforts of the urban contacts. Some respondents did not say they tried this method to search for a job, and yet they found a job through this method. Apparently, it is so prevalent and informal that some people take it as a given and do not mention it as one of the methods tried. The next most used method – approaching factories, worksites, etc. – was a dismal performer. This method was often used by migrants who were searching for jobs, but the number who actually got work through this rather direct method is relatively small. Jobbers and *chowk* were apparently quite successful methods according to this index, with the success rate being 89 and 64 per cent, respectively. Most of the other methods used were all less effective. Private employment

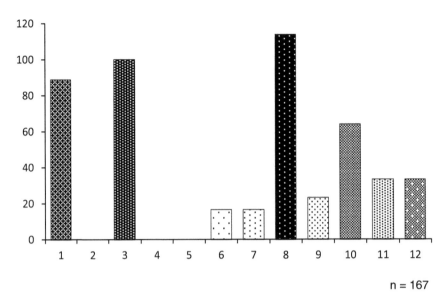

n = 167

Figure 4.9 Channels of recruitment – an index of their effectiveness

*The index is the % ratio of those who found a particular method useful by the number who tried it. For a description of channels indicated by numbers 1 to 12, see Table 4.4.

agencies, radio/television and newspapers were less used and less effective methods. The only method used by a very few but that was very effective was referrals, that is, recommendations from more resourceful people to the employer or manager for consideration.

It is not possible to do a chi-square test of the waiting period with each of the channels due to the 'expected frequency' problem. However, it is possible to do it with respect to the most used methods, viz, jobbers, search efforts of the urban contacts, approaching factories and worksites, etc., *chowk* and other channels. The results indicate that there was no significant difference between those using any particular one of these channels and those not using it with respect to the waiting time (the time from the start of the job search until a job was found in Delhi).

The evidence presented in this section shows labour demand is buoyant for the sort of skills these migrants bring. Contrary to the 'push' thesis, they are not driven from rural unemployment to urban unemployment.

Jobs in Delhi

Information was also collected on respondents' post-migration occupational history to see how migrants used skills to get jobs and in turn acquired skills from jobs and if and how they switched from one job to the other as time passed.

After going into detail on the migrants' first job in Delhi (such as the sectors of employment, the method of payment, the duration of the first job and the reasons for ending it), the first sub-section discusses why the construction sector was the main entry point into the urban labour market for migrant respondents of this study. The other two sub-sections give some idea of the subsequent occupations of the respondents.

The first job

This sub-section gives details about important aspects of the first jobs of the migrants in Delhi. It is divided into five parts. The first part of this sub-section points out the sectors where the migrants found their first job in Delhi, and the second part describes the methods of payment. About 86 per cent of the respondents had left their first jobs in Delhi before the being surveyed. For these migrants who had left their first jobs before the survey, the third part of this sub-section describes the duration of the first job, and the fourth part puts forth the reasons for ending the first job. The last part of this sub-section discusses why the construction sector was the sector of entry into the job market for the respondents of this survey.

Sectors of the first job

Table A-4.4 presents the details and Figure 4.10 gives an idea about the sectors where the migrants in Delhi found their first jobs.

The construction sector (Occupation codes 3 to 5 in Table A-4.4) was the biggest employer of migrants. It employed 37.5 per cent of them, mostly as unskilled workers. It was followed by the service sector (Occupation codes

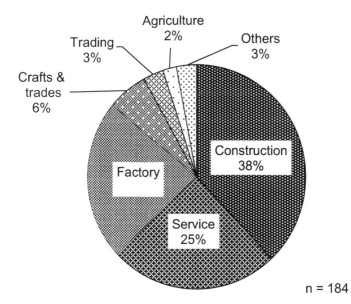

Figure 4.10 Sectors of migrants' entry into the urban labour market

14 to 20 in Table A-4.4), which accounted for about 25 per cent of the jobs of the new migrants. The factory sector (Occupation codes 6 to 10 in Table A-4.4) was closely behind the service sector. It accounted for about 23 per cent of the jobs of the new migrants. The trading sector provided employment to about 3 per cent. Six per cent worked as crafts and tradespersons. Two per cent worked in the agricultural sector. The other jobs like porter, chipping firewood, laying railway tracks, hawking for or picking up scrap paper or used bottles, para-medic and one describing himself as "assistant to prostitutes" accounted for the remaining 3 per cent of the first jobs.

Method of payment in the first job

The question on the method of payment was not applicable for thirteen respond-ents (about 7 per cent of the migrants) because they were not hired workers but were self-employed. Seven of them were vendors, two shopkeepers, one crafts-man, one animal husbandry and two 'other' occupations – one a scrap buyer and the other a paramedic.

Figure 4.11 presents the distribution for those to whom this question was rele-vant. Roughly half were paid by the day – 43 per cent were employed as casual daily labourers and about 5 per cent were regular workers employed on a daily basis.

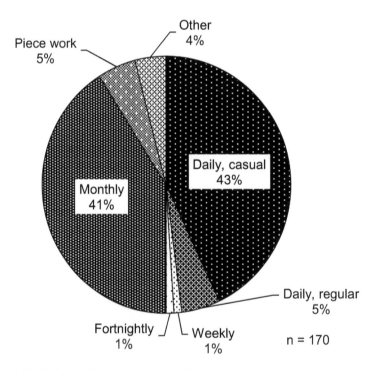

Figure 4.11 Methods of payment in the first job

*Number of valid cases used = 170; one missing case; excluded thirteen migrants who were self-employed and hence the question on method of payment was inapplicable to them

   The monthly basis was almost equal in importance to casual daily employment. Forty-one per cent of the new migrants' first jobs were paid on a monthly basis. Very few were employed on a weekly or fortnightly payment basis. However, piece work (work on the basis of piece rate) was important – about 5 per cent of the migrants (mostly tailors) were paid on this basis. 'Other methods' were reported by 3.5 per cent of the respondents. These 'other methods' included methods such as work in lieu of training, work for a stipend or basic expenditures and payment by number of pieces after deducting the commission.

   The greater proportion of wage workers in pre-migration rural jobs were employed on a daily basis (65 per cent) and a smaller proportion on a monthly basis (16 per cent) compared with urban jobs. This corroborates the description by the migrants that the post-migration jobs in Delhi were more regular and secure than the rural wage jobs.

Duration in first job

About 86 per cent had left their first jobs before being surveyed. Only 14 per cent were still in their first jobs. The total duration of the first job was ascertained for all the migrants.

   Table A-4.5 and Figure 4.12 present the results. For about two in ten it was less than one month. For a quarter, it was less than 3 months. For about half, it was less

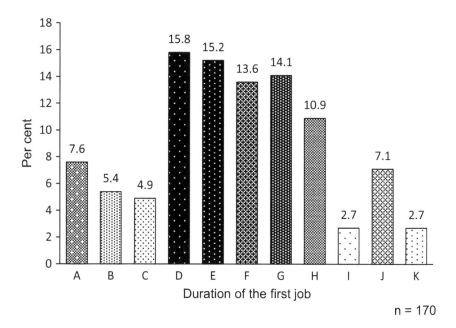

n = 170

Figure 4.12 Percentage distribution of migrants by the duration of the first job (months)

*(DURATION IN MONTHS) A: Up to 0.23; B: 0.24 to 0.50; C: 0.51 to 1.00; D: 1.01 to 3.00; E: 3.01 to 6.00; F: 6.01 to 12.00; G: 12.01 to 36.00; H: 36.01 to 72.00; I: 72.01 to 108.00; J: 108.01 to 180.00; K: 180.01 to 240.00

than 12 months. Up to three-quarters had less than 36 months in their first job. The average was 7.5 months (median).

Reasons for ending the first job

Eighty-six per cent of respondents had left their first jobs before this survey. They were asked the main reason for ending the first job. Table 4.5 provides the details.

If individual factors are considered, low income was the single most important reason for quitting. It was mentioned by 23 per cent of the respondents. Strictly speaking, the grouping is not possible because of the multiplicity of answers, and the sum in Table 4.5 does not add up to 100.

However, it is possible to make some generalisations. If the reasons are grouped into broad categories, being laid off (Reason codes 16 to 18 in Table 4.5) comes at the top, mentioned by 29 per cent of the respondents who had left their first jobs before the survey, followed by adverse factors associated with the employment (Reason codes 5, 6, 8, 9 and 10 in Table 4.5) that were mentioned by 27 per cent of the respondents. The next important group

Table 4.5 The main reasons for ending the first job in Delhi

	Reason	(Valid) Percentage of respondents mentioning the reason
1	Have not stopped	0.0
2	Got promotion/regularisation	1.3
3	Low income	22.3
4	Paid off debt	0.0
5	Unpunctual payment/cheating	3.2
6	Insecure nature of job	1.9
7	Went to village/absenteeism	12.1
8	Poor working conditions	14.6
9	Illness/accident related to job	7.0
10	Quarrel/dispute with the employer	3.8
11	To take another job	15.3
12	Apprenticeship/training over	5.7
13	To join training/to learn work	1.9
14	To set up business	0.6
15	Quit for other reasons	5.7
16	Laid off, no work	18.5
17	Laid off, factory/shop closed	4.5
18	Laid off, other reasons	5.7
19	Job completed	0.0
20	To get married	0.0
21	Pregnant	0.0
22	Wanted to move to another area	0.0
23	Other reasons	1.9

(n = 157)

* *Sum does not add up to 100.*

consists of positive factors like getting another job after acquiring new skills in the first job (Reason codes 2 and 11 to 14 in Table 4.5) that were mentioned by 25 per cent of the respondents who had left their first jobs before this survey. Absenteeism (Reason code 7 in Table 4.5), generally with the purpose of going to the village due to a work responsibility there and also due to lack of provision for holidays from the job, was mentioned by 12 per cent. The other reasons – like a family feud or chaos (like the riot that followed the then Prime Minister Mrs Indira Gandhi's assassination in 1984) were mentioned by about 2 per cent of the respondents. An alternative scheme to the one described earlier is to group factors as follows: laid off (mentioned in at least one of the reasons 16 to 18), adverse factors (mentioned in at least one of the reasons 5, 6, 8, 9 and 10) and positive factors (mentioned in at least one of the reasons 2, 11 to 14). The result is 29 per cent, 27 per cent and 18 per cent, respectively. This indicates that first jobs are usually the ones that end more as a result of adverse factors than positive ones.

In order to remove the overlapping manifest in Table 4.5, an exercise was carried out to determine the order of importance of the main reasons for ending the first job in the cases of respondents who mentioned more than one reason. The twenty-three categories of Table 4.5 were collapsed into five 'reason groups' for ending the first job in Delhi, and the results are shown in Figure 4.13.

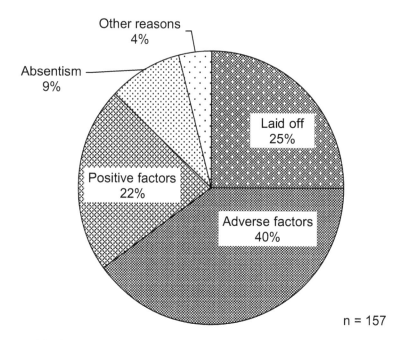

n = 157

Figure 4.13 First reason (group) for ending the first job in Delhi

From this it can be concluded that in the beginning, the migrants tended to get jobs that were less remunerative, had poor working conditions and often ended more as a result of negative conditions than positive ones. But it was equally likely that the jobs ended with the migrants having gained some skill and, as a result of it, they were in a better position to get another job which was at least as good as, if not better than, the first.

Why was the construction sector the entry point?

The results discussed in Chapter 3 indicate that the migrants from below-average families were more likely to have their first jobs in construction and service sectors, those from average families were more likely to be in the garment factories and those from above-average families were more likely to be in the nongarment factories.

Two points can be made:

1   Migrants from a low socioeconomic status and with low education levels matched the predominantly unskilled nature of the construction-sector jobs. Their relatively low socioeconomic status made them particularly suitable for the unskilled construction jobs, which are relatively hard and low paying. Piore's (1979: 17) description of migrant job characteristics would be particularly helpful in this interpretation.
2   Due to the low technology and labour-intensive nature of the unskilled construction jobs, there was more labour demand in this sector.

Subsequent jobs

All the later jobs, mainly understood in the sense of different occupations after the first, were recorded. The distribution of those who took up their second job is given in Table A-4.6. The regrouping by sectors is shown in Figure 4.14.

Compared to the distribution of the first jobs, here the construction sector lost 20 percentage points. Its position slipped to third place after the service and factory sectors.

Table A-4.7 and Figure 4.15 show the distribution of those who took up their third job in Delhi.

The share of the factory sector is now at the top. The construction and service sectors have an equal share. The construction sector improved its importance compared with the second job. However, within this sector, in the case of respondents doing their third job, the share of semi-skilled workers increased compared with the unskilled workers. Regarding the change from the first to the second and the third job, it can be observed that the importance of garments in the factory sector increased compared with the nongarment part of it.

Migrants changing jobs more often

An insignificant number of respondents changed jobs more than twice. The important thing to note about these frequent job changers is that they tended to switch

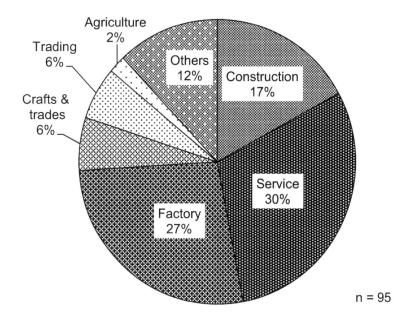

Figure 4.14 Sectors of the second job

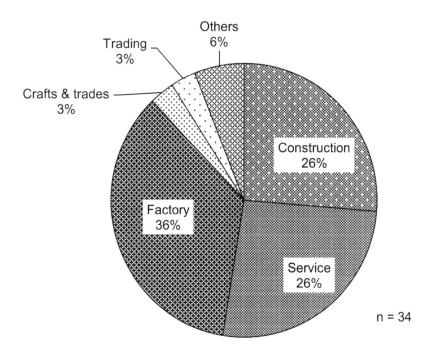

Figure 4.15 Sectors of the third job

to more skilled jobs. Table A-4.8 provides the details of fourth job of migrants. Only two migrants did a fifth job in Delhi – one as a helper in a nongarment factory and the other in the service sector. The sixth and seventh jobs were done by one person. The jobs were a semi-skilled garment factory job and shopkeeping, respectively.

Why not work in the village?

It is increasingly accepted that noneconomic considerations are important in migration decisions. To analyse these possible factors, all the respondents were asked if they would prefer to live in the village for the income and job similar to theirs when they joined their first job. Those replying in the negative were asked to state the reasons for it. The first sub-section explores why a similar income would not move a migrant back to the village; the second sub-section explores why a migrant would not do a similar job in the village.

Would they settle for a similar income in the village?

In the present sample survey, 91 per cent of the migrants said they would prefer to live in their villages if they could earn the same income as they earned in their first job in the city. The remaining 9 per cent said they would not. So, about one in ten would not go to the village even if they could earn the same income. The latter group (consisting of seventeen respondents) was asked the reasons for preferring not to live in the village even if they could earn the same income as they earned in their first job in the city. The results are presented in Table 4.6.

About half of the respondents said that in the city they were relatively free from the effects of social factors such as family feuds, social oppression and the considerations of caste and religion that bothered them in rural areas.

The wish to move to another area and the presence of other family members in the city were also important factors, which shows the relative attraction of the city. The category 'other reason', which accounted for 19 per cent, included factors such as the complaint that jobs in the village could be found only through favours,

Table 4.6 Reasons for not preferring to live in the village

Reason	Valid per cent	Cumulative per cent
Family feud	25.0	25.0
Social oppression/lawlessness	25.0	50.0
Wanted to move to another area	18.8	68.8
Other family member/relative lived here	12.5	81.3
Other reasons	18.8	100.0
	100.0	

Valid cases: 16 Missing cases: 1

there were insufficient places to live and the perception that in the city, even a low income is acceptable due to the benefits of training.

A t-test exercise was carried out to find if those who would be ready to live in their village for an income similar to what they received in their first job in Delhi differed from the ones who would not be ready to do so. It appears that the only significant difference that could be seen was regarding the ownership of bicycles and the number of children in the case of married migrants. The latter group scales better in terms of the ownership of bicycles, whereas the former group tended to have more children.

From among the people who had anything to do with land, the group which would not settle for the same income in the village had significantly higher pre-migration income from leasing-out, shopkeeping/vending and *naukari* ('service'). This gives a clear indication that this group had more diverse sources of income and a lower stake in agriculture as far as doing the job in the village was concerned.

The chi-square test results show that the latter group was not significantly different from the first in terms of the most important reasons for migration or the fact of having land or not. However, those describing their families as below average compared with the other families in the village tended to be more ready to go back.

Of those who were willing to settle in the village for the same income as they received in Delhi, significantly fewer had visited Delhi before migration compared with those who did not want to go back. This result can be interpreted due to the less connectivity with and lesser appreciation for the city life on the part of these migrants who were less exposed to the city life before migration. The group wanting to stay in the city was significantly more likely to have acquired the ability to read and been educated compared with the group willing to settle in the village for the income of their first job.

Cross-tabulation indicates that even among those who were ready to go back to the village, there were proportionately fewer ready to do a job in the village which was similar to their first job in Delhi. This group, which had a relatively better pre-migration economic status compared with fellow villagers, found the city more attractive due to family and social networks and their own wish to acquire a skill. They did not want to go back to the village for that would mean social and cultural deprivation.

Would they mind doing a similar job in the village?

About one in ten said they would not be prepared to do in the village a job similar to their first job in Delhi. From t-test results it emerges that the ones who were not ready to do a similar job in the village were better off in terms of the ownership of bicycles or radios. Chi-square results show that there was no significant difference between the two groups regarding their having an ability to read and having been to school. Cross-tabulation analysis suggests that those below average were more likely to do a similar job in the village. Those who were not willing to do a similar job in the village were more likely to have visited Delhi before migration compared with those who were willing.

Table 4.7 presents the reasons for not doing a similar job in the village. About three in ten said they would feel shame in doing a similar job in the village (status

Table 4.7 Reasons for not doing a similar job in the village

Reason	Valid per cent	Cumulative per cent
Would feel shy/shame	29.4	29.4
Well settled here	17.6	47.1
Family feud	5.9	52.9
Social oppression/landlessness	11.8	64.7
Wanted to move to another area	11.8	76.5
Other reasons	23.5	100.0
	100.0	

Valid cases: 17 Missing cases: 2

consciousness). This matched closely with their better social and economic status before migration. Family feuds and social oppression accounted for two out of ten cases.

Roughly two in ten said they would not do the same job in the village because they were well settled in the city, and one in ten said they wanted to move to another area. Other reasons such as a less lucrative job and lack of facilities in the village accounted for a quarter of such cases. The reasons described earlier indicate a positive bias on the part of this group towards urban jobs.

Additional observations on the process of migration

This section considers the responses of the migrants at different points during the structured interviews in this survey where they expressed their reasons for migration. The first sub-section is based on the results of a direct question during the listing survey. The main questionnaire of the survey allowed for a spontaneous remark, and there was a direct question to conclude the detailed interview. They are discussed in the second and third sub-sections, respectively.

Stated reasons for migration

Towards the end of the listing survey, all the respondents born outside Delhi (and not only the criteria migrants) were asked to give the most important reason for migration to Delhi. The results are given in the Table 4.8.

The job search and associational migration were the most important factors. The job search could be seen to have its causation in other factors mentioned in the table, like the insufficiency of work, unsatisfactory nature of work, unemployment and irregularity of work.

These comments apply to all the migrants. As mentioned in Chapter 2, one of the standards for choosing the criteria migrants was that they must have come in search of a job. The distribution of these respondents by the most important reason for migration is given in Table 4.9.

Because the bias is deliberately towards the economic factors, the pattern is different. A look at Table 4.9 reveals that with the exception of reasons 8, 9 and

Table 4.8 Most important reason for migration

Code	Reason	Per cent
2	In search of a job	0.2
3	Work was insufficient to support the family	7.2
4	Nature of the work unsatisfactory	1.6
5	Unemployment	4.0
6	Irregularity of work	0.9
8	To learn a skill	2.0
9	To seek better job/income	4.3
10	Offered better job/income	1.3
11	Landlessness	0.9
13	Poverty	5.6
14	Economic difficulty	0.9
15	Indebtedness	1.8
16	Bought land/business in Delhi	0.9
17	To get education for self	0.4
19	To get married	0.2
20	To accompany the family	15.5
21	Family/social feud in the previous place of residence	1.3
22	Caste violence/social oppression	0.2
23	Family tragedy	0.2
26	Illness	0.9
27	Natural calamities	7.8
28	Other reasons	2.7
		100.0

(n = 446)

Table 4.9 The most important reason for migration (criteria migrants)

Code	Reason	Per cent
2	In search of a job	50.0
3	Work was insufficient to support the family	11.4
4	Nature of the work unsatisfactory	2.2
5	Unemployment	4.9
6	Irregularity of work	1.1
8	To learn skill	0.5
9	To seek better job/income	7.6
10	Offered better job/income	1.6
11	Landlessness	1.6
13	Poverty	9.8
14	Economic difficulty	2.2
15	Indebtedness	3.3
16	Bought land/business in Delhi	0.5
21	Family/social feuds in the previous place of residence	0.5
22	Caste violence/social oppression	0.5
23	Family tragedy	0.5
27	Natural calamities	0.5
28	Other reasons	1.1
		100.0

(n = 184)

10 that account for 10 per cent of the criteria migrants' most important reason for migration, all other reasons are related to the job search or the causes that led to the job search.

The twenty-eight codes used in Table 4.9 were reduced to four categories as detailed at serial number 3 in Table G1 of Appendix G that provides details relating to the 'reduced dataset'. If 'in search of job' is considered to be 'neutral,' the results show a predominance of village job-related negative factors. Figure 4.16 presents the results more succinctly. The conclusion one can draw is that the negative village factors are the facilitating factor or the necessary conditions of migration.

Spontaneous remarks on migration

At the beginning of each main interview, the opening remark of the interviewer was followed by a deliberate pause to allow for any spontaneous remark from the respondents. The technique was successful because it evoked spontaneous remarks from about two-thirds of the respondents.

At the same time, there was a vast diversity of concerns. A female respondent had feared the train journey while travelling alone and hence said: "There was no problem in coming from home. Someone occupied a seat and no jostling took place". However, such concerns were not equally frightening to others, most of whom were males. Most of the respondents described how the unavailability

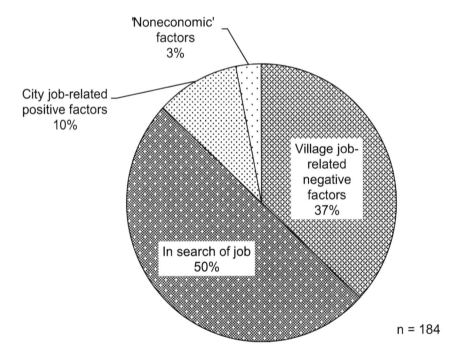

Figure 4.16 The most important reason for migration

or insufficiency of work in the village and lack of land or property made their position difficult in the village and so they came in search of a job. These early remarks emphasised the conditions at origin.

The landless agricultural labourers as a group tended to be more ready to leave. Aside from having no land or property, the cycles of low and high demand for their labour in the countryside made their lives not only economically difficult, but also socially vulnerable. For example, an agricultural worker mentioned that whereas the lean season would mean lack of income, the busy season would send the competing landlords and rich farmers rushing to his thatch house, sometimes applying brute force to pressure him into working for them. He said:

> My main problem, however, was that the people used to trouble me. Four people would come at a time. When the work started simultaneously, then the people would trouble – would trouble very much. (They) would threaten to beat me up, would storm the house and would abuse me. I wondered what to do in such conditions. It was because of this that I moved here.

Similar trouble was described by a person who, as a child labourer, had to do work which was very hard for his age until a friend of his said: "No. How long will you continue to suffer kicks like this? Come with me, I will get you work somewhere".

On the other hand, some people equally emphasised their problems at the origin and possibilities at the destination. A typical example is the following remark:

> My parents died while I was studying. Due to the economic hardship, I kept on wandering in my own district, looking for a job (*naukari*); I was getting small jobs that were not sufficient to subsist. That's why I had to come here. Somebody told me that the work of stitching clothes for export was flourishing and was well-paid. That's why I came to Delhi and started working in the 'export line'.

The gist of these subjective responses corroborates the main findings regarding pre-migration socioeconomic status and channels of recruitment given in Chapter 3 and the present chapter. It also matches the information received from the earlier question on the reasons for moving to Delhi, which has been discussed in the preceding sub-section.

The reasons on balance

A neat summary of most of the responses to the question "Looking on balance, why did you come?" is captured in a comment by one of the respondents: "The heart of the matter (was) work. If one can't meet expenses, what can one do?" Most of the respondents mentioned the need for a job and the conditions that made them think about the city. It seems from a reading of the responses that although the unavailability or insufficiency of work in the village might have been a necessary factor that made them think beyond their village, the possibility of a city job was the deciding factor that finally moved them. This direct question at the end of the interview brought the responses, which match and corroborate the findings of this study presented in Chapter 3 and the present chapter.

Conclusion

The evidence that a significant proportion of the respondents had visited Delhi before migration, most of them knew somebody in Delhi and the vast majority received information and advice from their contacts – many were brought along and a few were even given a work trial – goes to show that the connection with the urban area was quite active before migration.

The need to supplement earnings, diversify the earnings base of the family, find a solution to the problems of debt or economic difficulties or to strengthen their position, worry about the future of the family, etc., were the main concerns of the families. The family often provided food, fares and initial expenditures. These elements show the importance of family strategies in the process of rural to urban migration.

A few came with jobs arranged beforehand and the rest searched for jobs on arrival. The migrants had a realistic idea before arrival regarding what to look for in the urban job market and what to expect. The existence of close contacts resulted in an early start in job searching. After arrival, the time before the job search started was often used to learn the 'manners' of urban areas. The waiting period for the first jobs was a week for over half of the migrants, and 86 per cent got a job within one month.

The migrants received help from families, relatives, co-villagers and friends during the waiting period. They also used savings and found other ways to survive during this period.

They mainly got the first job through the search efforts of urban contacts and jobbers. The labour *chowk* was often the way to get unskilled construction jobs. The finding that migrants often got jobs in the sectors where their acquaintances worked corroborated the importance of the fact that the migrants had contacts in Delhi before they moved to the city.

The main sectors of migrants' entry into the Delhi labour market were construction, service, and factory, respectively. The construction sector emerges as the entry point for two-fifths of the migrants. Usually migrants from low socio-economic status and with low education started in unskilled construction jobs. Moreover, the low technology and labour-intensive nature of this work meant there was more demand for labour in this sector compared with others.

Migrants tended to leave their first jobs between 6 months and a year after starting. The first jobs often ended due to negative factors such as low remuneration, poor working conditions and being laid off. In later jobs, the service and factory sectors became more prominent. Within the construction sector in subsequent jobs, the share of skilled workers increased compared with unskilled ones.

Although most of the migrants would go back to their village for the same income or a similar job as in Delhi, about one in ten would not. The latter group was relatively better off before migration, and social factors and status consciousness were important issues for them.

It has been discovered that this majority group of the economically deprived would have rather worked and stayed in the village if they had a similar income and would not have cared for the social shame of doing any work in the village. When the opportunity of work arose in the urban areas and they learned of it, they were ready to move. However, a small group of the relatively better-off migrants would rather not go to the village and would not do in the village the work they did in the urban areas. These were the ones who had a relatively higher level of living in rural areas compared with other families. This group was deprived socially and culturally rather than economically.

On balance, it emerges that the possibility of getting a city job was the critical factor in their decision to move, and thus recruitment in the urban labour market is decisive in migration. Whether the pattern of change over time – in location, job and skill of migrants and in their retrospective look on why they migrated to Delhi – confirms or contradicts this thesis is the subject of the next chapter.

Note

1 The three migrants to whom the question on the attitude of the family was not asked were the only members in the family in the village and hence they thought this question was inapplicable to them. The attitude could not be ascertained for five cases (3 per cent of the sample).

References

Banerjee, B. (1986). *Rural to urban migration and the urban labour market: A case study of Delhi*. Delhi: Himalaya Publishing House.

Piore, M.J. (1979). *Birds of passage: Migrant labour and industrial societies*. Cambridge: Cambridge University Press.

Suri, P. (1991). *Housing for the urban poor: People's needs, priorities and government response – Case study of Delhi*. Unpublished doctoral thesis, School of Planning and Architecture, New Delhi.

5   Retrospective on the process of migration two decades later

Introduction

It is not merely misery in the countryside but also the demand for labour in urban areas communicated through channels of recruitment that determines rural to urban migration – this is the conclusion that emerges from the results reported in Chapters 3 and 4. In this context, the present chapter examines whether the pattern of change over time – in location, job and skill of migrants, as well as in their reflection on why they migrated to Delhi – confirms or contradicts the decisive role of labour demand in explaining migration. For this purpose, the chapter brings out changes in location, as well as demographic and occupational profiles of the respondents nearly two decades since the first sample survey was undertaken in 1992.

The prevalent models of migration, as well as policies, often assume migration to be a one-way ticket. Such assumptions often go unchallenged. The next section examines this assumption with the help of data on where the criterion migrants were two decades after they were initially interviewed in Delhi. The third section looks at occupational status as well as occupational mobility of the respondents. It does so in an intensive and focused manner by restricting itself only to the first city job and the current city job. It specifically and directly addresses the issue of whether the respondents experienced any occupational mobility during their stay in Delhi. With respect to those who in 2009 were in the same job as they were in 1992, the fourth section describes what changed in their jobs over these two decades. With respect to the respondents who in 2009 were in jobs different from those they were in 1992, the fifth section describes how their new jobs differed from their old jobs. The sixth examines if the migrants acquired any skill or education over the period. The seventh section provides a brief description of those who were not working in 2009. The eighth section considers some additional observations on rural to urban migration with the objective of uncovering any changes over these two decades in the migrants' reflection on their migration to Delhi. The final section concludes the chapter.

Whereabouts in 2009

The demographic profile of all 184 criterion migrants on the basis of the sample survey in 1992 was discussed in Chapter 2 and Appendix B. The present section presents information regarding the whereabouts of the criterion migrants in 2009.

Current updated status regarding location

As presented in Figure 5.1, whereas the whereabouts of nearly 7 per cent of the 184 criterion migrants could not be ascertained, 11 per cent were reported to be dead.

We can exclude these 18 per cent and look at the location of the remaining 152 criterion migrants who were living and whose whereabouts could be found out during the resurvey in 2009. Figure 5.2 presents the results. Whereas seven out of ten (105 out of 152) were in Delhi or the National Capital Region (NCR) of India, three out of ten (47 out of 152) had returned to their villages. Further, of the 105 found in Delhi or NCR, whereas six out of ten were reported to be living at the same place where they were surveyed in the 1992, four had moved to places elsewhere in Delhi or the NCR.

Regarding those who were no more

As reported in the preceding sub-section, 20 out of the 184 criterion migrants (11%) were reported to have died between the two fieldwork studies in 1992 and 2009. The following discussion regarding the age at which they died and the reasons for demise afford only an indicative picture because these could be ascertained only for a few cases.

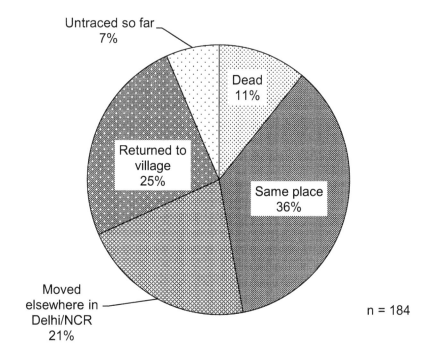

Figure 5.1 All the criteria migrants in 2009

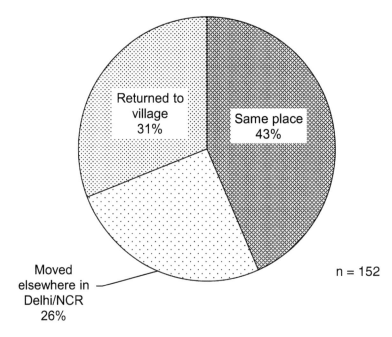

Figure 5.2 The living and traced criteria migrants in 2009

Age at death

The age at death could be determined only for one-third of the respondents (seven out of the twenty) who were reported to have died. The average (mean = 51.71 years, median = 51 years) was low compared with the norm (Mathur, 2009).

Reasons for death

The reasons for death could be ascertained only for the one-third of the respondents (eight out of twenty) who were reported to have died since the fieldwork in 1992. The results are presented in Table A-5.1. It is interesting to note that all eight were reported to have died due to illness. Although in three cases specific illnesses – tuberculosis (TB), cancer, heart attack – were mentioned, in the remaining five cases, merely the word 'illness' was spoken as the reason for death. In fact, due to fear and stigma of TB, people avoid mentioning the disease by its name and it is merely referred to as 'the illness'. Hence, there is a suspicion that a high incidence of TB might have been the cause of death. In any case, not a single respondent is reported to have died a 'natural death'. It certainly indicates the appalling health conditions to which labouring classes are exposed in the squatter settlements of Delhi.

Localities of the respondents in Delhi

Due to resource constraints, most of the fieldwork in 2009 was restricted to the localities where fieldwork was conducted in 1992. However, because one of the localities – Bengali Camp – was found to have been demolished, an effort was made to go to localities where the bulk of its residents had moved to try and contact the original migrant respondents of the study. Moreover, there were a few whom the researcher tried to interview over the telephone. In this context, Table A-5.2 provides the distribution of the respondents who were interviewed in 2009 to show how many of them were contacted at places other than those of their residence in 1992. About 85 per cent of the respondents lived in the same locality as they did in 1992; the remaining 15 per cent were found at other places not 'very far' from their old places.

Almost all the respondents said that they usually lived in Delhi since the fieldwork in 1992. Only one of them moved out of Delhi between the two points and then returned to Delhi, and he, too, mainly went out due to job-related reasons.

Occupational status and mobility of the respondents

The prevalent models of rural to urban migration that emphasise the excessiveness of migration often make a claim that the migrants are stuck in low-paying jobs with hardly any occupational mobility and that very few go up the ladder via 'lottery'. It would be interesting to see if the evidence from the two rounds of fieldwork lends any credence to this idea. The present section specifically and intensively examines if and what kinds of occupational changes have taken place in the profile of migrants' jobs compared with their first jobs in Delhi. The section attempts to deal with this question through the presentation of results in five respects: The first sub-section discusses the occupational status of the respondents. The next sub-section focuses on comparing the sector-wise distribution of respondents with respect to their first city job and their current city job in 2009 (i.e., inter-sector comparison). The third sub-section presents a flowchart analysis of movement of migrants from the sectors of their first jobs into the sectors of their current jobs and tests if the overall movement across sectors is significant. The fourth sub-section compares the distribution of respondents within sectors of economic activity (i.e., intra-sector comparison). The fifth sub-section discusses moves across sub-sectors (i.e., moves between sub-sectors). Hence, it allows the perception of moves across jobs at the level of sub-sectors, which means it is down almost to the level of individual jobs.

Occupational status

As given in Table A-5.3, whereas nine out of ten reported they worked, the remaining one said he did not – mostly due to sickness or disability. This result is important because, as with the reason for death, here, too, sickness or disability comes out to be an important indicator of the state of health of the migrant labouring classes. It may be pertinent here to mention that the average age of those reporting illness or disability (mean = 51 years, median = 48) is roughly same as the age at death in the case of those who were reported to have died between 1992 and 2009.

Physical observation also showed that these individuals look like a shadow of their former selves. It might look like a subjective – and at the same time a cynical and sad observation – but most of these people looked on their way out. In one of the cases the man had deteriorated to such an extent that it was hard to believe it was the same person when he brought out his Identity Card from the early 1990s. He detailed the many illnesses he had suffered and described how difficult it was for him to keep buying the medical prescriptions.

Sector-wise distribution of respondents in the first city job and the current city job

Figure 5.3 presents a comparative picture of sectoral shares both for the first jobs and the current jobs with respect to each of the five sector categories.

The service sector maintains its highest position, with the largest and constant share at both points of time. It has nearly one-third of the respondents in it. The shares of the two sectors of shopkeeping /shop worker and 'others' have increased and the shares of the two other sectors – construction and factory work – have decreased. The next sub-section analyses the precise nature of such sectoral shifts.

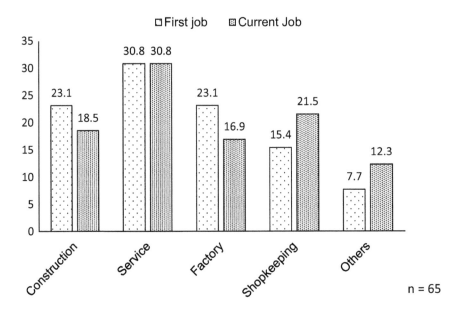

Figure 5.3 Sector-wise distribution of migrants' first jobs and current jobs

Is there a significant move across sectors of migrants' jobs? An analysis in terms of the first city job and the current city job

The preceding sub-section dealt with changes in the sectoral distribution of the migrants' jobs and found that although the service sector kept its top slot, there has been a shift away from construction and factory occupations towards trading and 'others'. Figures 5.4 to 5.8 show the movement from the first city job to the current city job for all seventy-one respondents interviewed in 2009. These figures correspond to each sector of the first job the movement or lack thereof of respondents to other sectors. As can be seen, a large number of respondents continued to be employed in their original sector.

It emerges from the cross-tabulation in Table A-5.4 and from the highly significant values of chi-square and phi that a significant number of respondents continue to be employed in the sector they entered with their first job in Delhi two decades earlier. On the one hand, this reinforces the argument that migrants were recruited into jobs that need the types of skills they possess. On the other hand, in the absence of evidence that the respondents had moved into better-paid and higher-skilled jobs within the sector, this can be interpreted as a lack of occupational mobility. For this to be confirmed, however, it is necessary to go to a more disaggregated level of analysis and look at the distribution of jobs within the sector, as well as to see the movement from old jobs to new jobs. This is done in the following two sub-sections.

Intra-sector distribution of respondents

The previous sub-sections discussed changes in the occupational structure of the migrants' jobs at two points of time, as well as the movement across sectors. In this context, let us now look at the structure of jobs within the sectors. The present sub-section reports changes across sub-sectors for each of the sector categories. A graph for each of the five sectors has been constructed to present these results.

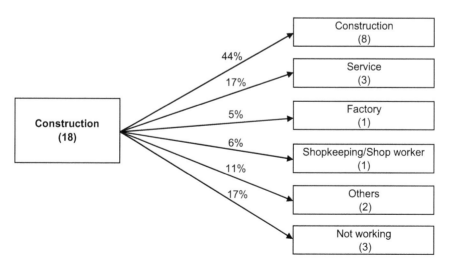

Figure 5.4 Occupational mobility in the construction sector

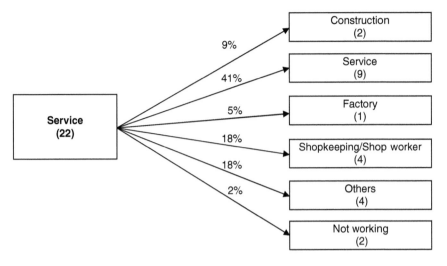

Figure. 5.5 Occupational mobility in the service sector

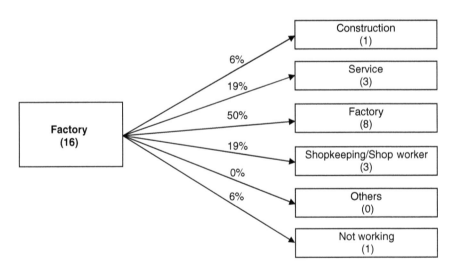

Figure 5.6 Occupational mobility in the factory sector

Changes in occupational structure of the construction sector

Figure 5.9 presents a comparative picture of the distribution of the first and current jobs in the construction sector. The increase in the proportion of the semi-skilled construction workers at the cost of the proportion of unskilled construction workers and 'other construction-sector workers' can be seen clearly from this figure. It can be deduced that there has been a definite change towards higher-skilled and better-paid jobs with respect to the jobs of the respondents in the construction sector.

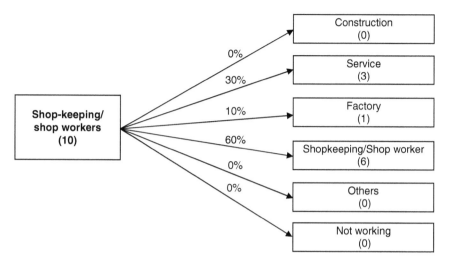

Figure 5.7 Occupational mobility in the shopkeeping/shop workers sector

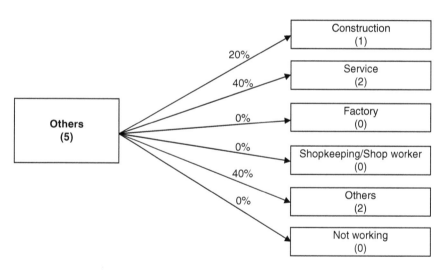

Figure. 5.8 Occupational mobility in the sector category 'others'

Changes in the occupational structure of the service sector

It emerges from Figure 5.10 that whereas the share in current jobs with respect to vendors, sweepers and security guards is higher compared with first jobs, for all other categories it is lower. This can perhaps be interpreted as a positive change – a move towards less informal and higher-paying jobs.

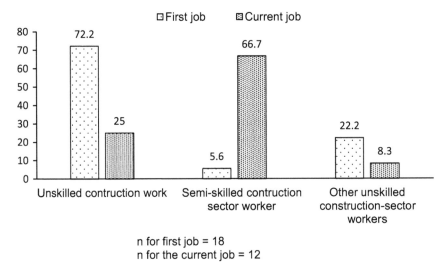

□ First job   ▣ Current job

n for first job = 18
n for the current job = 12

Figure 5.9 Sub-sectors of the construction sector: percentage distribution of first jobs and current jobs

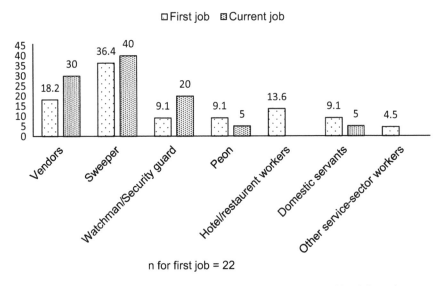

□ First job   ▣ Current job

n for first job = 22

Figure 5.10 Sub-sectors of the service sector: percentage distribution of first jobs and current jobs

Changes in the occupational structure of the factory sector

As presented in Figure 5.11, the share of helpers/labourers has gone down and the share of semi-skilled workers has increased in the garment and nongarment segments of the factory sector. It is noteworthy that the share of tailors has also

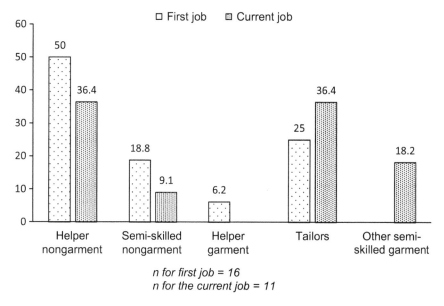

Figure 5.11 Sub-sectors of the factory sector: percentage distribution of first jobs and current jobs

increased. Overall, this provides a definite indication of a general improvement in the nature of the jobs in the factory sector.

Changes in the occupational structure of the shopkeeping/ shop workers sector

In this sector, there has been a definite move towards proper shopkeeping and a decline in the 'craft and trade' and 'shop worker' segments (Figure 5.12). This again is a case of improvement.

The small number of cases in the case of this category of 'others' does not permit much generalisation. Even then, the move away from animal husbandry and the increase in the sub-category of the 'other' jobs (consisting one each of sweeper, wood splitter and unskilled construction worker), as seen in Figure 5.13, was no indication of a worsening occupational structure.

Overall, the results presented in this sub-section show that within all sectors there has been a move towards relatively higher-skilled, better-paid and more secure jobs. Thus, these results indicate that staying in the same occupational sector did not amount to stickiness or stagnation.

Occupational moves at the sub-sectoral level and at more disaggregated levels

To continue our analysis, this sub-section indicates occupational moves of the respondents at a sub-sectoral level. Table D1 in Appendix D presents the

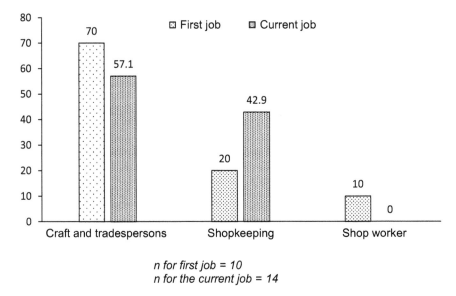

n for first job = 10
n for the current job = 14

Figure 5.12 Sub-sectors of the shopkeeping/shop-workers sector: percentage distribution of first jobs and current jobs

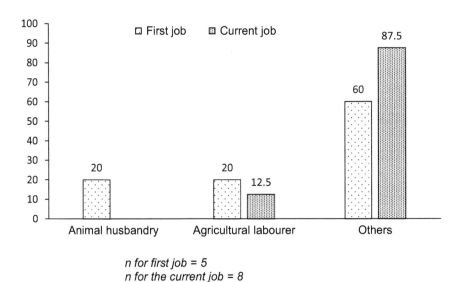

n for first job = 5
n for the current job = 8

Figure 5.13 Sub-sectors of the 'others' sector: percentage distribution of first jobs and current jobs

comparison of first jobs and current jobs at the sub-sectoral level in a comprehensive manner. A careful look allows one to say that the move of jobs towards better ones that was noted earlier is supported by Appendix D which goes beyond the sectoral occupational structure and shows all moves, indicating not only sectors but also sub-sectors of the first and latest jobs.

It emerges that three persons with their first jobs as *beldar* and two as sweepers had suffered health issues to the extent that they were unable to work due to their sickness. This corroborates the picture regarding mortality and morbidity presented in other sections of this chapter.

What has changed in the jobs?

Nearly three-fourths (forty-seven out of sixty-five of the migrant worker respondents said they were in the same job as they were when interviewed in 1992. These forty-seven respondents were asked what had changed in the job. Their responses with regard to this question are tabulated in Table 5.1. Seven out of ten respondents said there had been no change in their job over the period of nearly two decades. The remaining three out of ten mentioned some change in their respective jobs.

The responses regarding change in the same old jobs express, on the one hand, something about changes in the economy and the nature of jobs in Delhi, etc., and on the other, changes in the old jobs from the viewpoint of the welfare of the labourers.

Therefore, although the situation has to be read in its entirety, one can roughly group the responses into the following three groups from the labourers' angle: better off in the same job (Codes 2, 9 and 10 in Table 5.1) mentioned by 10 per cent; worse off in the same job (Codes 3, 6 to 8, 11 in Table 5.1) mentioned by 23 per cent; and change in the nature of the job (Codes 4 and 5 in Table 5.1)

Table 5.1 Change in the nature of the same jobs between 2009 and 1992

Code	What has changed in the job?	Number of respondents mentioning it	Per cent of respondents mentioning it*
1	No change	33	70
2	Has become less strenuous	1	2
3	Has become more strenuous	2	4
4	Has become more skill intensive	0	0
5	Has become more technology intensive	2	4
6	Has become less satisfactory	1	2
7	Work has shrunk	5	11
8	Have to go to farther places now	2	4
9	Now permanent/regular in the job	2	4
10	Earn higher	2	4
11	Earn less	1	2

* Sum does not add to 100.

mentioned by 4 per cent. Comparing the groups 'better off' and 'worse off', it seems clear that for those who in 2009 were still in the same job as they were in 1992, either there was no change in their respective jobs or the change had made them worse off. As for the change in the nature of the job itself, 4 per cent noted the increasing skill intensity.

How are new jobs different from the old ones?

A little over one-fourth (eighteen out of sixty-five) of the migrant worker respondents said they were not in the same job as they were when interviewed in 1992. These eighteen respondents were asked how their job was different from the 1992 job. Their mention of any of the positions with regard to this question is given in Table 5.2.

The results regarding new jobs being different from the old ones from the viewpoint of workers' welfare are as follows: not any different (Code 1 in Table 5.2; one respondent, 5.6 per cent); better off in current job compared to old job (Codes 2 to 4 and 6 in Table 5.2; twelve respondents, 66.7 per cent); worse off in current job compared to the old job (Code 8 in Table 5.2; four respondents, 22.2 per cent); difference in the nature of job (Codes 5, 7, 9, 10 and 11 in Table 5.2; five respondents, 28 per cent).

It clearly emerges that those who had changed jobs thought that things had changed. Only a minuscule (one respondent, 5.6 per cent) thought that the new job was not any different. The overwhelming majority said they are better off in the new jobs: two-thirds of the respondents. Those feeling worse off were only a few – less than one-fourth.

Nearly three in ten said that the nature of the job had changed. The responses were varied. Some of the responses were as follows: business expanded; job of

Table 5.2 Difference in the nature of work between 2009 and 1992

Code	How is the current job different (from the job in 1992)?	Number of respondents mentioning it	Per cent of the respondents mentioning it*
1	Not any different	1	5.6
2	Paid better in current job	2	11.1
3	Less strenuous	7	38.9
4	Expectation of becoming permanent in the job	1	5.6
5	Business has expanded and grown	1	5.6
6	Better income in present business	2	11.1
7	Job of lower skill than earlier	1	5.6
8	Less remunerative	4	22.2
9	Old job had threat of eviction from police/ municipal authorities	1	5.6
10	Current job more risky but better paid	1	5.6
11	More to learn in current job	1	5.6

* Sum does not add to 100

lower skill than earlier; old job had threat of demolition from Municipal Corporation of Delhi and the police; current job more risky but better paid; more to learn in the current job.

These results paint a mixed picture of changes in respondents' jobs during the nearly two decades between the first resurvey in 1992 and the resurvey in 2009. One section of respondents moved down to lower-skilled jobs, and the other section moved on to better-paid, albeit riskier, jobs. Another section found that their business had grown faster in the new job and there were now more opportunities to acquire skills. The arts and crafts persons amongst our respondents with no particular address to run the business from now faced a constant threat of eviction from places where they could make and sell their wares without many problems two decades earlier.

Change in skill

Studied or learned any job

During the fieldwork in 2009, all seventy-one migrant respondents were asked if they studied or learned any job since 1992. Most of them (sixty-five out of seventy-one; i.e., 92 per cent) had neither studied nor learned any work. Most of the respondents replied negatively in a matter-of-fact manner as if this were their fate. There were a few who could not initially understand the question. There were a few who at first thought that the question could only have been about their children and hence started lamenting their inability to get their children educated. At least one respondent expressed the desires and wishes as well as the stark reality and conditions of the working people, particularly those who left their studies midway just before or at the time of migration to Delhi: "This work (vegetable vendor) is such that one does not get an opportunity. I thought of studying part-time but I cannot spare any time for that." These results indicate that very few of such migrants had a chance to acquire new skills, either through education or training. This obviously has serious implications for their economic and social well-being.

Kind of study or work learned

Six (8 per cent) studied or learned work. They were further asked about the kind of study or learning they received. A look at Table A-5.5 reveals that it was mainly mechanical work (mechanic's work, making ovens) or service-sector work (learned how to operate photostat and printing machines, work of a painter, electrician's work). These facts indicate that given a chance, some migrants do get involved in learning what would be of use to them in the job market. Another type of job learned by one respondent was land rejuvenation work in conjunction with a society involved in such projects.

Only two persons were involved in learning in addition to the first. The one who learned land rejuvenation also tried to further learn more broad 'environmental work'. Another person learned masonry work.

Regarding those who were nonworkers in 2009

Out of the six respondents who were not working for living, three wanted to work. One each was without work for 1 month, 12 months and 36 months, respectively. Before stopping work, one was a semi-skilled nongarment factory worker, the second one was a vendor and the third one was a sweeper. These unemployed people were looking for work.

This also means they might have been sick and unemployed at the same time because they would have liked to work if they could have found something that they can do. In fact, one gentleman, the one who was suffering with illness and who showed his earlier Identity Card to illustrate his loss of health, when asked if he wished to work, almost retorted, albeit humorously and ironically, if the author could get him any work.

A retrospective on the process of migration by those who stayed in Delhi

Chapter 4 analysed the stated reasons for migration along with the spontaneous remarks and a concluding question asking for summing up of the 'why' of migration. This was for verbal corroboration of the other parts of the structured interviews during 1992.

The present section considers some additional observations on rural to urban migration to see if any changes have occurred over two decades in the migrants' reflection on their migration to Delhi.

Stated reasons for migration

Table 4.8 and Table 4.9 in Chapter 4 record the most important reasons for migration for the 446 respondents of the listing survey and the 184 criterion migrants, respectively. Figure 4.16 presents the results for the 184 criterion migrants in terms of the reclassification given in the reduced dataset as detailed at serial number 3 in Table G1 of Appendix G. Figure 5.14 does the same for the seventy-one respondents of the 2009 fieldwork in Delhi to see if their reasons are any different. It turns out that those who stayed, compared with the total sample of 184 criterion migrants, were, on the whole, more likely to have had a higher incidence of village job–related negative factors and a lower incidence of city job–related positive factors. Because we have interpreted the negative village factors as the facilitating factor or the necessary conditions of migration, this group appears to consist of those who were keener to migrate out of their relative deprivation.

Spontaneous remarks on migration

The whole idea and technique of eliciting spontaneous remarks was almost the same as reported in Chapter 4. In 1992, the technique was able to evoke spontaneous remarks from 62 per cent of the criteria migrants. However, during the resurvey in 2009, the technique evoked spontaneous remarks only

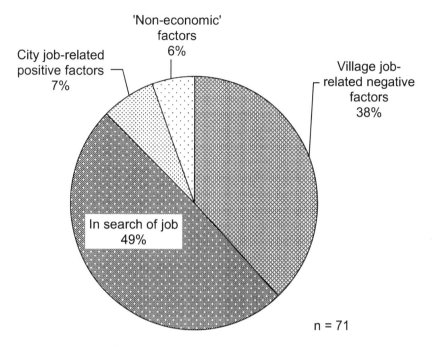

'Non-economic' factors 6%

City job-related positive factors 7%

Village job-related negative factors 38%

In search of job 49%

n = 71

Figure 5.14 The most important reason for migration

from 58 per cent- from forty one out of the seventy one respondents who were interviewed.

The spontaneous remarks in 2009 matched closely the ones from the earlier survey. Two typical groups were identified on the basis of the fieldwork in 1992: (1) agricultural labourers whose position at origin was difficult due to unavailability of work and/or that of land or property (they emphasised problems at the origin); and (2) those who were a bit better off, typically those who even got to study but their condition did not allow further study, and they even got jobs in rural areas, but these jobs were not very remunerative; they had a contact in the city and were helped to move (they emphasised problems at the rural origin *as well as* possibilities in the urban areas). In 2009, these two groups were distinct in terms of their spontaneous remarks. However, there were some differences. For example, compared with the earlier fieldwork, the open-ended remarks this time were generally less eloquent – perhaps having lived so long in the national capital of India, they were now more accustomed to the format of the surveys and so waited for questions to be put to them rather than speaking themselves. Perhaps with time they no longer felt or remembered as much. There were some in 2009 – about ten out of the forty-one – who matter of factly described that they came to Delhi for a job, with no emphasis on origin or destination! There was also a tendency to describe satisfaction at the achievement – 'regular job now'; 'house now'; 'children settled now', etc. – exhibited by seven out of forty-one, and similarly a tendency of describing channels of support in the city without mentioning anything about origin.

In conclusion, it can be said that although the analysis of the spontaneous remarks made in 2009 support the conclusions in Chapters 3 and 4, these remarks demonstrate a change in their mental location with time – they now saw more of the city and the process of their migration to and settlement in Delhi, and therefore the problems at the origin found a mere mention at the most, and not as much elaboration of the conditions at origin as was found in 1992.

Reasons on balance

The responses to the question "Looking on balance, why did you come?" were mostly in line with what was summarised in Chapter 4: the response to this direct question at the end of interview, as before, matched and corroborated the main findings of Chapter 4 and this chapter. There was a continued emphasis on the attractiveness of the destination, channels of recruitment and migration as part of their overall strategy, but there was also an interesting and striking mixture of caution and assertiveness, as if the interviewer was challenging their right to live and work in Delhi. One respondent from Tamil Nadu said, "I hope there isn't any trouble (*chakkar*) in it, (you) are talking so much *kanoon* (law) . . . that (I) feel fear". Another migrant from Eastern Uttar Pradesh asserted rather mischievously, "It is not a crime to do wage labour (*majoori*) and anyone can go anywhere." Although most looked back at their migration in a rather matter-of-fact manner, one respondent felt that but for the low wages, economic coercion and social oppression in his village he would not have left his village and that he had cried when he left. Although most felt happy and satisfied at their decision to migrate and at what they had been able to achieve in Delhi – that is, could raise families, meet social obligations, get a place to reside, etc. – at least one respondent felt he could not achieve what he thought when he first migrated: "thought would earn enough to make it . . . would get children educated and help them gain status . . . but that has not happened."

Conclusion

Contrary to the image suggested by the Harris–Todaro model of migrants thronging to cities and staying put there in an irrational manner, this chapter reveals that a significant proportion of our sample returned to their village and another significant proportion to other places in and around Delhi. The pattern of changing jobs and the nature of the new jobs corroborate the migrants' move towards better jobs but with limited investment in new skills or education. The general pattern of change in the nature of the respondents' jobs suggests an increasing role of skill and technology and reflects changes in the nature of the economy and the spread of urbanisation.

Reference

Mathur, O.P. (2009). *National urban poverty reduction strategy 2010–2020 A.D.: Slum-free cities*. New Delhi: The National Institute of Public Finance and Policy.

6 Discovering and characterising groups of migrants

Introduction

The issues of the *who* and *how* of migration were addressed in Chapters 3 and 4, respectively, to understand *what is decisive in the decision to migrate*. Although some groupings of migrants were explored and some emerged with regard to different variables and phenomena, an element of bias cannot be ruled out in a supervised analysis. In this context, it might be interesting to form clusters in an unbiased manner and see if and how these add to our knowledge. Therefore, the goal of the present chapter is to discover groups from amongst the migrant respondents. This is done with the help of k-means clustering. Using wisdom gained from analysis in earlier chapters, a data-reduction exercise involving selection of variables and recoding of values was carried out. The resulting dataset, the details of which are provided in Appendix G, has been used for clustering.

The second section briefly introduces the clustering technique used. The third section reports the results of the clustering exercise. The fourth section elaborates on the statistical significance of differences between groups. The phi coefficient and Cramer's V are used for this purpose. This exercise is helpful in further characterising the clusters. In the fifth section, the results are placed in their theoretical and empirical contexts.

Clustering analysis

Clustering is a multivariate exploratory data analysis technique that creates groups of individuals from within a dataset, based on a set of underlying variables (Han and Kamber, 2012: 444–445, 451–454; Witten and Frank, 2005: 136–138). Clustering algorithms of various kinds are being increasingly utilised by economists to discover groups from within datasets based on the similarity measures of individuals. In this chapter, the most commonly used clustering technique, k-means, is applied to form groups from the dataset. As an experiment for determining the number of groups, the dataset was sequentially split into two to five groups through four separate exercises. After considering the measures of the goodness of groups and their meaningfulness for the research problem, it emerged that the split of the cases into two groups made most sense. However, a brief analysis of the case with three groups is also included towards the end of the fourth section. For more technical details on the k-means clustering method, the reader may refer to Appendix E.

Groups emerging from the clustering exercise

The clustering was carried out using a set of thirty-two variables from across the two surveys. The sample is restricted to those migrants who could be traced and were alive in 2009.

The two clusters formed by the method of k-means clustering contain 83 cases (55 per cent of the 152 cases) and 69 cases (45 per cent of the 152 cases), respectively. Whereas for the nineteen variables listed in Table 6.1, the modal values were same for the two groups, for the thirteen variables listed in Table 6.2, the modal values were dissimilar. Even with similar modal values of a variable, it is possible for the two groups to differ with respect to the distribution of the variable. Hence, in Table 6.1, the relevant coefficient (the phi coefficient/Cramer's V) is calculated and indicates significant difference in the distribution of variables with similar modal values. In Tables 6.1 and 6.2, "**" denotes significance at the 1 per cent level and "*" significance at the 5 per cent level. In cases of significant difference, the phi coefficient /Cramer's V and the p-values are provided in brackets alongside. A 1 per cent level of significance has been used in discussions throughout this chapter unless otherwise stated. The significance is reported, interpreted and analysed in the next section.

Significance of differences between groups

The present section discusses the importance of differences between the groups in terms of statistical significance with respect to different variables. It further interprets, analyses and characterises the groups.

Statistical significance

Although the values of the phi coefficient or Cramer's V are significant with respect to all thirteen variables listed in Table 6.2 that have dissimilar modal values for the two groups, it is also so with the two variables with similar modal values, namely 'Being unemployed in the year before migration' and 'Livelihood compared to others in the village'. Thus, the values of fifteen variables in all are statistically significantly different between the two clusters. The values for these variables for both the clusters given in Tables 6.1 and 6.2 show that there is a pattern which can be used to denote, identify and characterise the two groups.

Interpretation and analysis

A closer look reveals that one of the variables (polrdist) pertains to the area of origin: being from the area of high out-migration (ahom) or not. The people from

Table 6.1 List of variables with similar modal values for the two groups

Sr. No.	Variable Name	**Signf at 1% level *Signf at 5%	Variable description	Cluster 1	Cluster 2
1	ageatarr				
2	mostimp				
3	age2009				
4	work_ybm				
5	unempld	**(0.355,.000)	Unemployed in year before migration	No (less likely to be Unemployed)	Yes (more likely to be unemployed)
6	famtype				
7	compare	**(0.298, 001)	Livelihood compared to others in the village	Above average	Below average
8	repmem	*(0.179,.028)			
9	indebt				
10	visit	*(0.198, .015)			
11	famatt	*(0.272, .011)			
12	livevill				
13	sjivill				
14	ss_exist				
15	whyquit1				
16	support1				
17	channel1				
18	endreason1				
19	cus_asu				

Note: Descriptions of each variable and its values are available in Table G1, Appendix G

this area can be termed *poorvees* (Easterners), called *poorbias* by the natives of north India, which means 'easterners'. This distinction is crucial to the reading of the results and underpins the following discussion. All other characteristics of these two groups are best understood in the context of this fundamental difference in their areas of origin.

The next two significant variables which characterise the groups are 'ability to read' and 'attended school or not'. The results indicate that the *poorvee* group scores significantly higher on literacy and education.

The next group of three variables pertains to the pre-migration job and its nature: 'main occupation before migration'; 'hired or not'; 'basis of hiring'. The *poorvee* group were mostly peasants, followed by workers. The non-*poorvee* group were mostly workers followed by the category 'artisan and traders'. Obviously, the *poorvees* (easterners) were more of the self-employed type than hired labour. On the other hand, the non-*poorvees* were wage labourers in the village before migrating to Delhi. The wage labourers mostly worked as day labourers. In addition, it also emerges that the non-*poorvees* were characterised by higher

Table 6.2 List of variables with dissimilar modal values for the two groups

Sr. No.	Variable Name	**Signf at 1% level *Signf at 5%	Variable description	Cluster 1	Cluster 0
1	polrdist	** (0.279, .001)	Area of origin	From area of high out-migration	Not from area of high out-migration
2	read	** (0.296, .000)	Ability to read	Able to read	Not able to read
3	school	** (0.354, .000)	Attended school	Attended school	Didn't attend school
4	mainjob	** (0.548, .000)	Occupation before migration	Peasants (and some workers)	Workers (and some artisans)
5	hired	** (0.507, .000)	Hired or own work before migration	Own work before migration (self-employed)	Worked for wages before migration (wage labourer)
6	hirebase	** (0.517, .000)	Basis of hiring	Self-employed	Day-worker
7	durunemp	** (0.369, 000)	Duration of unemployment	Low unemployment	Highly unemployed
8	ownland	** (0.812, 000)	Did family own land	Owned land	Didn't own any land
9	difflt	** (0.737, 000)	Difficulty in meeting family food requirement in off season	Off-season difficulty due to less food from own cultivation	No cultivation of food
10	fjindel	** (0.362, .001)	First occupation in Delhi	Factory	Construction
11	paymeth	** (0.311, .005)	Method of payment in first Delhi job	Monthly-salary worker in first Delhi job	Daily-wage worker in first Delhi job
12	oh_size	** (0.712, .000)	Size group of operational holding	Marginal farmer	Mainly nonfarmer
13	oh_tenure	** (0.814, .000)	Tenurial category of farmers	Wholly owned and self-operated	Mainly nonfarmer

Note: Descriptions of each variable and its values are available in Table G1, Appendix G

pre-migration unemployment, and for a greater duration, compared with *poor-vees*. This makes sense considering non-*poorvees* were workers as opposed to peasants.

The variable 'livelihood compared to other families in the village (compare)' reveals that although the *poorvees* were better off than others in their respective villages, the non-*poorvees* were worse off compared with other families in their respective villages. The next group of variables pertains to ownership and operation of land. It emerges that the *poorvees* also scored better in this respect. This group had more landowners than the other. The proportion of landowners amongst the non-*poorvees* was low, and even amongst the ones who owned any land, most were, in fact, the 'leased-in' type of operators. Although the first jobs in Delhi (fjindel) for *poorvees* were mostly in the factory sector, those for non-*poorvees* were in the construction sector. The predominant method of payment (paymeth) was by month in the case of *poorvees* and by day in the case of non-*poorvees*.

On the whole, the clear conclusion we can draw is that there are two distinct groups of migrants in the sample. The *poorvees* had higher pre-migration land ownership, lower unemployment and higher status in the village; this group was then able to obtain better post-migration jobs compared with non-*poorvees*. This obvious inference – pre-migration status affects post-migration prospects – can be suggestive of the greater resources better-off migrants (*poorvees*, in this instance) could invest in pre-migration capacity building and channels of communication. More research is required, however, to disentangle how pre-migration characteristics influence channels of recruitment.

The whole story can be reduced to the four characteristics that best describe the distinction outlined previously in this section. This characterization of migrants is portrayed in Figure 6.1. In words, a single descriptive line characterises each of the two clusters: (1) Above average livelihood, literate, and marginal peasant *poorvees* migrate to Delhi to join monthly-salary factory work; (2) Below average livelihood, illiterate, and daily-wage non-*poorvees* migrates to Delhi to join daily-wage construction work.

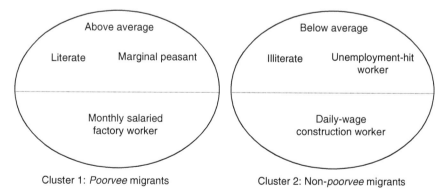

Figure 6.1 Characterization of migrants

Most of the variables relating to the channels of migration do not significantly separate the two groups. This indicates that channels are a common method among migrants for carrying information, advice and support to get jobs at their destination and, hence, these were available to most of the migrant respondents of our study, irrespective of status.

Briefly, it is also interesting to consider an extension to a three-group clustering exercise: whereas the *poorvee* group stays intact, the non-*poorvee* migrant group is further divided into two sub-groups. The bigger sub-group consisting of about two-thirds of this group arrived in Delhi at an older age but retains the characteristics of the group as a whole. However, the smaller sub-group consisting of younger non-*poorvee* migrants differs from the bigger sub-group in two respects. One, they were literate and went to school rather than working before migration. Two, with regard to the first city job in Delhi, this smaller sub-group entered the monthly-salaried service sector rather than the daily-wage construction sector. This hints at the importance of pre-migration literacy and schooling that subsequently led to relatively better post-migration jobs.

Conclusion

The remarkably distinct two groups that emerge from the clustering exercise are, in fact, the subject matter of empirical debate in India to which this book is anchored in the sense that the present research has tried to pick up its research question from the major assertion along the lines of what has been described in Chapter 1 as well as in Appendix A as the 'area argument of migration': that a highly out-migrating area sends more migrants because this area is poor and backward; the migrants from this area are poor and they move out *due to* misery. This assertion was also refuted earlier in Chapter 3 by comparing the migrants from the highly out-migrating region with those from the rest of India.

Thus, this clustering exercise not only confirms the validity of the research question of the present study, but also contributes to the entire debate on the interpretation of the Indian reality of a highly out-migrating area being or not being the fountainhead of 'poverty-driven' migration, the area which 'spills poverty' to some of the major urban centres of India and on poverty being or not being the decisive factor in the decision to migrate. It is also significant because the two groupings with respect to the area of origin by and large corroborate the refutation of the poverty hypothesis as well as its counterpart – the area argument of migration – that this book has done through the background literature review, as well as empirical analysis and through the description of results.

References

Han, J. and Kamber, M. (2012). *Data mining: Concepts and techniques* (3rd ed.). San Francisco: Morgan Kaufmann Publishers.

Witten, I.H. and Frank, E. (2005). *Data mining: Practical machine learning tool and techniques* (2nd ed.). New Delhi: Elsevier.

7 Who stays and who returns?

Introduction

The overall focus so far in this book has been on *what is decisive in the decision to migrate*. However, the goal of the present chapter is determining *who stays and who returns*. The second section describes and illustrates the conceptual framework of the decision-tree method. The third section interprets the decision tree of this study to describe the manner in which different variables influence the decision by migrants whether to stay or return. The fourth section analyses the dynamics of the decision to stay or return by the rural migrants once they reach their urban destination on the basis of the knowledge gained from the decision tree that was created using the data collected for this study. The fifth section juxtaposes the newer ideas discovered in this chapter with the gist of earlier chapters and discusses their relevance for our understanding of what drives rural to urban migration.

The concept and illustration of the decision-tree method

This section provides an essential background and lays out the conceptual framework required to understand decision-tree analysis.

A decision tree is a flowchart-like structure that represents several courses of action (i.e., decisions) based on tests on the underlying set of variables. A decision tree is constructed in a top-down recursive 'divide and conquer' manner. Of all the variables in a dataset, one of the variables is specified as the *decision* (i.e., class) variable. This is the variable on the basis of which the data instances are classified. The rest of the variables are called *predicting* variables (i.e., predictors). The objective of a decision-tree method is to evaluate the relationship or functional dependence of the *decision* variable on the *predicting* variables. Decision-tree induction is a widely used knowledge discovery tool for classifying data instances in relation to a decision variable (Witten and Frank, 2005: 62–69, 200–207; Han and Kamber, 2012: 330–343). Conceptually, this approach is similar to using logistic regression, but decision-tree analysis is a nonparametric method as opposed to a parametric one. Given the nature of the sample and variables, we opted for decision-tree analysis to present the results in an intuitive and reader-friendly manner. A brief illustration of this method follows.

For a dataset with three predicting variables (*A*, *B* and *C*) and two values of the decision variable (Decisions 1 and Decision 2), the decision tree would look something like Figure 7.1. Henceforth in this chapter, the word *variable* refers to a predicting variable unless indicated otherwise. Further, let us say that variable *A* can take three values: A_1, A_2 and A_3; variable *B* can take two values: B_1 and B_2; and variable *C* can have two values: C_1 and C_2. The ecliptic nodes are known as internal nodes and rectangular nodes are called leaf nodes. The topmost internal node in the decision tree is designated as the root node. The root node contains the whole dataset.

So, for instance, a split on variable *A* at the root node partitions the data along three branches, each corresponding to one of the values of the variable *A*. A leaf node is created only when all or almost all the instances in the data partition belong to the same category of the decision variable. Starting from the root node, there can be many internal nodes involving splits on one or the other of the remaining variables before reaching a decision node. The data keep getting partitioned into smaller and smaller sub-sets along the dimensions of predicting variables.

The interesting distinguishing feature of such a decision-tree model is that it is built by splitting variables in order of their relevance or significance to classify data instances in terms of the decision variable. The most significant variable, which creates the clearest and purest partitions, is considered on the top, that is, at the root node of the tree. Further successive splits on the remaining variables are made at various internal nodes in order of their significance. This significance for selection of variables for splits at various levels of a decision tree is based on a heuristic function, which determines the predictive power of variables. The predictive power of a variable is nothing but a measure of its association with the decision variable. The commonly used methods for selection of variables include gain ratio, chi-square and Gini index (Han and Kamber, 2012: 330–343). The decision-tree model J48 available in the data mining software *WEKA* (Machine Learning Group at the University of Waikato, 2016) applied in this chapter makes use of the concept of the gain ratio to determine the order of selection of variables for creating

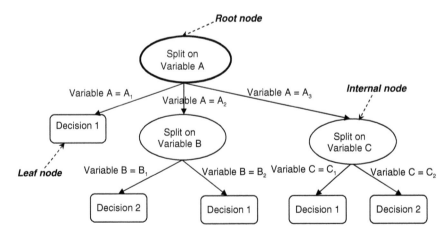

Figure 7.1 Illustration of a decision tree

splits at the internal nodes. The gain ratio of a variable indicates the amount of additional information acquired for classifying data with respect to the decision variable as a result of 'knowing' the values of this particular predictive variable.

The gain ratio is computed for all the variables at the root node, and the variable with the highest gain ratio is selected for the split. At the next level of internal nodes of the decision tree, the gain ratio of the remaining variables (i.e., excluding the one already used for the split at the root node) is computed based on the data instances left in the partitions at these nodes. The same process of selecting predicting variables is repeated in a top-down manner until either all the data instances in a partition belong to the same value of the decision variable or the number of instances in the partition goes below a user-defined threshold number of cases. In the latter case, a leaf node is created and labelled with the majority class of the data partition. More details about decision-tree induction are provided in Appendix E.

The decision-tree model with respect to the 'stay or return' dichotomy

The decision variable to test our hypothesis of who stays and who returns has two values: 'stay' and 'return'. All the other variables are treated as predicting variables.

The gain ratio was calculated for all thirty-one predicting variables with respect to the decision of the migrant to stay or return, and the values of this ratio are given in Table E-3. The decision-tree model that emerges from the primary data of the present study is shown in Figure 7.2.

According to this decision tree, whether the squatter settlement of the migrants' residence in 1992 existed or not in 2009 is the strongest factor influencing the decision to stay or return. Out of the total of ninety-seven migrants whose squatter settlement existed, eighty-four stayed and thirteen migrants returned.

Further, for the migrants whose squatter settlement did not exist, the next factor is the reason for the migrant ending his or her first job in Delhi. With respect to this factor, those mentioning lay-off or absenteeism or 'other reasons' (consisting mainly of seasonality and unfitness for the job) returned to their place of origin. Those who stayed in Delhi were the ones who had left their first jobs due to positive factors like taking another job, setting up business, completion of work training, etc.

For migrants whose first jobs ended due to adverse factors associated with employment, the next important variable turns out to be whether their family was in debt in the year before migration. Further in the sequence, those who were in debt were divided on the basis of their first occupation in Delhi. Whereas the migrants whose first job in Delhi was either in the service sector or in factories decided to stay, the ones with jobs in the category 'other jobs' went back.

The migrants with their first job in the construction sector are categorised further on the basis of their age at the time of the survey in 2009. This division shows that migrants who were in the age group of 32 to 51 years returned, whereas those in the age group of 52 to 61 years stayed.

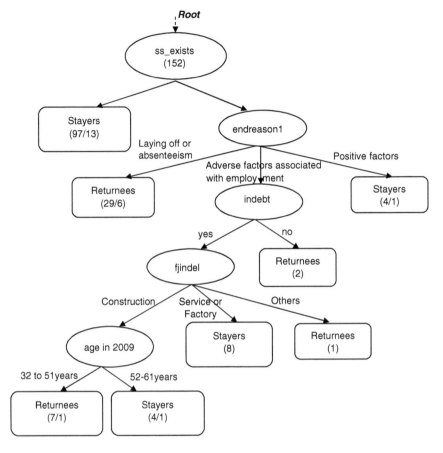

Figure 7.2 Decision tree created for the decision to stay or return

This interpretation largely describes how the migrants decide whether to stay or return. The next section tries to link this interpretation with the possible ways in which these relationships can be understood.

Analysis of the dynamics of 'stay or return' on the basis of knowledge gained from the decision tree

A few things can be understood from the interpretation of the decision tree described in the previous section.

Does demolition of squatter settlements lead to return migration?

The first and foremost point that emerges is the vital importance of the existence, availability and continuance of the community provided by a *basti* or a *jhuggi jhompari* area in the city where the labouring classes stay. This is in congruity and consonance with the pre-migration socioeconomic status of the migrants being largely miserable that has been described in Chapter 3. When displaced, they did not have any substantial resources to fall back upon. It also fits very closely with the fact that the channels of information that have been described in Chapter 4 are seen to be connecting the demand in urban areas for labour of a particular type and skill with the potential migrants who can meet this demand. The sense in the entirety of the process of migration is that the channels of recruitment embedded in these settlements provide not only the pre-migration information, contact and advice before the migrant leaves the village, but also the means of survival, support and sustenance on arrival; help and guidance in finding job; and later on, continuing social, cultural and psychological support for existence in the destination area.[1] In this context, the demolition of a squatter settlement can be understood as having such a significant influence on the decision of the migrant workers living there to return to their places of origin in the countryside.

This can also be understood at the level of the city economy: to constitute and run itself effectively, efficiently, profitably and competitively, a city economy requires more labourers than it might need in the short term. This can be seen in the context of the ideas of the classical economists on labour migration that have been discussed in Chapter 1. Karl Marx called it a 'reserve army of labour'. The political economy of this 'reserve army of labour' is corroborated by the existence or otherwise of its 'encampment' in the form of squatter settlements and the consequential decision of the workers inhabiting these settlements to stay or return.

This finding matches well with the experience in other developing countries of allowing or not allowing squatting to take place in the cities and the consequent effect on the extent of the 'reserve army of labour'. For example, China by and large does not let squatting take place in its cities and, thereby, it tries to allow only the 'army of labour' and restrict the 'reserve army of labour'. It tries to do so not only through its policy of restricting and regulating city-ward migration as an instrument to minimise the cost of mobilised labour, but also through periodic 'clean-ups' or threats thereof to ward off fears that parts of the 'reserve army of labour' may break the law to strengthen its position (Breman, 2010: 270–279). However, in most of the cities of the developing world, squatting is the norm, and one can understand that the rural to urban migration of the labouring classes in these countries is contingent, to a large extent, on the existence of such settlements. At a policy level, therefore, the results presented here highlight the vital role that squatter settlements play in facilitating rural to urban migration.

The importance of the reason for ending the first job, indebtedness, the first city job and age on return migration

Once the squatter settlement is broken, the next important factor determining whether to stay or return turns out to be the reasons for migrants ending their first job in Delhi. It emerged in the previous section how layoffs, absenteeism and 'other reasons' (consisting mainly of seasonality of and unfitness for a job) for ending the first job are associated with a return, whereas the positive factors that lead to ending the first city job are associated with staying in the city. This means that the migrant worker returns if he is laid off or goes off to the village to be absent from work or the season is over or he is unfit for the job. This indicates that the workers who mention any of these reasons had jobs in which they were a little too disposable. On the other hand, the positive factors that lead to ending the first jobs are associated with staying in the city; this indicates these are "fitter" migrants who were absorbed into the city economy.

However, as mentioned in the previous section, for migrants whose first jobs ended due to adverse factors associated with employment, the next important variable is whether their family was in debt or not. This means this group of migrants did not decide to stay or return in that simple a manner – they did not return simply because their first jobs ended on an unpleasant note. The additional factor that got included with this group of migrants was whether or not their family was in debt before they moved to Delhi. Although it not possible to generalise due to the small numbers, the group whose settlement had been demolished, who had faced adverse circumstances that ended their first jobs in Delhi and who were not in debt returned to their villages.

However, it was not possible to make a clear judgement regarding those who were in debt in the year before migration. There was an additional caveat in this situation: those with their first jobs in Delhi in the service or factory sector stayed.

In this context, it might be interesting to go a little further and say that those who had their first job in Delhi in the construction sector were not clear-cut returnees under the conditions of demolition of their settlement, losing their first jobs under adverse circumstances and being in debt. The additional variable of importance in their case comes out to be their age in 2009. Whereas those in the 32 to 51 year bracket returned, those in 52 to 61 year bracket stayed in Delhi. Although it is hard to conclude due to small numbers at this stage of the decision tree, this suggests that the return was associated with people who were between 15 and 34 years during the 1992 fieldwork and the decision to stay back was associated with people who were between 35 and 44 years at that time.

Conclusion

The analysis carried out in this chapter departed in some way from the rest of the book in that it focused specifically on return migration. The results presented should be treated with some caution given the small sample sizes. Nonetheless, the associations discovered via the decision-tree analysis paint an interesting and nuanced picture of return migration that presents many ideas for future research.

The demolition of the Bengali camp was treated at face value; that is, although it was in some ways an exogenous event, it can be argued it is in no way an anomaly in developing countries. The key finding in this regard was that the existence of residential facilities for migrants – which comprise not just physical space but social networks, including the channels through which migrants were recruited – remains a critical requirement for migrants long after the migration decision has been made. Other interesting associations highlighted in the chapter include the migrants' success in their first job. Understandably, success in the first job is associated with staying, whereas more negative outcomes are associated with a return. A positive association between indebtedness and staying, meanwhile, suggests that perhaps return migration is not an option for migrants working to pay off their village debts.

We concluded in earlier chapters that pre-migration relative deprivation in rural areas readies the potential migrants to move to the city. The decision-tree analysis complements this idea by showing that relative deprivation, as reflected by rural debts, prompts them to try and stay put there. Earlier in the book, it emerged that the labour demand at the destination is the decisive factor in the decision to migrate. In this context, the noteworthy finding of the decision-tree analysis is that the continuance of the squatter settlement is associated with the migrant staying in the city, and the destruction of the squatter settlement is associated with his return. More research into the political economy of squatting and labour migration might be necessary to examine whether breaking up of squatter settlements is an indicator signalling a lack of demand for labour or an expression of the intention to restrict and limit the 'reserve army of labour'. However, this finding certainly does not lend support to the idea that rural to urban migration is unresponsive to city conditions which lurks behind the theories of Hoselitz and Todaro. Thus, it can be said that our results do not support the case of 'urban bias' and 'over-urbanisation' that attribute rural-urban migration to conditions in the rural areas of origin and that deny any responsibility of urban destination for the migrants.

In view of the discussions so far in the book, a brief critique of the main propositions of Hoselitz and Todaro and the implications of the results of this study for policy are taken up next in Chapter 8 of this book, which is its concluding chapter.

Note

1 A comic illustration that conjures up the complexity of human motives for rural to urban migration *as well as* return migration is the short story *Annamalai* by R.K. Narayan (Narayan, 1985: 117–144).

References

Breman, J. (2010). *Outcast labour in Asia: Circulation and informalization of the work force at the bottom of the economy*. New Delhi: Oxford University Press.

Han, J. and Kamber, M. (2012). *Data mining: Concepts and techniques* (3rd ed.). San Francisco: Morgan Kaufmann Publishers.

Machine Learning Group at the University of Waikato (2016, January 9). *Weka 3: Data mining software in Java*. Retrieved from http://www.cs.waikato.ac.nz/ml/weka/

Narayan, R.K. (1985). Annamalai. In Narayan, R.K. (Ed.), *Under the Banyan Tree & Other Stories* (pp. 117–144). William Heinemann Ltd., U.K. (First Indian edition, (1992) Chennai: Indian Thought Publications).

Witten, I.H. and Frank, E. (2005). *Data mining: Practical machine learning tool and techniques* (2nd ed.). New Delhi: Elsevier.

8 Conclusion

When this study was conceptualised in 1991, theories and policies that viewed migration negatively held sway. One of our motivations was to bridge the disconnect between such theories and theories of capitalism – after all, significant increases in the mobility of labour were intertwined with this economic system. This led to the development of a multiphase fieldwork that integrated wisdom from classical works with the concepts and methods of the researchers who broadly respected this framework – ranging from Lenin (in FLPH edition 1956) and Buchanan (1966) to Breman (1996) and Stark (1991) who in their own ways firmly placed migration in the framework of the development of capitalism.

The academic consensus has moved on since then. Urbanisation, and by corollary, rural to urban migration, are now largely viewed as necessary conditions for long-term growth. Urbanisation via in-migration can lead to more efficient allocation of labour, increasing levels of productivity and participation, agglomeration economies and economies of scale that are a result of a spatial concentration of industries and technologies, and also an improvement in the quality of life of the migrants via beneficial effects on education and fertility levels (Clunies-Ross, Forsyth and Huq, 2009). Ellis and Harris (2004) survey diverse studies from rural and urban areas to argue that mobility can play a vital role, not just from the point of view of economic efficiency, but also leads to the exchange of ideas, skills and knowledge; the transfer of resources from more dynamic to less dynamic regions (via remittances); and ultimately to poverty reduction. The analytical work by Stark (2006) and its empirical follow-up by Stark, Micevska and Mycielski (2009) start off from the classical and Marxist ideas on migration and then conduct a closer exploration of the idea of relative deprivation and, in that sense, these studies corroborate the validity of the design of our work..

In this context, the primary micro-research on the 'recruitment versus expulsion' hypothesis of labour migration, as well as return migration reported in this book, may be of wide use particularly for further research, policy making, practice, consultancy and extension work on migration and urbanisation. The other research work on this question has often been based on secondary macro-data that has significant limitations. This study used a unique panel dataset to address the role of demand for labour in migration as well as return migration. The collection of primary data for different time points in the processes of migration and return migration spanning four decades collected from hundreds of representative migrants through two rounds of fieldwork, nearly two decades apart, and analysis of this panel data has revealed many interesting results and avenues for future research.

One of the key findings to emerge has been that information networks between prospective migrants and earlier migrants facilitate the exchange of information and advice, and thus play a decisive role in the formation of job expectations and the decision to migrate. In other words, migrants came for the jobs they knew could be attained without much wait – over half of the migrant respondents of this study got a job within a week of their arrival in Delhi, about three-quarters within a fortnight and 86 per cent within a month. Although relative deprivation predisposes people to look for better opportunities, the concrete decision to migrate is made on the basis of demand for labour in urban areas communicated through the 'channels of recruitment'. An earlier study by Buchanan (1966) highlighted the role of such channels while looking at the predominance of migrants from Ratnagiri in Bombay mills. This study adds much needed, newer evidence from India.

At an individual level, return migration can be understood as these migrants not being required in the production process. At the city level or at the level of national policy, it could largely be read as cost cutting with regard to urban infrastructure and, in a general sense, as a policy of not allowing too great a number of migrants than the 'active labour army' needs and thereby reducing the size of the 'reserve army of labour'. Breman (2010) discusses this in the context of China. In our study we find return migration to be most dramatically associated with the destruction of labourers' dwellings in the squatter settlements. The study found evidence of family strategies for diversification of sources of income and risk aversion. The process of migration is much more structured than the pessimistic models recognise. In this regard, we discuss in brief the results of the present study in relation to the logic of the pessimistic theories and policy.

The 'over-urbanisation' thesis based on the comparison by Hoselitz (1962) of the nineteenth-century urbanisation of Europe with Indian urbanisation of the mid-twentieth century is an example of urban pessimism bereft of historical analysis. Although propounding the idea that in both situations 'push' factors were preponderant, he singled out India for its less developed industry, small proportion of urban labour force in industry and large proportion in services, and fractionalised urban labour market. Apart from the question of the reliability of the data to be able to draw such drastic conclusions, this comparison assumed a fixed ratio between manufacturing and service employment regardless of the historical period. The idea of 'over-population' in the rural areas of India, based on the comparison of its 'man–land ratio' with that of nineteenth-century Europe, evades an analysis of poverty. This primitive index assumes that all rural people cultivate and all landless are poor. Our results indicate the contrary.

Two in five migrants of the present study had nothing to do with agriculture. Of those who worked on their own or others' land, very few were totally dependent on agriculture. Moreover, of our respondents who were involved in agriculture, the proportion of marginal operational holdings was lower, and the proportion of small and semi-medium holdings higher, compared with the all-India Agricultural Census figures. From this it appears that the propensity to migrate is greatest, not amongst the lowest stratum (marginal holdings) but the strata just above the lowest (small and semi-medium holdings). These results belie the belief that man–land ratio and migration have a direct and proportionate relation.

The pessimistic models of migration to cities reflect the policy assumption that overpopulation and deprivation in rural areas of developing countries drive people out, often into urban unemployment. This assumption has resulted in a deflection of attention from the questions of key importance: Why is it that not all or most of the poor living in the rural areas migrate to the cities and only a very small minority do? Of the overwhelming majority of the rural people in developing countries, which might be poor, how are the ones who migrate selected? And of all those who migrate, how are the ones who return selected?

Following Hoselitz, the 'poverty hypothesis' has been used widely to interpret rural to urban migration in India. States of India which are thought to be poor in terms of low per capita income, low availability of land per worker and low productivity in agriculture exhibit high rates of out-migration compared with other States of India. There have been attempts to argue that it is 'push' migration (Mohan, 1982; Ratnoo, 1987; Mallick, 2012). However, results of the present study show that there were a significantly larger number of people from average economic status and fewer from below average than expected among the migrants from a highly out-migration region of North and Central Bihar and Eastern Uttar Pradesh compared with the rest of the migrants. In fact, the results of an unsupervised clustering analysis carried out on a reduced dataset support these results quite strongly. The *poorvanchalis* get distinguished as 'above average' livelihood, literate and marginal peasants migrating to Delhi to join monthly-salary factory work. This sets them apart from the non-*poorvanchalis* who come out to be 'below average' livelihood, illiterate and daily-wage workers migrating to Delhi to join daily-wage construction work.

The remarks from respondents suggest that although the unavailability or insufficiency of work in the village may be a necessary factor making them think beyond their village, the possibility of a city job is the deciding factor that finally moved them. Deprivation is a necessary condition (a facilitating factor), but not a sufficient condition, of out-migration for most of the migrants. The sufficient condition is urban labour demand communicated through the channels of recruitment. This suggests that migration to urban areas is an option, not for all poor people, but only those who were recruited. Thus, recruitment in the urban labour market is decisive in terms of migration.

The decision-tree analysis of return migration carried out in Chapter 7 led to complementary findings. It indicated the importance of post-migration factors such as availability of residential and social spaces in the form of squatter settlements and the success migrants have in their first job, in addition to pre-migration indicators such as whether the migrants were in debt or not. Thus, whereas 'allowing' squatting is associated with staying, the destruction of squatter settlements is associated with a return. Whereas positive factors for ending the first job in

Delhi is associated with staying, layoffs, absenteeism and other reasons (mainly seasonality and unfitness for the job) are associated with a return. The other factors that have subsequent prominence are adverse factors for ending the first city job, indebtedness back in the village, sector of job in the city and age. Although the results of the decision-tree analysis need to be treated with abundant caution given the small sample sizes, and the picture that emerges is greatly nuanced, the least that can be concluded is that the thrust of these results does not support the case of 'urban bias' and 'over-urbanisation' that attribute rural-urban migration to conditions in the rural areas of origin and that deny any responsibility of the urban destination for the migrants.

The Todaro model included the role of income expectations in the migration decision. However, the way this was modelled has given rise to one of the biggest confusions about the process of rural to urban migration.

In this model, favoured jobs were to be allocated by lottery and migrants would earn lower incomes than nonmigrants. Our results show that there was no lottery involved in getting jobs. People with the right skills, education and age were recruited to *appropriate jobs* through reliable go-betweens. Yap (1976: 238) found that income differentials had less to do with the migrant status than with age and skills. Evidence from other studies also does not support the view that migrants earn less than nonmigrants (Yap, 1977; Nelson, 1979; Mohan, 1980). Potential migrants invest in education (Kochar, 2004), gather information about jobs from networks (Roberts, 2001) and search jobs from their rural base (Banerjee, 1991) in order to reduce the risk of unemployment and uncertainty of return after migration.

Although the concentration in the destination area of a pool of migrants from the same area of origin facilitated migration (Mora and Taylor, 2005), it has to be weighed against the possibility of the migrants from the same origin competing with each other for jobs (Yamauchi and Tanabe, 2003). This indicates that potential migrants assess the prospects of getting a job by weighing the conflicting effects of these two factors. The migration of young adults can be related to positive net expected returns due to larger remaining life expectancy or social norms (de Haan and Rogaly, 2002).

Another proposition of the Todaro model was that the potential migrant calculates the expected value of the lottery ticket and compares it with certain employment in rural areas. There was an accompanying assertion that migrants would have a higher incidence of unemployment. Our results contradict this belief. Labour demand was found to be buoyant for the sorts of skills these migrants brought. Contrary to the 'push' thesis, most of them were not driven from rural unemployment to urban unemployment. Migrants' expectations about city jobs were not wild, but rather they had a good idea of what jobs they would get. Such migration decisions were discovered to have been a part of family strategies to diversify income sources and risk – it is not an indefinite wait with a lottery ticket. This assertion is consistent with the earlier findings in the literature that unemployment rates among migrants were low (Papola, 1981: 99; Berry and Sabot, 1984: 111). Our results indicate that the duration of a job search is short for most of the labour migrants. Earlier studies on Delhi (Banerjee, 1986: 118–119; Suri, 1991: 250) and other studies (Sinclair, 1978: 50–51; Papola, 1981: 83–84; Bhattacharya, 2015: 3–4) reach similar conclusions.

The evidence does not back the Todaro view that wages in the modern sector are well above those in the informal sector, particularly for manual workers (Kannappan, 1985: 708–712). In fact, a study by Contreras, Gillmore and Puentes (2015) suggests that the very scheme of the Todaro model of dual markets is too extreme.

One key idea of the Todaro model is that of a sector of the urban economy with zero marginal productivity. Migrants in this informal sector are thought to be earning less in the city when they arrive than they earned in the rural areas they left. Our respondents maintained that this was not the case. Earnings in the first city job were higher than their pre-migration rural earnings. Some other studies reached a similar conclusion. Yap (1977) and others have found that migrants improve their income over their rural options immediately upon finding the first urban job. Williamson (1988a: 448) reported studies on American and British cities to make the point that historically, too, the process of migration has not been dismal, uncertain, random and blind as Todaro would like us to perceive for the developing countries. Ellis and Harris (2004), through a detailed analysis of evidence on location of economic activity and mobility, argued how migration is the best hope of getting out of poverty for individuals, families and societies.

In the light of these results, it would be pertinent to have a brief discussion on the policy approach of governments in India and other developing countries.

A snapshot of the Indian policies since its independence in the middle of the twentieth century gives a sense that the growth of big cities has, by and large, been viewed with disapproval and efforts made to stop their growth.

During the 1980s, a National Commission on Urbanisation (NCU) prepared a report on urbanisation in India and made policy recommendations. The attitude of the NCU towards migration reflected the 'too big city' syndrome of Hoselitz (1962) (GOI, Ministry of Urban Development, 1988, vol. 1, pp. 4–5). Development of "growth centres" and "counter-magnets" to stop the "avalanche" of rural to urban migration and prevent the "runaway growth of large cities and migration of rural people into metropolitan cities" were its prescriptions (GOI, Ministry of Urban Development, 1988, vol. 2, pp. 31–33).

The recommendation of the NCU matched what the government had already initiated during its Sixth Five Year Plan (1980–1981 to 1984–1985), a scheme called Integrated Development of Small and Medium Towns (IDSMT). The objective of the scheme was to slow down the growth of larger cities by developing small and medium towns through increased investments in these towns for the improvement of their infrastructure, in addition to other essential facilities and services. The idea was to place them in a position where they could "effectively serve the rural hinterland and ultimately help in checking the migration of people from rural areas and urban centres to big towns/metropolitan cities as a part of the National Policy of dispersed urbanisation" (GOI, Town and Country Planning Organisation, 1994: 25). It envisaged the development of towns that were headquarters of administrative divisions and districts. The aim was to 'generate employment' in small and medium towns in order to 'retard' rural to urban migration to large cities. The government ministries were thought to be the main 'generators' of such employment. One of the examples of this idea was the formation of the National Capital Region Planning Board to reduce 'population pressure' on Delhi by dispersing and diverting population and economic activity to other urban centres within the National Capital Region.

The idea that the size and 'hinterland' of urban centres can be determined fails to appreciate that the cost of production and distribution of goods and services is not determined by population size or geographical proximity to the point of consumption, but by the economies in the sphere of production. The 'generation' of employment by government ministries can hardly be a substitute for the functioning of economic laws. This policy approach failed to appreciate the need to study the comparative advantages of particular regions and urban centres in terms of their productive power to compete with other cities on a larger, possibly global, scale. It did not recognise heterogeneity within the categories 'big', 'medium' or 'small'. That is why it talked about each category as an aggregate. The idea that a city can be 'too big' is false unless proven that it is out of tune with the logic of accumulation and production. The belief that government can decide the 'optimal' city size is difficult to justify except at a heavy economic cost in lost productivity. The cities in India grew despite government efforts to stop them. A gist of the studies reported in a UN/UNFPA workshop (UN, 1981: 18, 40, 122, 126) and the ones reported by Ellis and Harris (2004) suggests a negligible effect of such policies. Another problem with this approach is the belief that the bureaucracy can decide which cities to develop. Otherwise, what justification could there have been for choosing political capitals of the provinces and other administrative headquarters for 'development'?

The Town and Country Planning Organisation (TCPO) of the government of India in one of its reports implicitly accepted the inevitable failure of the efforts to resist the power of labour demand as a factor determining migration:

> It is also true that migration from smaller urban areas to bigger urban areas has been taking place in the past with a view to find better employment facilities. One simple but major factor for such movements has been the belief that bigger cities offer more employment opportunities and better living standards.
>
> (GOI, Town and Country Planning Organisation, 1994: 26)

Following the launch of the economic liberalisation policies in 1991, the Eighth Five Year Plan of India (1992–1997) expressed the need to link urban growth with economic development, and it sought convergence of the IDSMT with its other urban-sector schemes to create the desired impact on small and medium towns (Batra, 2009: 18).

However, the Ninth Plan (1997–2002) more explicitly recognised the failure of the ISDMT scheme in achieving 'dispersed urbanisation' (Batra, 2009: 23). This is an admission that it is the recruitment in the urban labour market – and not a blind and random flow of 'push' migrants – that is responsible for migration to cities. It was this realisation of the strength of economic dynamism over bureaucratic directives that led to the development during this period of the schemes of employment for the poor (even though these were feeble ones) through self-employment and wage employment, as well as to the policy of allowing 100 per cent foreign direct investment (FDI) in urban projects and in infrastructure more generally.

The 2001 population census reported a decline in urban population growth. The Tenth Plan document celebrated this decline and attributed it to the "success of rural development programmes along with the limited availability of land for squatting in central urban areas" (Batra, 2009: 27). It indicated the faith of the national authorities in India in 'rural development' as an instrument to halt rural-urban migration. Even then the force of the economic dynamism prevailed and the failed vision behind the IDSMT scheme led to its eventual merger in 2005 with a scheme called the Urban Infrastructure Development Scheme for Small and Medium Towns (UIDSSMT). Of course, the small and medium towns need much more policy attention than they have been given so far, not only for improvement of the quality of life in these towns, but also in the realisation of their role in economic growth and poverty alleviation, and therefore, our criticism of the IDSMT scheme ought not be misunderstood as undermining this need. The only point being made here is that jockeying and selling of the IDSMT scheme as an instrument to stop migration to big cities was neither justified nor plausible.

The decades of neo-liberal 'reforms' have seen an unprecedented spurt in the growth of the urban population, as well as in rural to urban migration (Sainath, 2011). This has made it completely untenable for anyone to claim measures to halt, or blunt or manipulate or even ignore the processes of urbanisation and migration to cities.

Past failures did not deter the government of India, in 2005, from positioning yet another scheme – the Mahatma Gandhi National Rural Employment Guarantee Act (MNREGA), as a policy to discourage rural to urban migration. An effective and immediate deterrence of distress migration arising out of natural calamities (like drought, flood, earthquake, etc.) or social oppression (like feudal discriminations, atrocities, etc.) may be a legitimate target of such policies. In the short term, such schemes may also remove for a certain section of rural poor the facilitating factor of 'relative deprivation' in rural areas, and hence a section of potential migrants may be partially or temporarily out of the pool of rural labour that is ready to move. The overall rural population still being large, it is quite likely that there may be no insufficiency of those ready to move to cities in case urban labour demand warrants it. So, although MNREGA may be a legitimate tool for rural development, to claim that it will deter economic migration to cities is to daydream. Rural development leads to an increase in the demand for education and health, as well as aspirations for diverse skills and jobs that urban areas are more capable of offering. Rural development also increases demand for industrial and service products, which in turn, increases urban demand for labour in these sectors. Given these dynamics, rural development could in fact lead to an increase rather than a decrease in rural to urban migration. The belief that rural develop-ment leads to a decline in the rural to urban migration of labour indicates a persis-tent and perhaps wilful inadequacy in understanding the dynamics of migration to cities. For example, Dasgupta (2013: 96) reports that there had been no significant change in migration since the implementation of the National Rural Employment Guarantee Act and that with the exception of the women interviewed, all the men said that they still had to go to nearby big cities to look for work.

The early signs following a change of central government in 2014 indicate almost an abdication of responsibility to even reflect on the question of rural to urban migration. The Smart Cities Mission is now the latest pet urban scheme of the government. Its 'Mission Statement & Guidelines' do not contain any verb or noun or adjective that has anything to do with the word 'migration' (GOI, Ministry of Urban Development, 2015). This seems to be the beginning of a more exclusionary urbanisation, where it would be harder for the poor people to get a foothold in cities. It is ironic that at a time when the increasing role of urban areas in economic and social development is being recognised almost universally and the role of migration in the economic vibrancy of the cities in India is being acknowledged (IOM, 2015: 50), the central government does not even mention it in its most propagated urban 'mission'.

Although the Smart Cities Mission shows the priorities of the government are skewed, its flawed political mind-set has been evident during the latest elections to the Indian Parliament and the Bihar State Legislative Assembly where the pre-sent head of the government of India persistently berated internal migration in India, blaming it on a lack of development in the sending areas (Ashok, 2013; "Nitish Kumar and Lalu Yadav turned Bihari youths into migrants: Modi", 2015, October 25). The situation on the ground in destination areas already mirrors this negative outlook towards migrants. A study that used evidence from fieldwork in Mumbai and Kolkata shows that internal migrants experience a lesser citizenship status and curtailed citizenship rights because of their migrant status. In Maha-rashtra, for instance, the bureaucracy and local politicians have been shown to restrict migrant rights by allocating ration cards preferentially to ethnic Maha-rashtrians rather than to migrants (Abbas, 2015).

It seems clear that official government policies in India continue to reflect a lack of clarity and focus with respect to migration. This is particularly alarm-ing given future projections. By 2050, it is estimated that the urban population in developing countries will rise by over 3 billion, a whopping 135 per cent rise compared to 2005 (UNFPA, 2007). Sadly, the lack of understanding or acceptance of the economic dynamics of migration seems to extend beyond India into much of the developing world.

For example, based on a survey of forty-eight Poverty Reduction Strategy Papers (PRSPs), Black, Sabates-Wheeler and Skeldon (2003: 18–19) report how migration was widely portrayed in a negative light. Of the forty-eight PRSPs, twenty-one did not even mention migration, and almost all the remaining ones referred to migration in negative or pejorative terms. As reported in a 2013 UN report, the percentage of governments that regarded the spatial distribution of population in their countries as satisfactory declined from 29 per cent in 1996 to 10 per cent in 2013; the percentage of governments keen for a major change in the spatial distribution has increased from 42 per cent to 60 per cent. In 2013, a much greater proportion of governments in less developed regions (70 per cent) preferred a major change in the spatial distribution of population than in more developed regions (29 per cent) (UN, 2013: 108). In recent years, more governments have seen the need to devise policies to slow rural to urban migration. According to this UN report, from amongst the 185 countries for which data were available in 2013, 80 per cent of governments had policies to lower rural to urban migration, an increase from 38 per cent in 1996. In 2013, the proportion of governments that had policies to lower rural to urban migration was higher in less developed regions (84 per cent) than in more developed regions (67 per cent). This proportion was even higher in least developed countries (88 per cent). Between 1996 and 2013, the proportion of governments with policies to lower rural to urban migration is reported to have increased in both more and less developed regions, as well as in all world regions (UN, 2013: 109). In fact, the policymakers in low-income countries tend to consider rural-urban migration as the main contributor to overcrowding, congestion, increasing exposure to environmental hazards and to shortfalls in basic infrastructure and services. (IOM, 2015: 19)

Examples of policies motivated in such a way abound. Apartheid in South Africa used harsh measures to monitor what was aimed to be temporary migration to the cities. Indonesia tried resettling people from high-density to low-density areas through its policy of 'transmigration'. The Mexican government tried restricting migration by discouraging certain types of investment in large cities (Cole and Sanders, 1983). Like India, Malaysia, Thailand and Peru also adopted policies to discourage migration to big cities (Waddington, 2003). Malaysia's attempt to stem urbanisation through rural development failed (Skeldon, 1997). The potential of a rural sector to supply a mass of labour to cities is so high in China (Henderson, 2005) that there are questions if city-ward migration can be impeded. Bangladesh has been following similar policies of reducing congestion in large cities through promoting industry and services in peri-urban and secondary cities (Skeldon, 2003). Waddington (2003) finds significant challenges to such policies of decentralisation in India, Malaysia and Tanzania.

Talking of the term 'floating population' in the context of his fieldwork in Xiamen in China, Breman (2010: 241) observes that this term indicates that this is how authorities treat the newcomers who flock to the city, but this stubbornly held belief that they are dealing with a mass of transient workers is diametrically opposed to the desire of the migrants themselves to settle in Xiamen, at least for the duration of their working lives, if not for good. He describes the *hukou* system in China as a wall preventing migration to maintain the 'rural-urban apartheid'. Breman astutely notes that what is presented as an administrative practice, is in fact, an instrument to minimise the costs of mobilised labour and thereby bolster the position of the Chinese economy in the global market (Breman, 2010: 271–272).

Interestingly, Ellis and Harris (2004: 9–17) report how Chinese public authorities in certain sending areas started realising the potential benefits of migration and began to promote migration. In this regard, they cite an example of Anhui Province going to the extent of training would-be migrants at the locations of origin. They conclude that the urbanisation of the poor implicit in general urbanisation has the potential to bring many more of the poor to the locations most favourable to overcoming poverty. They argue that because most of the world's poor live in rural areas and the patterns of economic growth, dynamism and opportunity vary across both rural and urban areas, no single formula can guarantee poverty reduction and therefore, there is no point in stopping people from moving to areas they find more remunerating and rewarding. They rue the instinct to control as reflected in the tendency of the governments to block mobility of people as overriding any thoughts of the positive contribution to economic dynamism that people on the move make. In policy terms, Ellis and Harris (2004: 18) warn against the simplistic tendency of rushing to residential locations where high concentrations of poor are found and instead advocate a better understanding of how the 'routes out of poverty' involve exchange and mobility.

It is high time the governments at different levels realise the key role that migration can play to benefit the sending and receiving areas, the country as a whole and the migrants themselves. It is better if the poor have more options. Ellis and Harris (2004: 18) rightly observe that more options are created in the 'vortex of dynamic growth processes' and not in the declining sectors that the migrants leave behind.

The results of our study leave no doubt that migrants make moves that are best for them and their families. An emerging body of research brings out how mobility is good both for the sending and receiving areas. Hence, the governments at different levels need to recognise and build this wisdom into all their policies.

References

Abbas, R. (2015). Internal migration and citizenship in India, *Journal of Ethnic and Migration Studies*. 42(1), 150–168. Retrieved from http://dx.doi.org/10.1080/1369183X.2015.1100067

Ashok, A.D. (2013, November 22). Why is Narendra Modi pitying migrants from UP? *India Today*. Retrieved from http://indiatoday.intoday.in/story/why-is-narendra-modi-pitying-migrants-from-up/1/326058.html

Banerjee, B. (1986). *Rural to urban migration and the urban labour market: A case study of Delhi*. Delhi: Himalaya Publishing House.

Banerjee, B. (1991). The determinants of migrating with a pre-arranged job and the initial duration of urban unemployment: An analysis based on Indian data on rural to urban migrants, *Journal of Development Economics*, 36(2), 337–351.

Batra, L. (2009). *A Review of urbanisation and urban policy in post-independent India*. Working Paper Series. New Delhi: Centre for the Study of Law and Governance, Jawaharlal Nehru University.

Berry, A. and Sabot, R.H. (1984). Unemployment and economic development, *Economic Development and Cultural Change*, 33: 99–116.

Bhattacharya, P.C. (2015). *A model of optimal development*. Working Paper No. 2015–04. Edinburgh: Department of Economics, Heriot-Watt University.

Black, R., Sabates-Wheeler, R. and Skeldon, R. et al. (2003). *Mapping study of migration issues*. Sussex Centre for Migration Research, March, processed.

Breman, J. (1996). *Footloose labour: Working in India's informal economy*. Cambridge: Cambridge University Press.

Breman, J. (2010). *Outcast labour in Asia: Circulation and informalization of the work force at the bottom of the economy*. New Delhi: Oxford University Press.

Buchanan, D.H. (1966). *The development of capitalist enterprise in India*. London: Frank Cass & Co. Ltd.

Clunies-Ross, A., Forsyth, D. and Huq, M. (2009). Migration and urbanization. In Clunies-Ross, A., Forsyth, D. and Huq, M. (Eds.), *Development economics* (Chapter 14, pp. 403–432). Maidenhead: McGraw-Hill Education.

Cole, W. and Sanders, R. (1983). Interstate migration and in Mexico: Variations on the Todaro theme, *Journal of Development Economics*, 12(3): 341–354.

Contreras, D., Gillmore, R. and Puentes, E. (2015). Self-employment and queues for wage work: Evidence from Chile, *Journal of International Development*, DOI: 10.1002/jid.3074.

Dasgupta, P. (2013). *Employment generation programs and long term development: The case of India's National Rural Employment Guarantee Act*. PhD dissertation, University of Missouri, ProQuest, Kansas City and Ann Arbor.

de Haan, A. and Rogaly, B. (2002). Migrant workers and their role in rural change, *Journal of Development Studies*, 38(5): 1–14.

Ellis, F. and Harris, N. (2004). *Development patterns, mobility and livelihood diversification*. Keynote paper for DFID Sustainable Development Retreat, University of Surrey, Guildford. Retrieved from http://www.researchgate.net/publication/255039830

GOI, Ministry of Urban Development (1988). *Report of the national commission on urbanisation, Volumes 1 and 2*. New Delhi: Ministry of Urban Development, Government of India.

GOI, Ministry of Urban Development (2015). *Smart cities mission statement & guidelines*. New Delhi: Ministry of Urban Development, Government of India.

GOI, Town and Country Planning Organisation (1994). Integrated development of small and medium towns: Revised guidelines. In *IDSMT: At a glance*. New Delhi: Town and Country Planning Organisation, Government of India (Unpublished).

Henderson, J.V. (2005). Urbanization and growth. In Aghion, P. and Durlauf, S. (Eds.), *Handbook of economic growth* (Volume 1, Part B, pp. 1543–1591). Amsterdam: North Holland.

Hoselitz, B.F. (1962). The role of urbanisation in economic development: Some international comparisons. In Turner, R. (Ed.), *India's urban future* (pp. 157–181). Berkeley and Los Angeles: University of California Press.

International Organization for Migration (IOM) (2015). *Migration report 2015: Migrants and cities: New partnerships to manage mobility*. Retrieved from http://publications. iom.int/system/files/pdf/wmr2015_en.pdf

Kannappan, S. (1985). Urban employment and the labour market in developing nations, *Economic Development and Cultural Change*, 33: 669–730.

Kochar, A. (2004). Urban influences on rural schooling in India, *Journal of Development Economics*, 74(1): 113–136.

Lenin, V.I. (1956). *Development of capitalism in Russia: The process of formation of home market for large scale industry*. Moscow: Foreign Languages Publishing House.

Mallick, S.K. (2012). *Disentangling the poverty effects of sectoral output, prices and policies in India.* New Delhi: Subregional Office for South and South-West Asia (SRO-SSWA), Economic and Social Commission for Asia and the Pacific (ESCAP).

Mohan, R. (1980). *The people of Bogata: Who they are, what they earn, where they live.* World Bank Staff Working Paper No. 390. Washington, DC: World Bank.

Mohan, R. (1982). *The morphology of urbanisation in India: Some results from the 1981 census.* Paper presented in the seminar on Urbanisation and Planned Economic Development – Present and future perspectives, organised by the Centre for the Study of Regional Development, Jawaharlal Nehru University, New Delhi.

Mora, J. and Taylor, E.J. (2005). Determinants of migration, destination, and sector choice: Disentangling individual, household, and community effects. In Ozden, C. and Schiff, M. (Eds.), *International migration, remittances and the brain drain* (pp. 21–51). New York: The World Bank and Palgrave Macmillan.

Nelson, J.M. (1979). *Access to power: Politics and the urban poor in developing nations.* Princeton, NJ: Princeton University Press.

Nitish Kumar and Lalu Yadav turned Bihari youths into migrants: Modi. (2015, October 25). *Firstpost.com.* Retrieved from http://www.firstpost.com/politics/nitish-kumar-and-lalu-yadav-turned-bihari-youths-into-migrants-modi-2481776.html

Papola, T.S. (1981). *Urban informal sector in a developing economy.* New Delhi: Vikas Publishing House.

Ratnoo, H.S. (1987). *Migration, urbanisation and economic development: Rajasthan in the all India context (1961–81).* Unpublished MPhil dissertation, Jawaharlal Nehru University, New Delhi.

Roberts, K. (2001). The determinants of job choice by rural labor migrants in Shanghai, *China Economic Review*, 12(1): 15–39.

Sainath, P. (2011, September 27). Decadal journeys: Debt and despair spur urban growth, *An OP-ED in The Hindu*, Delhi, p. 11.

Sinclair, S.W. (1978). *Urbanization and labour markets in developing countries.* London: Croom Helm.

Skeldon, R. (1997). Rural-to-urban migration and its implications for poverty alleviation, *Asia-Pacific Population Journal*, 12(1): 3–16.

Skeldon, R. (2003). *Migration and migration policy in Asia: A synthesis of selected cases.* Paper presented at the Conference on Migration, Development and Pro-Poor Policy Choices in Asia, Dhaka, Bangladesh.

Stark, O. (1991). *The migration of labour.* Oxford: Basil Blackwell.

Stark, O. (2006). Inequality and migration: A behavioral link, *Economics Letters*, 91: 146–152.

Stark, O., Micevska, M. and Mycielski, J. (2009). Relative poverty as a determinant of migration: Evidence from Poland, *Economics Letters*, 103: 119–122.

Suri, P. (1991). *Housing for the urban poor: People's needs, priorities and government response – Case study of Delhi.* Unpublished doctoral thesis, School of Planning and Architecture, New Delhi.

United Nations (1981). *Population distribution policies in development planning.* Papers of the United Nations/UNFPA workshop on population distribution policies in development planning, Bangkok, September 4–13, 1979, United Nations, New York.

United Nations (2013). *World population policies 2013.* New York: United Nations. Retrieved from http://www.un.org/en/development/desa/population/publications/pdf/policy/WPP2013/wpp2013.pdf#zoom=100

United Nations Population Fund (UNFPA) (2007). *State of world population 2007: Unleashing the potential of urban growth.* New York: UNPF. Retrieved from http://www.unfpa.org/publications/state-world-population-2007

Waddington, C. (2003). *National policy and internal migration.* Paper presented at the Regional Conference on Migration, Development and Pro-Poor Policy Choices in Asia, June 22–24.

Williamson, J.G. (1988a). Migration and urbanisation. In Chenery, H. and Srinivasan, T. (Eds.), *Handbook of development economics* (Volume I, pp. 425–465). North Holland: Oxford.

Yamauchi, F. and Tanabe, S. (2003). *Nonmarket networks among migrants: Evidence from Bangkok, Thailand.* International Food Policy Research Institute, Food Consumption and Nutrition Division (FCND) Discussion Paper No.169. Washington: International Food Policy Research Institute.

Yap, L. (1976). Rural-urban migration and urban underemployment in Brazil, *Journal of Development Economics*, 3: 227–243.

Yap, L. (1977). The Attraction of cities: A review of migration literature, *Journal of Development Economics*, 4(3): 239–264.

Appendix A

Empirical backdrop of starting the present longitudinal study in the early 1990s: a detailed note on then-prevalent interpretation of inter-State rural to urban migration in India

(In support of Chapter 1)

The present study was planned, designed and started in the early 1990s. Therefore, the situation regarding migration and urbanisation up to that point formed the empirical backdrop to the study. Although it is important, it would sound 'historic' to place its details in Chapter 1 that introduces the work. Therefore, although some important parts have gone into Chapter 1, the whole has been kept as this appendix.

This appendix presents the prevalent interpretation of the trends of inter-State rural to urban migration in India with the goal of providing a macro-empirical context to the key issue of this study – migration to Delhi. Therefore, it provides a general picture of inter-State rural to urban migration in India and its interpretation from the angle of the conventional wisdom at the time the present study was initiated.

Inter-State migration: the conventional wisdom

Due to an imbalance in the relative size of the two sectors, rural and urban, a relatively small movement from the rural sector is able to account for a significant increase in the population of urban areas. In such a situation of low urbanisation and high urban population growth, the perception of the national urbanisation policymakers in India was ambivalent. Hence they stressed the need to 'check urban growth' and 'bring order' to 'this chaos'. At the same time, however, they wanted to aim for 'higher urbanisation to reach economic prosperity' (GOI, Town and Country Planning Organisation, 1975: 7–8). And of course, the villain of the piece was migration: "the gains of economic development should not be washed away by the flood of migrating population to the cities creating squalor, discord, heterogeneity and urban ugliness in all its facets" (GOI, Town and Country Planning Organisation, 1975, p. 7). Apparently they seem not to have agreed amongst themselves that it was not possible to achieve higher levels of urbanisation without a substantial transfer of population from rural to urban areas.

At the same time, it was very common to find the view that mobility in India was low and declining. Bose (1980) noted that rural to rural is the main stream of migration and that the rural to urban stream is dominant only in inter-State movements. He states that only 3 per cent of the male population was enumerated outside the State of birth. Kundu (1986) stated that mobility was declining in India, particularly over long distances. Earlier on, Bogue and Zachariah (1962: 31, 45) had noted that return migration was substantial in India, and close ties with rural origin fostered it.

According to the Census figures, the percentage of inter-State migrants[1] in India's rural and urban male population (inter-State migrant ratios) declined during the sixties and seventies[2] (Table A-1.1)[3]. Some argued that this was expected because there was an increase in the urban population and, with this, the contribution of the natural increase tended to become greater than the contribution of migration (Keyfitz, 1980; Rogers, 1984). Moreover, as Bogue and Zachariah noted, the tendency of the birth place data is to understate migration.

Contrary to the fears of a decline in inter-State mobility, the relative importance of inter-State migration, especially in urban areas, seemed to be increasing. The number of inter-State migrants as a percentage of total internal male migrants increased in urban areas during both the decades and in rural areas during the sixties (Table A-1.2). Looking at the State level, we found that the inter-State component of the total internal male migrants, particularly in urban areas, increased over these two decades for all the States except for some decline for Haryana and Maharashtra and West Bengal. The concerns that long-distance migration was declining needed a careful re-examination in the light of this fact.

Bogue and Zachariah had suggested, on the basis of a study of 1941–1951, that a rising tempo of rural to urban migration existed throughout India (Bogue and Zachariah, 1962: 30). Their experimental work showed that State of birth statistics had an built-in bias towards understating the volume of movement that has taken place (Bogue, 1960). They estimated the rate of net in-migration to the cities equivalent to 20 per cent of the 1941 population. It amounted to a rate of net out-migration from rural areas equivalent to 3 per cent of their 1941 population. The problem with the Bogue and Zachariah estimates was that they were not able to take into account the reclassification of towns and international migration during the decade. The figure for the latter was particularly high during that decade due to the partition of the country in 1947.

Mehrotra (1974) was one of the first comprehensive studies of migration in India. Apart from the mostly usual results about the characteristics of migrants, the findings on the measurement of migration showed how migration during the decade 1961–1971 fell in terms of the migrant ratios and growth rates, particularly in the urban areas.

Table A-1.1 reveals that there was considerable variation in the proportion of inter-State migrants in the male population among the States of India. Tables A-1.3 and A-1.4 show the broad magnitudes of inter-State out-migration for each major

State of India. States with a low proportion of migrants in the rural population and greater out-migration from their rural and urban areas shared certain common features. These features were low availability of land per agricultural worker, higher share of net State domestic product originating in the primary sector, low productivity of agriculture and high rate of unemployment. Bihar, Uttar Pradesh and Rajasthan were understood to be most typical of such States (Ratnoo, 1987). Apparently it was because of the combination of these factors that many felt that the rural 'push' factor was the explanation for the areas of origin of the migrants. There had been a decline in the female–male ratio in the highly out-migrating States of India and a particularly heavy decline in Bihar, during 1981–1991. There was some speculation that this decline is due to return migration (predominantly of males), supposedly a sign of worsening 'employment problems'.

The most common anxiety in many of the analyses of the level and pattern of rural to urban migration in India had been regarding employment growth. It was noted that only a marginal decline had occurred in the dominance of the primary sector in the occupational structure of the workforce, despite a significant decline in its share in the net domestic product of India. The higher growth rates of income and employment in the tertiary sector compared with those in the secondary sector had been observed since the seventies. It was being interpreted as the failure of the secondary sector to generate additional employment (Rao, 1987). The 'informal sector' was perceived as absorbing poor rural migrants in low-paying, low-productivity jobs. Mitra, Mukherji and Bose, et al. (1980) thought that despite the concentration of investment in a few metropolitan nodes, proliferation of jobs in them was mostly of tertiary sector, low-grade trade and services. Scarcity of land was thought to be 'pushing' the migrants out of the rural areas (Hoselitz, 1962: 169), and rural poverty was thought to be 'spilling over' into urban areas. Dandekar and Rath (1971: 35) thought that

> [t]he character of urban poverty is the consequence of the continuous migration of the rural poor into the urban areas in search of a livelihood, their failure to find adequate means to support themselves there and the resulting growth of pavement and slum life in the cities.

Thus, migration was seen as a process that simply transformed rural poverty into urban poverty. It was thought that due to the limited job opportunities in the modern industrial sector, workers were being forced into the tertiary sector on unfavourable terms. These views were very commonplace in much of the literature on migration in India. Mitra (1990) was just an example of writings of this type.

The tempo of urbanisation in India declined during 1981–1991 for the first time since 1961 (GOI, Census of India, 1991a: 13). We found that at the all-India level, the rate of growth of the population living in rural areas increased slightly from 1.78 per cent during 1971–1981 to 1.80 per cent during 1981–1991. The urban growth rate, however, declined from 3.83 per cent to 3.09 per cent (GOI, Census of India, 1991a, p. 51). It was argued that because natural growth had remained more or less the same during the seventies and the eighties (GOI, Census of India,

1991a, p. 52) and reclassification did not account for it[4], the decline in urban growth was due to a decline in migration.

At the State-level, the seventies saw a tapering off of urban growth in the more urbanised States and a sharp increase in the urban growth rate in backward States. This sharp dichotomy did not appear to hold so well for the decade 1981–1991. Nevertheless, it could be said that most of the major States with a higher proportion of the urban population registered lower decennial growth in their urban population, and the ones with relatively lower proportions registered comparatively higher growth rates in their urban population (GOI, Census of India 1991, 1991a: 15, 171–361).

Talking about the newly urbanising States, Mohan (1982) suggested that with the exhaustion of land that could be brought into additional cultivation and with low increases in productivity, the agricultural incomes in the States like Andhra Pradesh, Bihar, Madhya Pradesh, Orissa and Uttar Pradesh were not rising; nor could additional labour be absorbed as in earlier times (Mohan, 1982: 36). Hence the acceleration of urbanisation seemed to be the result of a push from rural areas. Because of small existing urban population, a small decline in labour demand in rural areas caused a large proportional change in the population in urban areas. Given the large size of these States, the absolute magnitude of the urban population was also large (about 55 million in 1981). Mohan argued that unless there was a significant productivity change in agriculture in these areas, and one that was labour using, this trend could be magnified over the next decade. He thought that the combination of demand-pull in the richer group of States and push in poorer States caused the acceleration in urbanisation during the eighties. The author suggested the need for employment generation in urban areas "for the increasing number of people who will tend to be pushed out from the rural areas – either because of immiseration or because of technological change."

• *Subregional analysis*

Mohan has suggested that within these States there were parts that are 'pushing' the rural population and others that were not.

The sub-regions of these States where population growth was highest were the ones where there had been heavy public investment in industry and mining or the ones where high agricultural growth took place. It seemed likely that in these regions incomes were rising fast, creating a demand for urban goods and services.

In contrast to the relatively dynamic regions mentioned earlier were the particularly poor and generally stagnant regions such as Northern and Central Bihar and Eastern Uttar Pradesh, which were geographically contiguous regions then accounting for a population of 100 persons. Table A-1.5 provides the names of the administrative districts for each of these sub-regions. In these regions the rural population growth was high, and a significant proportion of the urban population growth was due to the reclassification of many villages as towns. In Eastern Uttar Pradesh, medium-size towns (all district headquarters) such as Ballia, Gazipur, Azamgarh, Deoria, Basti and Sultanpur had all grown rapidly, whereas the larger cities of Allahabad, Gorakhpur, Varanasi and Faizabad were growing slowly. The level of urbanisation was still low in these regions: 6 per cent in Northern Bihar, 10 per cent in Eastern Uttar Pradesh and about 14 per cent in Central Bihar (which was dominated by Patna). The relatively high rates of urbanisation in these areas were accompanied by high rates of rural population growth. Mohan (1982) concluded:

> It seems fairly clear that whatever urbanisation is taking place here is of the 'rural push' variety: the high rural growth also indicates that, were opportunities of urban employment in this region to exist, very high rates of rural-urban migration can be expected.

The 'poverty hypothesis' had been used widely to interpret rural to urban migration in India. As a matter of fact, Hoselitz used India as a case of 'over-urbanisation'. This interpretation of the Indian case through its regional approach based on aggregate data, along with the research problem that emerged from the theoretical and analytical studies, has helped the statement of hypotheses in Chapter 1 of this book.

Notes

1 In the tables of this appendix, migrant is defined as one enumerated at a place different from his place of birth. Admittedly, it is no more than a partial indicator of population movement. Mehrotra (1974) discusses the data limitations following this concept. Since 1971, the place of last residence criterion has been used in migration tables extensively, although population is still classified by the place of birth as well. A large part of female migration in India is associational (related with family move) or is due to marriage. Classification by reason for migration was available for the 1981 Population Census only at the time this study was being planned. Hence, studies of economic migration based on census data were restricted to male migration only. Only the male population is considered in the tables of this appendix.
2 The migration tables of the 1991 Census, which gave data for the 1980s, were not out at the time the present study was initiated.
3 All table numbers with the prefix 'A' (e.g., Table A-1.1) are in Appendix F that contains the statistical tables.
4 Although fewer places emerged as new towns in 1991 is a factor accounting for the decline in the growth rate of urban population during 1981–1991 compared with 1971–1981, the 1981–1991 urban growth rate was lower than the 1971–1981 urban growth rate, even when we count out the effect of reclassification. For details, see GOI, Census of India 1991 (1991a), statement 30, p. 54.

References

Bogue, D.J. (1960). The use of place-of-birth statistics and duration-of-residence data for measuring internal migration. In *Seminar on evaluation and utilisation of census data.* Bombay: Demographic Training and Research Centre.

Bogue, D.J. and Zachariah, K.C. (1962). Urbanisation and migration in India. In Turner, R. (Ed.), *India's urban future* (pp. 27–54). Berkeley and Los Angeles: University of California Press.

Bose, A. (1980). *Studies in India's urbanisation (1901–2001)*. New Delhi: TMH.

Dandekar, V.M. and Rath, N. (1971). *Poverty in India*. Bombay: Indian School of Political Economy.

GOI, Census of India 1991 (1991a). *Series-1, India – provisional population totals: Rural-urban distribution, paper-2 of 1991*. New Delhi: Registrar General and Census Commissioner, Government of India.

GOI, Town and Country Planning Organisation (1975). *National urbanisation policy: Proceedings of the meeting of expert group*. New Delhi: Town and Country Planning Organisation, Government of India.

Hoselitz, B.F. (1962). The Role of urbanisation in economic development: Some international comparisons. In Turner, R. (Ed.), *India's urban future* (pp. 157–181). Berkeley and Los Angeles: University of California Press.

Keyfitz, N. (1980). Do cities grow by natural increase or by migration? *Geographical Analysis*, 12: 142–156.

Kundu, A. (1986). Migration, urbanisation and inter-regional inequality: The emerging socio-political challenge, *Economic and Political Weekly*, 21(46): 2005–2008.

Mehrotra, G.K. (1974). *Birth place migration in India*. Special monograph No. 1; Census of India, 1971. New Delhi: Registrar General and Census Commissioner.

Mitra, A. (1990). Duality, employment structure and poverty incidence: The slum perspective, *Indian Economic Review*, XXV(1): 57–73.

Mitra, A., Mukherji, S. and Bose, R. et al. (1980). *Indian cities: Their industrial structure, immigration and capital investment 1961–71*. New Delhi: Abhinav.Mohan, R. (1982). *The morphology of urbanisation in India: Some results from the 1981 census*. Paper presented in the seminar on Urbanisation and Planned Economic Development – Present and future perspectives, organised by the Centre for the Study of Regional Development, Jawaharlal Nehru University, New Delhi.

Rao, V.K.R.V. (1987). Growth and structural change in the Indian economy. In Brahmananda, P.R. (Ed.), *Development process of the Indian economy* (pp. 1–41). New Delhi: Himalaya Publishing House.

Ratnoo, H.S. (1987). *Migration, urbanisation and economic development: Rajasthan in the all India context (1961–81)*. Unpublished MPhil dissertation, Jawaharlal Nehru University, New Delhi.

Rogers, A. (1984). *Migration, urbanisation and spatial population dynamics*. Boulder, CO: Westview Press.

Appendix B

**Methodological details of the sample surveys and
demographic profile of the criteria migrants**

(In support of Chapter 2)

*Method in estimating the percentage of the squatter population in
different parts of Delhi*

First the decision had to be made regarding which part of Delhi to sample. The
organisations that kept and collected data on Delhi used different classifications. For instance, the Municipal Corporation of Delhi divided Delhi into four-
teen Zones; the Delhi Administration into five Districts; the Delhi Development
Authority into eight Planning Divisions and the Slum Wing of the DDA into five
Zones. Unfortunately, there was hardly any compatibility with each other. The
data were often incomparable.

During the information hunt we discovered an updated list of 929 *jhuggie jhonpari* clusters (squatter settlements), disaggregated for each of the five Zones of
the Slum Wing of the Delhi Development Authority (DDA) (Delhi Development
Authority, Slum Wing, C. 1990). The list also gave the number of *jhuggies* for
each cluster. In order to estimate the Zone-wise squatter population, it was necessary to estimate the average number of persons per *jhuggie* for each Zone. For this,
the Food and Supplies Department of the Delhi Administration were approached.
Their Circle offices located in different parts of the city had to be visited for data
on the number of *jhuggie* ration cards and number of sugar units. The average
number of sugar units per *jhuggie* ration card was estimated for each Zone of the
DDA (Slum Wing) by taking the average of the number of sugar units per *jhuggie*
ration card for Food and Supplies Department Circles serving a particular Zone
of the Slum Wing as an average for that Zone. Multiplying this figure of average
number of sugar units per *jhuggie* ration card by the number of *jhuggies* as given
in the DDA (Slum Wing) list, it was possible to estimate the population living in
squatter settlements for each Zone. But no data for the total population and area of
these Slum Wing Zones exist. However, the area figures and the population figures
for 1971 and 1981 could be found for the eight Planning Divisions of the DDA.
The area-related information was collected from the unpublished records of the

Zonal Planning Division of the DDA, and the population figures were taken from the Master Plan for Delhi (GOI, Ministry of Urban Development, 1990: 120). The estimates for the 1991 population were made, assuming that the 1971–1981 trends of population growth continued in the eighties. These 8 Planning Divisions could be regrouped into the 5 Slum Wing Zones, although the latter needed some adjustments for this because the Slum Wing Zones included some areas that were outside the DDA Zones.

With these steps, it was possible to estimate the percentage of squatter populations in different parts of Delhi (Table A-2.1).

Examination of density criterion: South Delhi or East Delhi?

This part of the appendix examines the evidence to see if population density meant poverty in the context of Delhi.

According to an unpublished *Report of the Committee on Poverty Line in Delhi* by the Delhi Administration, Bureau of Economics and Statistics (1982: 40–41), the availability in per capita terms of water, sewerage and hospital beds was low in East Delhi. According to an unpublished document on a development plan for higher education facilities in Delhi, the 'population/college ratio' was high in East Delhi compared with the other parts of Delhi (DDA, Perspective Planning Wing, 1983: 5). On the other hand, South Delhi stood highest in terms of most of these facilities in per capita terms. However, these indicators did not mean that the people living in the squatter settlements of South Delhi were any better off than those of East Delhi because the area averages have the tendency to hide the group differences.

The provisional results of the Economic Census of the Union Territory of Delhi, conducted in September 1990, showed that Shahdara Zone of the Municipal Corporation of Delhi (about the same as the East Zone of the Slum Wing of the DDA) topped in terms of its percentage share of the enterprises as well as that of the persons usually working in Delhi (Bureau of Economics and Statistics, Delhi Administration, 1991: 8–9). However, in this part of Delhi more enterprises were without premises than those with premises (Delhi Administration, 1991, p. 11) and more own-account (those using household labour only) than establishments (those working with the assistance of at least one hired worker on a fairly regular basis). It lagged behind in terms of its percentage share of the hired persons usually working in Delhi (Delhi Administration, 1991, p. 13). Moreover, this Census did not cover certain kinds of employment opportunities, for example, those of the domestic servants, which were greater in the case of South Delhi. In this context, it was useful to take into account the studies by the Perspective Planning Wing of the DDA (1986: 9), and Suri (1991: 258) that indicated that the squatter settlement dwellers predominantly depended on cheap means of transport and tended to live near their place of work. This corroborated the intuitive understanding that the higher employment opportunities attract labourers and these labourers tend to settle as close as possible to the places of their work. A survey by the Institute for Socialist Education (1989: 13) showed that 76 per cent of the squatter settlement dwellers of Delhi walk to their work and the rest used bicycles (12 per cent) and buses (12 per cent).

One more objection to the South Zone being chosen was that the squatter population is very highly concentrated in a part of it and South Zone of Delhi was usually perceived as a 'rich area'. This concentration of squatter settlements matched closely with the fact that the South Zone had the biggest industrial belt of Delhi. It was hoped that the sampling scheme would take care of this problem by allocating the greater probability of choosing squatters from this area of concentration (because of the very reason of this concentration). Moreover, this 'rich area' provided a lot of domestic employment and offered the best pay. Finally, the South Zone was selected because the notion that the poor and the rich do not live side by side and the conceptualisation by area were mainly responsible for the popular perception of rich and poor areas.

Index for selection of squatter settlements in Delhi

The following weights (given in brackets) were applied to the selected indicators for the calculations of the 'index of poverty and recentness of migration' for the 159 squatter settlements of South Delhi for which information was available:

1   The percentage of 5 to 12 years not going to school (0.1666)
2   The percentage distribution by occupation of those above 18 years (0.1669).
    The weight was further distributed as follows:

    i   *Mazdoor* (unskilled worker) (0.0534)
    ii   *Karigar* (skilled worker) (0.0267)
    iii   Service (0.0134)
    iv   Business (0.0134)
    v   No occupation (0.0601)

3   The percentage of 12 to 18 years working (0.1666)
4   The percentage of the scheduled caste in the population (0.1666)
5   The percentage distribution of households according to year of migration (0.3333). The weight was further distributed as follows:

    i   1960–1965 (0)
    ii   1966–1973 (0)
    iii   1974–1976 (0.0400)
    iv   1977–1980 (0.0667)
    v   1981–1985 (0.0933)
    vi   1986–1989 (0.1333)

Two clusters with the highest values of the index from each of the five size-groups (up to 100, 100 to 250, 250 to 500, 500 to 1000, 1000 to 3600) were selected.

These ten sites were visited for physical verification and observation. It was found that one of these settlements had been demolished, and hence the cluster with the next highest value of index in that size-group was substituted for it. The observations made during this round of the selected clusters corroborated the expectation that poor migrants can be found in 'rich areas'.

The selected census blocks

The following census blocks were the selected (Census of India, 1991, 1992):

1   Charge No. 109, Enumeration Block 87, Subhas Camp T. Huts Nos. (1–137)
2   Charge No. 109, Enumeration Block 92, Subhas Camp T. Huts Nos. (686–822)
3   Charge No. 110, Enumeration Block 70, Okhla Industrial Area Phase II Sanjay Colony T. Huts Nos. Block F181–300 and Block G 1–72
4   Charge No. 110, Enumeration Block 83, Okhla Industrial Area Phase I T. Huts of Bengali Camp at Plot No. A-197 Behind Punjab and Sindh Bank. T. Huts Nos. 1–139.
5   Charge No. 110, Enumeration Block 62, Okhla Industrial Area Phase II Sanjay Colony Census No. T. Huts Nos. 1201–1400 or Municipal Nos. Block – C 201–367.

It was difficult to locate any particular selected census block and to identify the households covered by it from among a large number of *jhuggies*. This was due to the lack of systematic numbering and the very nature of the settlement in the squatter areas. The maps of the census blocks were hard to get. Photocopying or tracing was not allowed. The copies were made by observation. Even the maps were not very accurate. The household list of the 1991 Census for the selected census blocks was of greater use. The respondents were located and traced with the help of household list, a map and purchase of the 'local expertise'.

The pre-testing of the questionnaires

The pre-testing of the Hindi translation of questionnaire I on seventeen heads of the household and of questionnaire II on four migrant heads of household, living in the *jhuggies* situated on both sides of the railway tracks near the Azadpur Railway station in the Azadpur-Wazirpur industrial area of North Delhi gave the impression that although the questionnaires were working well, some changes in translation were necessary. The questionnaires were finalised and printed after a review of the pre-testing. The questionnaire used in the listing survey (stage I) and the questionnaire used to further interview the migrant heads of the households (stage II) are given in Appendix H. The finalised questionnaires proved to be reasonably successful in eliciting the right information, except for the wording of a question on the place of last residence which, it was realised soon after the actual survey started, was being commonly misunderstood. This question (number 5(a) of the Questionnaire I) on the last residence before migration to Delhi was misunderstood as a question on the last residence in Delhi. Its wording was changed appropriately.

Other languages in interviewing

The questionnaires had to be translated into Bengali because most of the respondents in one of the squatter settlements could best understand that language. In some cases, interpretation became necessary while interviewing the respondents whose languages were Bengali, Tamil and Nepali.

The settings for data collection

Every head of the household residing in the selected census blocks was approached with the questionnaire designed for the listing survey (phase I of the sample survey). The opening remark of this questionnaire contained, apart from the introduction of the purpose of the survey as well as the surveyor, a request to agree to answer a few questions. If the person was prepared for this conversation, questionnaire I was used. If the person refused, a request for an appointment at some other time was made. Most of the respondents would at least agree to another time, although some of them did not keep the appointments and had made the appointment only to avoid and evade the interviewer.

If the respondent agreed to spare a few minutes, we would complete this part of the survey (listing). If the respondent turned out to be a criteria migrant, we would immediately request him or her to agree to be interviewed for the stage II survey. If the person agreed, we would continue the interview and try to finish the second stage of the interview, which, on average, took about 24 minutes. If the respondent refused to be interviewed further, we would try to set an appointment for some other time. The last part of the questionnaire I contained questions regarding the persuasion for the second-stage interview.

Where and when the interviews took place

The interesting contrast is that the proportion of criteria migrants was quite low in Subhas camp. We can see from Table A-2.2 that the proportion of migrants amongst the total number of households was half in this locality compared with the other two. Table A-2.3 provides similar distribution by census blocks.

- *Date, day and time of data collection*

The interviewing for the survey was done between 14 March 1992 and 29 April 1992. About two-fifths of the interviews took place on weekends. The tempo of work would start to build on Friday and reach its peak on Sunday, the day on which a quarter of the total interviewing was done. The tempo would start falling on Monday, and the mid-week was a period of 'underemployment' for the researcher (Table A-2.4). A quarter of the interviews were conducted before 8:00 in the morning. The results show that the forenoon contributed more than the afternoon in terms of the proportion of interviews conducted during the day (Table A-2.5). The case was similar with the listing survey.

- *Interview duration for the main survey*

The measures of the central tendency show that the average duration of the phase II interview was around 24 minutes. On the basis of mean (24.33) and standard deviation (8.46), we can say that in two-thirds of the cases the interview duration was between 16 and 31 minutes.

The interview duration was recorded for 163 out of the 184 criteria migrants. The quarter of the interviews took less than or equal to 20 minutes. The next quarter took between 20 and 24 minutes. The third quarter of the interviews took between 24 and 30 minutes. The last quarter took between 30 minutes and 55 minutes. The minimum duration was 9 minutes and the maximum 55 minutes. Table A-2.6 provides the distribution.

Demographic profile of the criteria migrants

Most of the migrants (98 per cent) were males, a higher proportion that than found among the sample population of 506 in the listing survey (94 per cent).

The criteria migrants were younger (median = 32 years) compared with the heads of the household in squatter settlements in general (median = 33 years). Table A-2.7 provides the distribution.

About 56.5 per cent of the criteria migrants had the ability to read, which was slightly higher than the figure of 55.3 per cent for the sample population of the heads of household of the listing survey. Regarding the ability to write in any language, the criteria migrants were better than the general sample population of the squatter settlements, as revealed by the listing survey. The survey showed that 55.4 per cent of the criteria migrants could write compared with 52.8 per cent for the heads of the household of the squatter population in general. With 52.7 per cent having been to school, the criteria migrants turned out to be better off than the general squatter heads of the household, the figure for the latter being 51.2.

Ninety-seven people reported having been to school. The years of schooling could be determined for ninety-five only. Table A-2.8 gives the distribution of the respondents according to the years of schooling they had.

About 92 per cent were married and 6.5 per cent unmarried. The proportion of others (divorced, windowed, etc.) was higher among the criteria migrants (1.5 per cent) (Table A-2.9) than was among the sample population in general (1 per cent). The question on number of children was not asked of unmarried people. However it was asked to the people in the category 'others' – the divorced, widow, etc. On the average, the criteria migrants had three children, which is similar to heads of household in the squatter settlements. The average number of male children (mean = 1.59, SD = 1.047) was higher than female children (mean = 1.40, SD = 1.13). It shows an adverse gender ratio (more adverse compared to the general sample population).

The profile of mobility

• *Duration of stay in Delhi*

Table A-2.10 presents the distribution of the criteria migrants according to the total duration of their stay in Delhi. The median duration of their stay in Delhi was 132 months compared to the average of 162 months observed in the case of migrants in general. This means our criteria migrants were more recent than the migrants in general. The proportion of recent migrants was also high among the criteria migrants compared to the migrants in general. Seven per cent of the criteria migrants had arrived in the past 7 months (compared to 4 per cent in the case of the migrants in general). Because we had selected the migrants of a particular duration only (those who have come in past 20 years), the two are not comparable. The point made here is that our preference for more recent migrants, in fact, is reflected in the distribution here.

Table A-2.11 presents the distribution of the respondents by the years since migration. This dummy variable corroborates the conclusion based on the direct question on duration of stay in Delhi.

• *Arrival in Delhi*

Only two-thirds of the criteria migrants could recall the exact month of their arrival in Delhi. However, the rate of recall was higher than the migrants in general – only half of them could recall it. The seasonal pattern that was observed in the case of migrants in general was also discernible in the case of our criteria migrants: March to May and November to January seem to be two peaks. The off-season in the countryside seemed to coincide with arrival in the city. However, the more interesting thing to observe here was that despite the peaks there is a year-round migration (Table A-2.12).

Table A-2.13 provides the distribution of the respondents by the calendar year of arrival in Delhi. There seems to be a greater concentration in post-1977 (the 'post-Emergency') period culminating in 1982 (the Delhi Asian games' year). The modal year of migration was 1982. The median year was 1981. The other year of high migration seems to be 1984. The recent migrants were well represented in the sample – about 10 per cent having arrived within one and half years before the survey.

Table A-2.14 presents the distribution of criteria migrants by the age at arrival in Delhi. The average age at arrival was around 21, slightly higher than the migrants in general (which included associational and other types of migrants).

• *Places of last residence*

Table A-2.15 provides the distribution by the type of the place of last residence. For 97 per cent of the criteria migrants, the type of the place of last residence was a village. The others with a place of last residence other than the village were, in fact, rural-born step-migrants.

To a certain extent, by the very logic of our selection, all the migrants had their last residence within India. The State of Uttar Pradesh contributed the highest. At the district level, Purnia (Bihar) contributed the highest. About 16 per cent of our criteria migrants came from this district. Maldah (West Bengal), with its contribution of about 7 per cent in the sample of the 184 criteria migrants, occupied second place. The other significant ones were Sawai Madhopur (Rajasthan) and Bulandashahar (Uttar Pradesh), each contributing about 5 per cent of the sample.

Area of last residence: area of high out-migration (ahom) and the rest of India

Two-fifths of the criteria migrants of the sample survey came from rural areas of the area of high out-migration as specified by Mohan (1982), which has been used as an important variable in analysis in this study. The details of the area of high out-migration (ahom) are available in Table A-1.5, Appendix F and shown in Map 3.1. The remaining came from the rest of India.

Ascertaining the whereabouts of the criterion migrants in 2009

Broadly, the efforts were designed as follows:

1   Preparing the complete list of the respondents of the earlier listing survey of four census blocks conducted in 1992 (containing the name, the address in Delhi in 1992 and the address of the area of origin with regard to each of the 506 respondents).
2   While searching for 184 migrants who were interviewed in detail in 1992, if any one of them was found, conducting a semi-structured interview with the help of a questionnaire/interview schedule.
3   With respect to the migrants who had left the earlier place of residence in the selected squatter settlements of Delhi, administering a questionnaire/interview schedule to a neighbour/relative/friend/community leader to find out the whereabouts of these migrant respondents of the earlier survey.
4   With respect to the migrants who had left the earlier place of residence in the selected squatter settlements of Delhi and whose whereabouts could not be ascertained by fieldwork in Delhi, writing a letter to the *Sarpanches* of their respective villages requesting information about the migrants.

First of all, the tools mentioned earlier were prepared and pre-tested. Then, the aforementioned design was implemented.

Whereas nearly 10 per cent of the 184 migrants surveyed during the fieldwork in Delhi in 1992 were reported to have died, nearly 35 per cent were revisited in Delhi and interviewed. This is despite the further intra-city migration of some of the respondents belonging to the three of the four census blocks surveyed earlier, as well as the complete displacement of all the residents of the locality consisting of the fourth census block because it had been demolished in 1997. Efforts were made to retrace twenty-six migrants of the earlier survey who were reported to be living in a locality other than the locality of their residence in 1992. Nearly a dozen such localities were reported, but it proved very difficult to get adequate information to be able to trace them with any degree of ease.

Although efforts were made to match as much as possible the period of resurvey in Delhi with that of the earlier survey (March–April) in order to take care of the seasonality and periodicity factors in migration and these efforts succeeded to a large extent, it was not easy. Multiple visits were necessary due to the growing absence of the respondents from the places of their residence during most days of the week which could be attributed to increased hours of work of those in employment, jobs at far-off worksites, changes in social and personal lives, etc. Moreover, the proportion of migrants still living in Delhi appeared to be nearly double the one-fourth that was anticipated on the basis of some report of an old survey (Banerjee, 1986: 12).

The resurvey involved fieldwork in the squatter settlements that were surveyed seventeen years ago and in the new localities where the migrant respondents of the earlier survey were reported to have moved. It was a helpful experience in terms of understanding the worlds of labour migrants, squatters and the land mafia. It also gave some sense of the new social, economic and political processes in Delhi.

Some interesting details of the exercise conducted in 2009 in order to ascertain the whereabouts of the criteria migrants who had been interviewed in detail earlier during the survey in 1992 are as follows:

1   The questionnaire meant for the neighbour/relative/friend/community leader (to find out the whereabouts of the migrant respondents of the earlier survey) did not prove to be a useful tool because the respondents were more comfortable and forthcoming without it! Hence, it was used for only a few cases, and information was sought and received in a rather open-ended fashion. This questionnaire is given in Appendix H.
2   With respect to the eighty-four migrant respondents who had left their earlier place of residence in the selected squatter settlements of Delhi and whose whereabouts could not be ascertained by the 2009 fieldwork in Delhi, a letter was written to the *Sarpanches* of their respective villages requesting information about the migrants. In the case of the migrants with their place of origin in the villages of non-Hindi States, the letter to the *Sarpanches* was sent both in Hindi and English. The format of the letter is given in Appendix H. Seventy-four *Sarpanches* were sent registered letters, with confirmation of receipt, about these eighty-four migrants along with self-addressed pre-stamped envelopes for reply by registered post. About one-third of these envelopes could not be delivered by the postal department and these were returned.
3   In response to the two-thirds (of the previously mentioned seventy-four) envelopes delivered, the whereabouts of about one-fourth of the relevant migrant respondents were ascertained. Even while some information about the migrant respondents kept coming (from the village *Sarpanches*, the respondents and their family, with whom contact was made through post and telephone), the priority became consolidation of the work of the migrant resurvey in Delhi, and this exercise had to be wound up at that point.
4   The information gathered about the 'missing migrant respondents' who were reported in 2009 to be scattered among diverse localities of Delhi (about 10 per cent of the 184 respondents of the 1992 survey) was used to chart out their respective locations in Delhi. A plan of fresh fieldtrips in Delhi in this regard was also prepared. However, due to the relatively high

cost involved in covering the scattered and nebulous addresses in addition to the more pressing tasks related to data handling and analysis, the task was not undertaken.

5   The postal and telephone responses from the village *Sarpanches* contained 'other information' about the return migrants that matched the responses of their friends, relatives and neighbours in Delhi.

References

Banerjee, B. (1986). *Rural to urban migration and the urban labour market: A case study of Delhi*. Delhi: Himalaya Publishing House.

Delhi Administration, Bureau of Economics and Statistics (1982). *Report of the committee on poverty line in Delhi*. Delhi: Bureau of Economics and Statistics (Unpublished).

Delhi Administration, Bureau of Economics and Statistics (1991). *Union Territory of Delhi: Economic census 1990 (provisional results)*. Delhi: Bureau of Economics and Statistics (Unpublished).

Delhi Development Authority, Perspective Planning Wing (1983). *Higher educational facilities: Development plan for Delhi 2001* (Unpublished).

Delhi Development Authority, Perspective Planning Wing (1986). *Transportation for Delhi* (Unpublished).

Delhi Development Authority, Slum Wing (n.d., C.1990). *List of identified jhuggie clusters in Delhi* (Unpublished).

GOI, Census of India 1991, (1992). *Delhi, Series 31, Occasional Paper No. 1 of 1992, provisional total population and scheduled caste population*. Delhi: Director of Census Operations, Delhi, Government of India.

GOI, Ministry of Urban Development (1990). *Master plan for Delhi*. The Gazette of India (Extraordinary), No. 437. New Delhi: Ministry of Urban Development, Government of India.

Institute for Socialist Education, New Delhi (1989). *Socio-economic baseline survey of 457 J.J. clusters in Delhi* (Unpublished).

Mohan, R. (1982). *The Morphology of urbanisation in India: Some results from the 1981 Census*. Paper presented in the seminar on Urbanisation and Planned Economic Development – Present and future perspectives, organised by the Centre for the Study of Regional Development, Jawaharlal Nehru University, New Delhi.

Suri, P. (1991). *Housing for the urban poor: People's needs, priorities and government response – Case study of Delhi*. Unpublished doctoral thesis, School of Planning and Architecture, New Delhi.

Appendix C

Ownership, leasing-in and leasing-out of land

(In support of Chapter 3)

This appendix is concerned with the people who owned land or leased-in land.

Economic position in terms of the ownership of land

Whether they owned land or not was ascertained for each of the 184 sample migrants. It was found that just under half of them had land and the rest did not.

One-quarter of the landowners had less than 1.25 acres, and half of them had less than 1.88 acres. Table A-3.3 gives some idea of how much land the migrants had in the countryside before they came to Delhi. The positive skewness of the distribution of total land in this table (skewness = 4.23) shows the tendency is towards lower-than-average acreage. However, what really counts in agriculture is cultivable land rather than the total land owned. It appears that the tendency to low acreage was stronger with respect to cultivable land. A quarter had less than 1 acre, half had less than 1.72 acres.

The distribution of cultivable land in Table A-3.3 and Figure C1 shows a greater positive skewness (+ 5.47) than the one with respect to the total land that has been provided in Table A-3.3.

• About the land owned and employment of labour

The size of the landholding in itself is not an adequate indicator of its economic worth. Important questions to be considered were the proportion of cultivable to total land, how fragmented or consolidated was the cultivable land owned and if and how much were the operators dependent on employment of others' labour.

Figure C2 shows the distribution of the cultivable to total land ratio for the land-owning migrants. For about 8 per cent of the landowners, less than half of their land was cultivable. For another 20 per cent, the extent of cultivable land was between half and three-quarters of their total land. It is clear that for three out of five landowners, all land was cultivable. On average, 82 per cent of the land was cultivable. The all-India average for operational holdings a comparable point in time was 90 per cent.[1]

Further, it was discovered that the land was fragmented in the case of three-fourths of all the respondents who had any cultivable land. A quarter had their land in one piece.

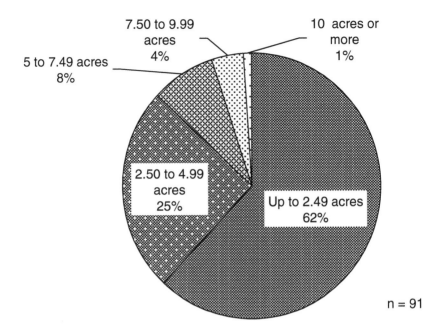

Figure C1 Ownership distribution of cultivable land (in acres)

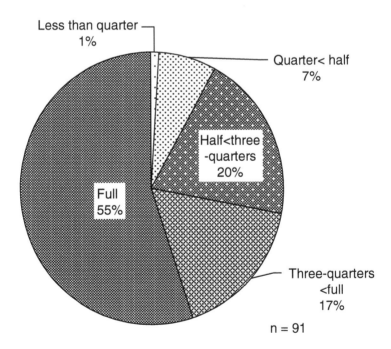

Figure C2 Extent of cultivable land

Figure C3 shows the distribution of single plot owners by the size of their plots of cultivable land. In the case of those with a single plot of cultivable land, only a third owned plots of area less than 1 acre. The comparable situation with respect to those with fragmented land was that four-fifths of them had plots of less than 1 acre.

For those who had fragmented land, the average number of pieces was five (median). Only one-third had two or three pieces. The rest had more than three pieces. For one-quarter of the respondents, the land was fragmented into nine or more pieces. In terms of the percentage of irrigated to cultivable land, the median of 67 per cent was much higher than the weighted average of 43 per cent based on official data. This average was arrived as follows:

i   Calculating percentage of area under irrigation for States (i.e., net irrigated area as percentage of net cropped area).
ii Taking an average of State-level figures, with weights being assigned in proportion to the migrants in our sample from that State.

[**Weight for a particular State** = Percentage contribution of the State to the sample by *place of last residence* (POLR) concept of migration + percentage contribution of the State to the sample by *place of birth* (POB) concept \ (2)]

The unweighted all-India average was 61 per cent (GOI, Ministry of Agriculture, 1987: 36), Table 3.27A.

The landowners were asked if they employed any labour for agricultural purposes. Only a quarter of the respondents did so. Even those who employed labour did so very occasionally.

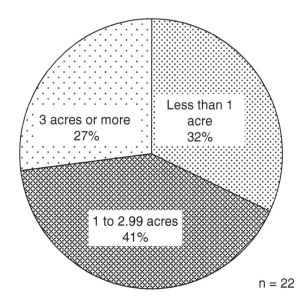

Figure C3 Distribution of single-plot cultivable holdings

It leads to the conclusion that most of the landowners had small amounts of acreage, and for many the land was not cultivable. Most of the migrants did not employ other people for work.

Extent of self-cultivation and leasing-out

Most of them (92 per cent) were from households who cultivated all their land by themselves. The remaining 8 per cent (seven respondents) did not cultivate all their land.

Those who leased out land were, by and large, similar to others in terms of the amount of land owned. The lack of resources to manage inputs was the main reason for leasing-out because four out of these seven gave this reason. Two said they did not know agriculture, and one gave a vague reason that the sharecropper needed to be helped!

The t-test shows that those who leased out land did migrate at an age that was significantly higher than those not leasing out. Moreover, these were people who had income from diverse sources – they were getting, on average, a significantly greater proportion of income from shopkeeping/vending, loans and mortgaging/sale of property in the year before migration compared to those who did not lease-out. Looking at this profile, those who were leasing out appear mostly to be the middle-income and more skilled people compared to others and reported a decline in the business of shopkeeping. The results show that most of the landowners cultivated their land themselves. Those who leased-out were a small group.

Leasing-in

This sub-section considers how many migrants leased in land from others. It also discusses the amount of leased-in land and aspects like fragmentation and irrigation. It considers the landowners among the migrants who lease in. The purpose is to find out how dependent this group was on the leasing-in of land.

The survey results show that about three in ten migrants leased in land. The average leased-in area was 1.25 acres (median). Table A-3.4 provides the distribution. In fact, a quarter of them leased in fewer than 0.63 acres.

The survey results show that two in five had more than one piece of leased-in land. The average size of a single plot of leased-in land was 1.25 acres (median). Table A-3.5 and Figure C4 present the distribution of single leased-in plots. More than half of the respondents who had more than one plot of leased-in land had more than three pieces.

The average size of plots of leased-in land was 0.52 acre (median). The average size of the plots of irrigated leased-in land was 0.63 acre (median).

The overall conclusion is that although some of the leased-in holdings (twenty out of fifty-five) were comparatively compact, the rest of them were very tiny pieces.

The survey also noted how much of the leased-in land was irrigated. Figure C5 provides the distribution.

For 58 per cent, all of it was irrigated, and another 11 per cent had more than half of the area irrigated. For a quarter, all the leased-in land was unirrigated.

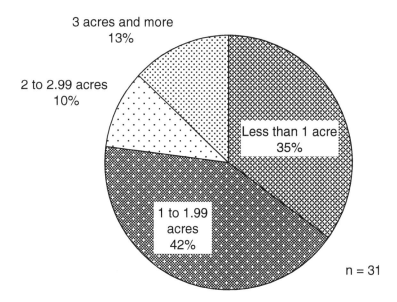

Figure C4 Size distribution of single plots of leased-in land

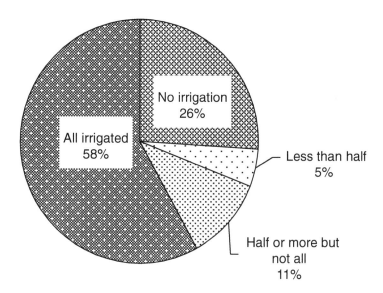

Figure C5 Extent of irrigation in the leased-in land

Thirty-four migrants owned as well as leased in land. To put the number into context, they were 37 per cent of the land-owning migrants, 62 per cent of those leasing-in and 18 per cent of all the sample migrants. On average, they leased in land equivalent to half of the land they themselves owned.

One of these thirty-four did not have any cultivable land. For the remaining thirty-three respondents, the percentage of leased-in to own cultivable land was 66, on average. It shows that the typical land-owning migrant who leased in any land leased in an amount of land equivalent to two-thirds of what he or she owned. About two in five of these respondents leased in land equivalent to or more than what they themselves owned. The distribution is given in Table A-3.6.

Note

1 GOI, Ministry of Agriculture (1987: 33), Table 3.25A.

Reference

GOI, Ministry of Agriculture (1987). *All India report on agricultural census 1980–81.* New Delhi: Ministry of Agriculture, Government of India.

Appendix D

Occupational moves at the sub-sectoral level

(In support of Chapter 5)

Table D1 Occupational moves at the sub-sectoral level

First Job		Current Job	
Sector	Sub-sector	Sector	Sub-sector
Construction (18)	Unskilled construction work (*beldari*) (13)	Construction (6)	Unskilled construction work (1)
			Semi-skilled construction sector work (5)
		Service (2)	Vendor (1)
			Sweeper (1)
		Factory (1)	Other semi-skilled garment sector factory (1)
		Shop-keeping/ Shop worker (1)	Shop-keeping (1)
		Not working due to sickness (3)	–
	Semi-skilled construction sector work (1)	Construction (1)	Semi-skilled construction sector work
	Other unskilled construction sector workers (4)	Construction (1)	Unskilled construction work (1)
		Service (1)	Watchman (1)
		Others (2)	MCD *beldar* (1)
			Car washing and gardening (1)

(*Continued*)

Table D1 (Continued)

First Job		Current Job	
Sector	Sub-sector	Sector	Sub-sector
Service (22)	Vendor (4)	Service (1)	Sweeper (1)
		Factory (1)	Labourer in non-garment sector factory (1)
		Shop-keeping / shop worker (2)	Shop-keeping (2)
	Sweeper (8)	Construction (1)	Other unskilled construction sector work (1)
		Service (5)	Sweeper (4) Peon (1)
		Not working due to sickness (2)	–
	Watchman/ Security guard (2)	Service (2)	Sweeper (1) Security guard (1)
	Peon (2)	Others (2)	Car driver (1) Helper in a printing press (1)
	Hotel/restaurant/Bar and related work (3)	Construction (1)	Semi-skilled construction sector work (1)
		Shopkeeping/shop worker (2)	Shopkeeping (2)
	Domestic servant (2)	Service (1)	Domestic servant (1)
		Others (1)	Driver (1)
	Other service sector work (1)	Others (1)	Security officer (1)
Factory (16)	Helper/labourer in nongarment sector factory (8)	Construction (1)	Semi-skilled construction worker (1)
		Service (1)	Watchman/security guard (1)
		Factory (3)	Helper/labourer in nongarment sector factory (2) Other semi-skilled garment sector factory work (1)
		Shop-keeping/shop worker (3)	Craft and tradespersons (3)
	Semi-skilled nongarment sector factory work (3)	Service (1)	Vendor (1)
		Factory (1)	Semi-skilled nongarment sector factory work (1)
		Not working because doing 'social service' (1)	–
	Helper/labourer in garment sector factory (1)	Service (1)	Watchman/security guard (1)
	Tailors (4)	Factory (4)	Tailors (4)

Table D1 (Continued)

First Job		Current Job	
Sector	Sub-sector	Sector	Sub-sector
Shopkeeping/ Shop worker (10)	Craft and tradespersons (7)	Service (1)	Vendor (1)
		Factory (1)	Helper/labourer in nongarment sector factory (1)
		Shop-keeping/shop worker (5)	Craft and tradespersons (5)
	Shop-keeping (2)	Service (1)	Vendor (1)
		Shopkeeping/ Shop worker(1)	Shopkeeping (1)
	Shop workers (1)	Service (1)	Vendor (1)
Others (5)	Animal husbandry (1)	Service (1)	Vendor (1)
	Agricultural labourer (1)	Others (1)	Agricultural labourer
	'Others' (3)	Construction (1)	Unskilled construction work (1)
		Service (1)	Sweeper (1)
		Others (1)	Splitting fire wood in a wood stall (1)

Appendix E

Methodological details relating to data-mining techniques applied in Chapter 6 and Chapter 7

What and how of clustering analysis

K-means clustering, used in Chapter 6, measures the similarity and dissimilarity between individuals and places the most similar individuals into the same cluster. The variants of k-means clustering can work on various types of variables, including interval scaled, binary and categorical variables. However, the method to compute the distance between two instances varies from one type of variable to another. For interval scaled variables, the most popular distance measure is computing the Euclidean distance between two instances. In this work, all the variables are categorical. Let us assume that the number of states for a variable is M. These states can be coded with letters or a set of integers from 1 to M. In such cases, the dissimilarity/similarity between two instances i and j is computed based on the ratio of mismatches as shown:

$$d(i, j) = \frac{p - m}{p} \tag{1}$$

$$s(i, j) = 1 - d(i, j) \tag{2}$$

In this equation, m is the number of matches (i.e., the number of variables for which i and j are in the same state) and p is the total number of variables. The dissimilarity is high when the number of matches m is low and similarity is high when the number of matches is high (Han and Kamber, 2012: 68–69, 451–454).

In this work, the k-means clustering algorithm available in *WEKA* data-mining software was used to form clusters. This algorithm computes the dissimilarity between instances using the previous equations while handling categorical variables. It uses modal values instead of mean values to compute the centroids. We also used the k-mode algorithm (a variant of k-means that handles categorical variables) provided in R, a free software environment for statistical computing and graphics, to form clusters for our data. The results from both algorithms were found to be corroborating each other.

Determining the number of clusters

The k-means algorithm has a parameter k, which denotes the number of clusters to be made. The value of k has to be determined based on some measure of the quality of clustering and the domain knowledge. Clustering is an unsupervised machine learning technique and, therefore, domain knowledge is essential in interpreting the meaning and relevance of the different clusters. One of the commonly used methods for measuring the quality of clustering is the silhouette width of the clusters.

The silhouette width of a cluster measures average intra-cluster homogeneity (cohesion) and inter-cluster heterogeneity (separation) of all the instances placed in it. The value of the silhouette width for an instance in a cluster varies from −1 to +1. A higher silhouette value for an instance means that this point is classified with less amount of uncertainty. An instance with a zero value belongs to the boundary of two clusters. A negative value signifies that an instance is placed in a wrong cluster. The average of the silhouette width of all the instances in a cluster becomes the cluster silhouette width (Rousseeuw, 1987).

A decision on the number of clusters appropriate for this study is made on two considerations: 1) the silhouette width of clusters, and 2) the meaningfulness of the groups in the light of the research problem.

In general, good quality of a clustering exercise is indicated by positive value of silhouette width for the clusters that emerge from it. However, it is also important that the silhouette widths of the different clusters from that exercise are not too dissimilar. K-means was run for values of k ranging from 2 to 5. The values of the silhouette width of clusters for various values of k are given in Table E1.

The silhouette values indicate the three-cluster exercise is producing a better grouping compared to the two-cluster exercise. However, the domain knowledge in terms of the hypothesis of the present study indicates that the clustering exercise with two groups produces the most meaningful groups. One group consists of migrants from North and Central Bihar and Eastern Uttar Pradesh that has been considered as an area of high out-migration in the context of internal migration in India. The other group consists of migrants from the rest of India. Because this is precisely the empirical context in which the contention of 'recruitment versus expulsion' is being examined in this study, the clustering exercise with two groups was preferred for a detailed interpretation and analysis. However, because the clustering exercise producing three groups further divides the group from 'the rest of India' into two sub-groups in a meaningful way, its results also add meaning

Table E1 The values of silhouette widths for different values of k

#k	Silhouette with Cluster1	Silhouette with Cluster2	Silhouette with Cluster3	Silhouette with Cluster4	Silhouette with Cluster5
2.	0.17	0.14	–	–	–
3.	0.17	0.16	0.32	–	–
4.	0.23	0.06	0.18	0.08	–
5.	0.11	0.04	0.00	0.14	0.02

to our analysis. Therefore, this three-group exercise has also been briefly discussed in the chapter. The rest of the clustering exercises (i.e., those with four and five clusters, respectively) were not found to be suitable on any of the two considerations.

Decision-tree induction

The variables used for decision-tree learning in *WEKA* are given in Table E-2. For the rest of this appendix, the variables will be called attributes, as it is common for the data-mining and machine learning literature to use the term *attribute* instead of the term *variable*. One of the attributes is designated as the decision or class attribute. The remaining attributes are called predicting attributes.

Table E2 Attributes used for the decision tree

	Predicting Attributes	*Decision Attribute or Class label*
1	ageatarr	cus_asu
2	polrdist	
3	mostimp	
4	age2009	
5	read	
6	school	
7	work_ybm	
8	mainjob	
9	hired	
10	hirebase	
11	whyquit1	
12	unempld	
13	durunemp	
14	ownland	
15	oh_tenure	
16	oh_size	
17	difflt	
18	famtype	
19	compare	
20	repmem	
21	indebt	
22	visit	
23	famatt	
24	support1	
25	fjindel	
26	channel1	
27	livevill	
28	sjivill	
29	paymeth	
30	endreason1	
31	ss_exist	

Note: Descriptions of each attribute and its values are available in Table G1, Appendix G

Several decision trees like ID3 (C4.5, C5.0, J48 and later versions of ID3), Classification and Regression Trees (CART) and Chi-squared Automatic Interaction Detection (CHAID) were developed for the purpose of classification and prediction. Here, in this analysis decision tree J48 is used. All of these decision trees are constructed by adopting a top-down recursive approach, which starts from a training dataset along with their decision labels (Witten and Frank, 2005: 62–69). This dataset is partitioned further and further on the basis of attribute tests until a leaf node is reached where the partition holds the instances belonging to only one of the values of the decision variable. The order of attribute tests at various levels of the decision tree is determined via a set of attribute selection criteria. An attribute selection method is a heuristic for selecting a splitting criterion that induces the best (i.e., pure) partitions in the dataset with respect to the values of the decision variable, that is, class labels (Han and Kamber, 2012: 330–343). The attribute selection method *gain ratio* used in J48 is as given here:

$$Info(D) = -\sum_{i=1}^{m} p_i \log_2(p_i) \tag{3}$$

$$Info_A(D) = \sum_{j=1}^{v} \frac{|D_j|}{D} \times Info(D_j) \tag{4}$$

$$Gain(A) = Info(D) - Info_A(D) \tag{5}$$

$$SplitInfo_A(D) = -\sum_{j=1}^{v} \frac{|D_j|}{|D|} \times \log_2 \frac{|D_j|}{|D|} \tag{6}$$

$$GainRatio(A) = \frac{Gain(A)}{SplitInfo(A)} \tag{7}$$

In equation 3 *Info (D)* gives the expected information needed to classify an instance in dataset D – that is, it is the average amount of information needed to identify the class label of any instance, m signifies the number of class labels and p_i is the probability that an arbitrary instance in dataset D belongs to class label C_i and is estimated by

$$P_i = \frac{|C_{i,d}|}{|D|}, i \in 1...m \tag{8}$$

The log function used is to the base 2 because information gain measured here is in bits.

In equation 4, let us assume that A is the attribute under consideration for split and it has $(a_1, a_2, a_3 ... a_v)$ distinct values observed in the dataset. A test on attribute A would induce v partitions $(D_1, D_2, D_3 ... D_n)$, each corresponding to a single branch growing out of the test split on attribute A. Further $|D|$ and $|D_j|$ denote the cardinality of the dataset D and the set D_j containing the instances that have a_j outcome. The second term in equation 4 is the expected information required to classify an instance from dataset D based on a partition induced by attribute A. Ideally, we would like each partition to be pure. The purer the partitions induced by attribute A, the smaller the value for the second term. Overall equation 4 measures how much more information would still be needed to arrive at an exact classification after partitioning at attribute A.

Equation 5 defines the information gain as the difference between the information required to classify a data instance only on the basis of the proportion of class labels and information needed after making test splits on attribute A. In other words, equation 5 calculates the reduction in the information requirement caused by knowing the values of attribute A.

The attributes are chosen for split in order of highest information gain. This is equivalent to saying that we want the partition on attribute A that would produce the best classification so that the information required to finish the classification is minimal.

Information gain is a good criterion for selecting attributes for test splits. However, it is biased towards tests with more outcomes, that is, it prefers the attributes that have a large number of values. The gain ratio given in equation 7 overcomes this bias by applying a kind of normalisation to information gain by using split information as defined in equation 6.

Ranking of predicting variables in terms of their association with the 'stay or return' dichotomy at the root level

The ranking of thirty-one predicting variables in descending order with respect to the decision of migrants to stay or return at the root level is given in Table E3. The first variable highlighted in this table has the highest gain ratio and, therefore, it is the most relevant of all the variables. That is why the first split in the decision-tree model induced in Chapter 7 occurs on this particular variable.

The decision-making rules and fitness of the model that emerged from the primary data of the present study

The decision-tree model can also be used to extract the rules for decision making. Table E4 shows the rules for migrants with regard to their decision to stay or return. These rules reflect the fitness of the model. The values in the table shown in boldface font are the number of cases correctly classified as 'stayers' or 'returnees'. The values shown in normal font are the incorrectly classified instances, that is, a 'stayer' misclassified as a 'returnee' or a 'returnee' misclassified as a 'stayer'. Overall, the sum of all the values in boldface denotes the correctly classified instances, and the sum of values in normal font gives the number of misclassified instances.

Table E3 Ranking of variables using the gain ratio attribute
evaluation method

Variable Name	Ranking	Gain Ratio
ss_exist	**1**	**0.193215**
polrdist	2	0.06794
sjivill	3	0.059247
indebt	4	0.042878
fjindel	5	0.040921
endreason1	6	0.036896
hirebase	7	0.030138
support1	8	0.029896
paymeth	9	0.029138
age2009	10	0.025806
unempld	11	0.023561
channel1	12	0.021181
oh_size	13	0.018845
mainjob	14	0.018106
work_ybm	15	0.01795
read	16	0.016469
ageatarr	17	0.013351
whyquit1	18	0.012123
mostimp	19	0.011196
oh_tenure	20	0.010729
famtype	21	0.010631
hired	22	0.008227
famatt	23	0.008223
durunemp	24	0.07862
livevill	25	0.004847
school	26	0.004203
visit	27	0.003945
difflt	28	0.003471
compare	29	0.000972
ownland	30	0.000939
repmem	31	0.000667

Note: Descriptions of each variable and its values are available in
Table G1, Appendix G

The decision-tree model classifies 130 cases correctly as stayers or returnees;
only 22 cases are classified incorrectly. Overall, the decision-tree model classifies
85.52 per cent of instances correctly. Out of the actual 105 stayers in the data, the
model classifies 98 correctly and 7 stayers are wrongly classified as returnees. The
level of correctly classified instances is lower in the case of returnees where out of
the 47 actual returnees, only 32 are classified correctly. That means 15 returnees
are wrongly classified as stayers. This lower accuracy in the case of returnees may
be attributed to the complex decision-making process regarding 'stay or return'
being made in the situation arising out of the demolition of their squatter settlement. Even with a slightly higher error rate in the case of returnees, the decision
tree gives sufficient indications of who stayed and who returned from amongst
those whose squatter settlements were demolished.

Table E4 Decision rules induced with respect to the decision to stay or return

Sr. No.	Decision Rule	No. of stayers covered by the rule	No. of returnees covered by the rule
1	If *ss_exist*=yes Then Stay	**84**	13
2	If *ss_exist*=no and *endreason1*= 1 or 4 or 5 or 8Then Return	6	**23**
3	If *ss_exist*=no and *endreason1*=3 Then Stay	**3**	1
4	If *ss_exist*=no and *endreason1*=2 and indebt=2 Then Return	0	**2**
5	If *ss_exist*=no and *endreason1*=2 and *indebt*=1 and *fjindel*= 2 or 3 Then Stay	**8**	0
6	If *ss_exist*=no and *endreason1*=2 and *indebt*=1 and *fjindel*=5 Then Return	0	**1**
7	If *ss_exist*=no and *endreason1*=2 and *indebt*=1 and *fjindel*=1 and *age2009*=1 Then Return	1	**6**
8	If *ss_exist*=no and *endreason1*=2 and *indebt*=1 and *fjindel*=1 and *age2009*=2 Then Stay	**3**	1

* *ss_exists:* squatter settlement of 1992 existing or not?; *endreason1: reason for ending the first job in Delhi; indebt: family in debt; fjindel: first occupation in Delhi; age2009: age at the time of survey in 2009.*

Note: The values in the table shown in boldface font are the number of cases correctly classified as 'stayers' or 'returnees'. The values shown in normal font are incorrectly classified instances.

References

Han, J. and Kamber, M. (2012). *Data mining: Concepts and techniques* (3rd ed.). San Francisco: Morgan Kaufmann Publishers.

Rousseeuw, P.J. (1987). Silhouettes: A graphical aid to the interpretation and validation of cluster analysis, *Computational and Applied Mathematics*, 20: 53–65.

Witten, I.H. and Frank, E. (2005). *Data mining: Practical machine learning tool and techniques* (2nd ed.). New Delhi: Elsevier.

Appendix F

Statistical tables

Table A-1.1(i) Lifetime internal male migrants as a percentage of the internal male population in the States and Union Territories of India – 1961, 1971, 1981

State / UT	Migrants			Rural			Urban		
	1961	1971	1981	1961	1971	1981	1961	1971	1981
1 Andhra Pradesh	21.18	21.25	20.46	17.52	17.80	15.80	38.24	35.42	35.50
2 Assam	23.43	24.38	N.A.	21.50	22.40	N.A.	47.82	45.01	N.A.
3 Bihar	12.20	9.48	8.38	9.45	6.59	4.93	39.65	33.65	31.16
4 Gujarat	19.91	19.67	20.18	13.99	13.61	13.51	36.85	34.99	34.69
5 Haryana	N.A.	13.93	14.28	N.A.	10.23	9.07	N.A.	28.26	34.18
6 Himachal Pradesh	N.A.	18.04	19.10	N.A.	14.74	16.02	N.A.	59.29	53.79
7 Jammu and Kashmir	12.02	11.07	9.61	10.56	9.90	8.36	19.25	16.16	14.28
8 Karnataka	23.59	23.15	22.28	19.61	19.38	17.05	37.01	34.51	34.35
9 Kerala	20.07	16.93	15.54	19.34	16.44	14.38	24.12	19.41	20.55
10 Madhya Pradesh	22.63	20.57	19.33	19.27	17.20	15.08	42.30	37.40	35.60
11 Maharashtra	31.08	29.39	31.99	21.64	20.30	23.71	53.33	48.08	46.43
12 Manipur	13.53	15.50	10.73	13.66	15.76	10.05	12.11	13.83	12.63
13 Meghalaya	N.A.	28.07	23.89	N.A.	26.20	20.26	N.A.	39.33	40.41
14 Nagaland	12.07	16.96	26.83	9.24	9.34	20.20	57.99	76.71	59.98
15 Orissa	13.63	17.02	15.60	11.46	14.17	11.44	42.72	45.95	44.60
16 Punjab	18.89	13.49	17.19	13.53	12.12	12.11	43.49	35.70	30.92
17 Rajasthan	12.20	12.73	12.81	9.50	10.10	9.66	26.38	25.22	24.41
18 Tamil Nadu	18.67	19.96	19.04	13.12	14.36	12.74	33.70	32.66	31.86
19 Tripura	22.87	17.53	14.30	23.23	17.56	14.05	18.21	17.21	16.52
20 Uttar Pradesh	11.66	9.02	7.18	8.47	6.21	4.46	32.63	25.86	19.43
21 West Bengal	22.24	14.91	14.53	14.24	9.84	8.90	47.06	29.98	30.25
22 Delhi	52.05	42.79	43.13	18.95	23.45	22.58	57.07	45.28	44.86
India	18.93	17.49	16.64	14.37	13.07	11.39	40.17	34.95	33.22

Table A-1.1(ii) Lifetime internal male migrants as a percentage of the internal male population in the States and Union Territories of India – 1961, 1971, 1981

State / UT	Inter-State migrant			Inter-State rural			Inter-State urban		
	1961	1971	1981	1961	1971	1981	1961	1971	1981
1 Andhra Pradesh	1.40	1.42	1.32	0.66	0.68	0.64	4.81	4.44	3.49
2 Assam	5.82	4.97	N.A.	4.54	3.56	N.A.	21.99	19.62	N.A.
3 Bihar	1.63	1.28	1.10	0.85	0.50	0.39	9.38	7.79	5.75
4 Gujarat	2.83	3.09	3.51	0.98	0.98	1.19	8.13	8.45	8.56
5 Haryana	N.A.	6.38	6.56	N.A.	4.23	3.49	N.A.	14.98	18.31
6 Himachal Pradesh	N.A.	3.87	3.92	N.A.	2.37	2.67	N.A.	22.57	18.08
7 Jammu and Kashmir	0.86	1.70	1.33	0.56	1.35	0.90	2.39	3.19	2.90
8 Karnataka	4.32	3.76	3.96	2.44	2.18	2.13	10.67	8.53	8.34
9 Kerala	1.47	1.22	1.36	1.26	0.99	1.19	2.67	2.39	2.10
10 Madhya Pradesh	4.32	3.83	3.44	2.12	1.69	1.41	17.21	14.50	11.20
11 Maharashtra	7.51	7.40	7.65	1.38	1.46	1.93	21.97	19.62	17.64
12 Manipur	1.54	3.05	2.28	1.17	2.82	1.66	5.36	4.58	3.99
13 Meghalaya	N.A.	6.86	7.07	N.A.	3.62	3.92	N.A.	26.33	21.39
14 Nagaland	4.56	11.40	11.52	3.10	5.30	7.60	28.34	58.59	38.14
15 Orissa	1.73	2.09	2.29	0.95	1.04	1.11	12.16	12.78	10.47
16 Punjab	3.24	4.05	4.74	1.52	1.82	2.38	11.14	11.81	11.11
17 Rajasthan	2.37	2.24	2.38	1.60	1.38	1.43	6.42	6.30	5.87
18 Tamil Nadu	1.80	1.92	1.69	0.61	0.63	0.52	5.03	4.84	4.05
19 Tripura	3.05	2.83	2.19	2.69	2.44	1.87	7.87	6.71	5.06
20 Uttar Pradesh	1.09	0.97	0.80	0.47	0.45	0.42	5.12	4.06	2.50
21 West Bengal	9.34	6.61	5.08	3.27	2.88	1.42	28.17	17.82	15.29
22 Delhi	46.61	41.52	41.04	16.76	19.49	20.13	51.15	44.36	42.80
India	3.56	3.44	3.24	1.40	1.35	1.20	13.25	11.68	9.68

Table A-1.1(iii) Lifetime internal male migrants as a percentage of the internal male population in the States and Union Territories of India – 1961, 1971, 1981

State / UT	Intra-district migrants ratio			Intra-district migrant ratio in rural areas			Intra-district migrant ratio in urban areas		
	1961	1971	1981	1961	1971	1981	1961	1971	1981
1 Andhra Pradesh	14.32	14.38	13.12	13.47	13.82	11.83	18.31	16.68	17.28
2 Assam	13.64	15.33	N.A.	13.53	15.26	N.A.	15.12	16.06	N.A.
3 Bihar	7.17	5.28	3.64	6.44	4.66	2.99	14.49	10.44	7.91
4 Gujarat	10.91	9.92	11.25	9.83	9.25	8.71	14.00	11.61	11.33
5 Haryana	N.A.	5.46	4.41	N.A.	4.58	3.45	N.A.	8.53	8.09
6 Himachal Pradesh	N.A.	10.18	10.71	N.A.	9.76	10.21	N.A.	15.44	16.39
7 Jammu and Kashmir	7.43	6.36	5.38	7.25	6.43	5.36	8.30	6.05	5.48
8 Karnataka	13.86	13.81	12.13	13.53	13.70	11.38	14.98	14.14	13.94
9 Kerala	13.32	10.04	12.17	13.34	10.26	12.51	13.20	8.92	10.69
10 Madhya Pradesh	13.46	11.96	10.62	13.66	12.16	10.41	12.31	10.98	11.45
11 Maharashtra	14.15	12.65	13.77	15.66	14.24	16.04	10.59	9.39	9.82
12 Manipur	11.99	10.84	6.14	12.49	11.33	6.50	6.76	7.64	5.12
13 Meghalaya	N.A.	20.80	14.01	N.A.	22.12	14.42	N.A.	12.65	14.11
14 Nagaland	6.41	6.92	10.72	5.00	6.24	9.34	29.39	13.72	17.59
15 Orissa	9.28	11.77	9.25	8.63	11.25	8.14	18.06	17.10	17.01
16 Punjab	8.68	7.99	7.38	7.70	7.02	6.57	13.16	11.38	9.73
17 Rajasthan	6.66	7.35	6.83	5.95	6.86	6.13	10.37	9.61	9.41
18 Tamil Nadu	11.40	11.57	10.29	10.16	10.89	9.40	14.76	13.12	12.17
19 Tripura	19.83	12.21	9.41	20.54	17.56	9.68	10.33	6.78	6.94
20 UttarPradesh	6.27	4.64	3.26	5.66	4.11	2.66	10.32	7.80	5.97

(Continued)

Table A-1.1(iii) (Continued)

State / UT	Intra-district migrants ratio			Intra-district migrant ratio in rural areas			Intra-district migrant ratio in urban areas		
	1961	1971	1981	1961	1971	1981	1961	1971	1981
21 West Bengal	8.35	6.80	5.73	8.63	7.72	5.77	7.47	4.06	5.63
22 Delhi	5.43	1.27	2.09	2.19	3.96	2.46	5.93	0.93	2.06
India	10.35	9.31	8.23	9.88	9.06	7.67	12.47	10.28	9.99

Sources:
1 GOI, Census of India, 1961. *Vol. 1 India; Migration Tables, part II-C (iii)*.
2 GOI, Census of India, 1961. *India: General population tables, Vol. 1, Pt. II-A (i)*.
3 GOI, Census of India, 1971. *Series 1 — India, Migration Tables, Part II-D (i)*.
4 GOI, Census of India, 1981. *Series-1, India; Migration Tables, Part V — A & B*.
5 GOI, Census of India, 1981. *Series 1 — India, Part II B (i) Primary Census Abstract General Population*.
6 Ratnoo, H.S. (1987: 30).

Notes:
1 Population and migrant figures for this table exclude international migrants and are not corrected for any boundary changes.
2 The figures for migrants in NEFA and Goa, Daman and Diu, as well as Himachal Pradesh, are excluded. Haryana and Meghalaya were not in existence as separate States in 1961.
3 The census in 1981 could not be held in Assam due to disturbed conditions.

Table A-1.2(i) Male migrants of different categories as a percentage of the total internal male migrants – 1961, 1971, 1981*

State / UT	Migrants in rural areas			Migrants in urban areas		
	1961	1971	1981	1961	1971	1981
1 Andhra Pradesh	68.10	67.41	58.96	31.90	32.59	41.04
2 Assam	85.04	83.86	N.A.	14.96	16.14	N.A.
3 Bihar	70.40	62.06	51.03	29.60	37.94	48.97
4 Gujarat	52.04	49.57	45.85	47.96	50.43	54.15
5 Haryana	N.A.	61.84	50.34	N.A.	38.16	49.66
6 Himachal Pradesh	N.A.	75.68	77.07	N.A.	24.32	22.93
7 Jammu and Kashmir	73.07	72.74	68.53	26.93	27.26	31.47
8 Karnataka	64.14	62.96	53.99	35.86	37.04	46.01
9 Kerala	81.59	81.24	75.10	18.41	18.76	24.90
10 Madhya Pradesh	72.71	69.70	61.86	27.29	30.30	38.14
11 Maharashtra	48.89	46.48	47.12	51.11	53.52	52.88
12 Manipur	92.28	88.23	68.95	7.72	11.77	31.05
13 Meghalaya	N.A.	80.00	69.53	N.A.	20.00	30.47
14 Nagaland	72.18	46.80	62.71	27.82	53.20	37.29
15 Orissa	78.27	75.78	64.17	21.73	24.22	35.83
16 Punjab	58.80	54.25	51.41	41.20	45.75	48.59
17 Rajasthan	65.37	64.44	59.37	34.63	34.56	40.63
18 Tamil Nadu	51.28	49.92	44.58	48.72	50.08	55.42
19 Tripura	94.48	91.04	88.42	5.52	8.96	11.58
20 Uttar Pradesh	63.01	59.06	50.80	36.99	40.94	49.20
21 West Bengal	48.40	49.39	45.11	52.60	50.61	54.89
22 Delhi	4.80	6.26	4.07	95.20	93.74	95.93
India	61.38	59.62	51.99	38.62	40.38	48.01

Table A-1.2(ii) Male migrants of different categories as a percentage of the total internal male migrants – 1961, 1971, 1981*

State / UT	Inter-State migrants			Inter-State migrants in rural areas			Inter-State migrants in urban areas		
	1961	1971	1981	1961	1971	1981	1961	1971	1981
1 Andhra Pradesh	6.59	6.67	69.43	2.57	2.59	2.40	4.02	4.08	4.03
2 Assam	24.84	29.40	N.A.	17.96	13.24	N.A.	6.88	16.14	N.A.
3 Bihar	13.32	13.53	13.10	6.32	4.74	4.07	7.00	8.79	9.03
4 Gujarat	14.22	15.73	17.40	3.63	3.56	4.03	10.58	12.17	13.37
5 Haryana	N.A.	45.81	5.94	N.A.	25.58	19.35	N.A.	20.23	26.50
6 Himachal Pradesh	N.A.	21.43	0.55	N.A.	12.17	12.84	N.A.	9.26	7.71
7 Jammu and Kashmir	7.18	15.33	13.79	3.84	9.95	7.40	3.34	5.38	6.39
8 Karnataka	18.32	16.23	17.76	7.99	7.08	6.25	10.33	9.15	31.01
9 Kerala	7.33	7.21	8.75	5.30	4.90	6.29	2.03	2.31	2.54
10 Madhya Pradesh	19.10	18.62	17.80	7.99	6.07	5.80	11.11	11.75	12.00
11 Maharashtra	24.16	25.18	23.92	3.11	3.34	3.83	21.05	21.84	20.09
12 Manipur	11.35	19.70	21.23	7.93	15.80	11.41	3.42	3.90	9.82
13 Meghalaya	N.A.	24.45	9.58	N.A.	11.06	13.45	N.A.	13.39	16.13
14 Nagaland	37.79	67.21	42.95	24.19	26.58	23.59	13.60	40.63	19.36
15 Orissa	12.67	12.28	14.66	6.49	5.54	6.25	6.18	6.74	8.41
16 Punjab	17.17	23.29	27.57	6.62	8.15	10.12	10.55	15.14	17.45
17 Rajasthan	19.42	17.55	18.56	11.00	8.92	8.79	8.42	8.63	9.77
18 Tamil Nadu	9.66	9.61	8.88	2.40	2.19	1.83	7.26	7.42	7.05
19 Tripura	13.34	16.16	15.34	10.96	12.66	11.79	2.39	3.50	3.55
20 Uttar Pradesh	9.34	10.72	11.16	3.53	4.29	4.83	5.81	6.43	6.33
21 West Bengal	42.00	44.30	34.97	11.11	14.21	7.22	30.89	30.09	27.75
22 Delhi	89.56	97.02	95.16	4.24	5.20	3.63	85.32	91.82	91.53
India	18.76	19.64	19.46	6.05	6.15	5.47	12.13	13.49	13.99

Table A-1.2 (iii) Male migrants of different categories as a percentage of the total internal male migrants – 1961, 1971, 1981*

State / UT	Intra-District migrants (all)			Intra-District migrants in rural areas			Intra-District migrants in urban areas		
	1961	1971	1981	1961	1971	1981	1961	1971	1981
1 Andhra Pradesh	67.61	67.69	32.41	52.33	52.35	12.44	15.28	15.34	19.77
2 Assam	58.23	62.89	N.A.	53.50	57.13	N.A.	4.73	5.76	N.A.
3 Bihar	58.82	55.67	43.44	48.00	43.90	30.92	10.82	11.77	12.52
4 Gujarat	54.78	50.43	47.26	36.56	33.70	29.57	18.22	16.73	17.69
5 Haryana	N.A.	39.20	30.91	N.A.	27.68	19.15	N.A.	11.52	11.76
6 Himachal Pradesh	N.A.	56.42	56.08	N.A.	50.08	49.09	N.A.	6.34	6.99
7 Jammu and Kashmir	61.81	57.44	56.03	50.19	47.23	43.96	11.62	10.21	12.07
8 Karnataka	58.78	59.67	54.45	44.27	44.49	36.05	14.51	15.18	18.40
9 Kerala	66.38	59.30	78.30	56.31	50.68	65.35	10.07	8.62	12.95
10 Madhya Pradesh	59.48	58.14	54.95	51.54	49.25	42.68	7.94	8.89	12.27
11 Maharashtra	45.52	43.04	43.05	35.37	32.59	31.87	10.15	10.45	11.18
12 Manipur	88.65	69.90	57.19	84.35	63.40	44.62	4.30	6.50	12.57
13 Meghalaya	N.A.	73.99	60.12	N.A.	67.55	49.48	N.A.	6.44	10.64
14 Nagaland	53.15	40.82	39.94	39.05	31.30	29.01	14.10	9.52	10.93
15 Orissa	68.12	69.14	59.30	58.93	60.13	45.64	9.19	9.05	13.66
16 Punjab	45.93	46.02	42.95	34.46	31.43	27.66	12.47	14.59	15.29
17 Rajasthan	54.59	57.67	53.31	40.99	44.50	37.65	13.60	13.17	15.66
18 Tamil Nadu	61.05	57.99	54.07	39.71	37.87	32.90	21.34	12.12	21.17
19 Tripura	86.66	69.65	65.81	83.52	66.12	60.95	3.14	3.53	4.56

(Continued)

Table A-1.2 (iii) (Continued)

State / UT	Intra-District migrants (all)			Intra-District migrants in rural areas			Intra-District migrants in urban areas		
	1961	1971	1981	1961	1971	1981	1961	1971	1981
20 Uttar Pradesh	53.78	51.42	45.42	42.08	39.08	30.31	11.70	12.34	15.11
21 West Bengal	37.54	45.60	39.46	29.35	38.75	29.25	8.19	6.85	10.21
22 Delhi	10.44	2.98	4.84	0.56	1.06	0.44	9.88	1.92	4.40
India	54.66	53.22	49.45	44.67	41.35	35.01	11.99	11.87	14.44

Sources:

1 GOI, Census of India, 1961. *Vol. 1 India; Migration Tables, part II-C (iii).*
2 GOI, Census of India, 1961. *India: General population tables, Vol.1, Pt. II-A (i).*
3 GOI, Census of India, 1971. *Series 1 — India, Migration Tables, Part II-D (i).*
4 GOI, Census of India, 1981. *Series-1, India: Migration Tables, Part V — A & B.*
5 GOI, Census of India, 1981. *Series 1 — India, Part II B (i) Primary Census Abstract General Population.*
6 Ratnoo, H.S. (1987: 40).

Notes:

1 Population and migrant figures for this table exclude international migrants and are not corrected for any boundary changes.
2 The figures for migrants in NEFA and Goa, Daman and Diu, as well as Himachal Pradesh, are excluded. Haryana and Meghalaya were not in existence as separate States in 1961.
3 The census in 1981 could not be held in Assam due to disturbed conditions.

Table A-1.3 Lifetime inter-State male migrants from rural and urban areas (per cent) and their growth rates – 1971–1981

States	Rural out-migrants to population		Urban out-migrants to population		Growth rates for migrants			
	1971	1981	1971	1981	Rural to rural	Rural to urban	Urban to rural	Urban to urban
1 Andhra Pradesh	1.84	1.81	4.07	3.42	3.33	23.72	15.65	27.31
2 Bihar	4.06	3.50	5.90	6.66	-29.08	37.60	71.68	72.20
3 Gujarat	2.61	2.34	4.60	3.82	19.17	7.81	21.39	16.30
4 Haryana	5.11	5.12	10.76	9.36	22.09	22.00	37.20	39.08
5 Himachal Pradesh	5.47	5.67	27.28	25.60	18.14	29.76	54.69	19.09
6 Jammu and Kashmir	0.96	0.87	4.96	3.88	55.76	-8.75	63.22	5.58
7 Karnataka	2.39	2.84	6.39	5.00	40.06	42.05	11.09	18.37
8 Kerala	3.59	3.29	14.67	12.42	-3.05	8.53	-9.70	20.29
9 Madhya Pradesh	1.21	1.66	3.49	2.95	53.88	80.20	43.68	27.11
10 Maharashtra	1.43	1.47	2.81	2.57	5.15	37.46	14.82	29.95
11 Manipur	1.03	1.33	2.96	1.06	30.08	72.11	63.95	247.72
12 Meghalaya	1.89	0.25	8.61	3.75	-89.53	-27.56	-66.59	-3.15
13 Nagaland	1.04	0.72	3.76	2.61	-39.25	92.17	-29.58	114.81
14 Orissa	1.93	1.63	4.43	3.60	-32.76	35.69	-8.57	50.19
15 Punjab	6.98	5.67	13.00	10.28	-0.87	-10.59	-5.52	17.51
16 Rajasthan	3.97	3.52	7.82	5.80	-3.01	20.96	3.42	20.16
17 Tamil Nadu	1.99	2.08	4.27	4.53	2.19	34.99	38.66	34.54
18 Tripura	1.73	0.83	4.88	3.15	-54.91	11.31	155.29	37.34
19 Uttar Pradesh	3.52	4.00	8.17	7.23	2.75	45.80	19.38	42.80
20 West Bengal	0.96	0.88	2.69	2.72	-9.48	42.92	13.55	33.22
India	2.69	2.76	5.49	4.99	-1.20	31.91	20.80	31.91

Source
1 GOI, Census of India, 1971, Series 1, India, Migration Tables, Part II, Table D-I
2 GOI, Census of India, 1981, Series 1, India, "Report and Tables based on five per cent data", Table D-I
3 Kundu, A. (1986: 2005–2008)
4 Ratnoo, H.S. (1987: 45)

Table A-1.4 Lifetime inter-State male net migrants and the decadal rates 1971–1981

States	Net migrants 1971	Net migrants 1981	Estimated net decadal migrants	Decadal rate of migrants
1 Andhra Pradesh	−178721	−237170	−74784	0.34
2 Bihar	−908347	−976053	−165099	−0.57
3 Gujarat	64740	190140	129016	0.93
4 Haryana	278873	289926	29183	0.54
5 Karnataka	62808	92256	33630	0.22
6 Kerala	−449054	−455482	−51574	−0.49
7 Madhya Pradesh	634144	510968	−62767	−0.29
8 Maharashtra	1596912	1977008	494611	1.89
9 Orissa	17785	113175	97273	0.88
10 Punjab	247583	276520	44918	0.62
11 Rajasthan	−217530	−186174	19277	0.14
12 Tamil Nadu	−90327	−153669	−72114	−0.35
14 Uttar Pradesh	−1362285	−2053328	−835908	−1.78
15 West Bengal	2825443	2821105	207118	0.88

Sources:
1 GOI, Census of India, 1971, Series 1, India Migration Tables, Part II-D(i), Table D-I
2 GOI, Census of India, 1981, Series 1, India, "Report and Tables based on five per cent data".
3 Kundu, A. (1986: 2005–2008)
4 Ratnoo, H.S. (1987: 47)

Note: Net migrant figures were obtained by subtracting the out-migrants from the in-migrants. Survivors among the 1971 migrants were computed by multiplying the net migrants by the survival ratio of 1971–1981, with the latter being the proportion of males aged 10 and above in 1981 to the total male population in 1971. Net decadal migrants were then obtained by subtracting the survivors among the migrants of 1971 from the net migrants of 1981. Decadal rate of migrants is the percentage of decadal migrants to the population of the states.

Table A-1.5 Areas of high out-migration as specified by Mohan (1982: 42)

Sr. No.	Region	Districts
1	Eastern Uttar Pradesh	Bahraich, Gonda, Basti, Gorkhpur, Deoria, Ballia, Azamgarh, Faizabad, Sultanpur, Jaunpur, Ghazipur, Varanasi, Mirzapur, Allahabad, Pratapgarh,
2	Northern Bihar	Purnea, Kathihar, Darbanga, Samastipur, Madhubani, Muzarffarpur, Sitamarhi, Vaishalli, Champaran, Saran, Siwan, Gopalganj,
3	Central Bihar	Bhagalpur, Moghyr, Begusarai, Saharsa, Patna, Nalanda, Gaya, Aurangabad, Shahabad, Bhojpur, Rohtas

Table A-2.1 Population of *jhuggie jhonpari* clusters (squatter settlements) in different parts of Delhi

Slum Wing (DDA) Zones	Population in jhuggie jhonpari clusters 1991	Population 1991	Percentage of J. J. to total population	Area (Hect.)	J. J. Population/ Area
East	195,944	2,108,616	9.29	5,396.3	36.31
Central	92,540	1,050,586	8.81	8,286.1	11.17
North	261,627	2,069,785	12.64	8,217.0	31.84
West	182,212	2,170,655	8.39	12,292.7	14.82
South	356,844	1,404,564	25.41	11,039.0	32.33
DELHI	1,089,167	8,804,206	12.37	45231.1	24.08

Notes on sources:
1 The population figures for Planning Divisions of the DDA are from GOI, Ministry of Urban Development (1990: 120).
2 The squatter population was estimated by taking the average size of the household in squatter settlements in different parts of Delhi using the unpublished data from the various Circles of the Food and Supplies Department of the Delhi Administration.
3 Figures for areas of Planning Divisions of the DDA were collected from the unpublished records of the Zonal Planning Division of the DDA.
4 GOI, Census of India, 1991 (1991b).

Table A-2.2 Percentage of criteria migrants from different squatter settlements

Name of the locality	Per cent of criteria migrants	Criteria migrant proportion*
Subhas Camp	33.7	0.24
Sanjay Colony	31.0	0.47
Bengali Camp	35.3	0.50
	100.0	

(n =184)

*Criteria migrants as proportion of all sampled heads of household of the listing survey.

Table A-2.3 The percentage distribution of criteria migrants among census blocks and the migrant proportion

S. No.	Census block	Per cent	Migrant proportion*
1	Subhas Camp, (E. B. 87)	18.5	0.25
2	Subhas Camp, (E.B. 92)	15.2	0.24
3	Sanjay Colony, (E.B. 70)	31.0	0.47
4	Bengali Camp, (E.B. 83)	35.3	0.50
		100.0	

(n =184)

*Criteria migrants as a proportion of all sampled heads of household of the listing survey.
E.B.: Enumeration Block

Table A-2.4 Percentage distribution of the phase I interviews with the criteria migrants by day of the week

Day of the week	Percentage of phase I interviews of the criteria migrants
Monday	14.1
Tuesday	14.1
Wednesday	9.2
Thursday	9.8
Friday	12.5
Saturday	16.6
Sunday	23.4
	100.0

(n =184)

Table A-2.5 Phase II interview in the forenoon or afternoon

Part of the day	Valid per cent
Forenoon	53.0
Afternoon	47.0
	100.0

(n = 183) Missing cases: 01

Table A-2.6 Interview duration in minutes (Phase II)

Duration	Valid per cent
up to 9	0.6
10 to 14	6.1
15 to 19	16.6
20 to 24	28.2
25 to 29	22.7
30 to 34	13.5
35 to 39	5.5
40 and over	6.7
	100.0

Valid cases 163   Missing cases 21

Table A-2.7 Age at the time of the interview in 1992

Age in years	Valid per cent
15 to 19	0.5
20 to 24	13.6
25 to 29	16.3
30 to 34	31.5
35 to 39	13.6
40 to 44	15.2
45 to 49	5.4
50 to 54	1.1
55 to 59	2.7
	100.0

Valid cases 95   Missing cases 2

Table A-2.8 Years of schooling

Schooling	Valid per cent
Below primary	15.8
>= Primary but < middle	27.4
>= Middle but < matric	26.3
>= Matric but < graduate	27.4
Graduate and above	3.2
	100.0

Valid cases 95   Missing cases 2

Table A-2.9 Marital status

Marital status	Per cent
Married	91.8
Unmarried	6.5
Others	1.6
	100.0

(n = 184)

Table A-2.10 Total duration of stay in Delhi (in months)

Duration	Valid per cent
Up to 6	5.5
7 to 12	1.6
13 to 48	6.0
49 to 119	24.6
120 to 179	39.3
180 to 239	21.3
240 and over	1.6
	100.0

Valid cases 183   Missing cases 1

Table A-2.11 Years since migration

Years	Valid per cent
Up to 1	3.8
1 to 4	10.3
5 to 9	22.3
10 to 14	39.1
15 to 19	22.3
20	2.2
	100.0

Valid cases 184   Missing cases 0

Table A-2.12 The distribution of the criteria migrants
by calendar month of arrival in Delhi

Month	Valid per cent
January	12.1
February	3.4
March	9.5
April	10.3
May	11.2
June	9.5
July	6.0
August	5.2
September	6.9
October	8.6
November	11.2
December	6.0
	100.0

(n = 116) Missing cases 68

Table A-2.13 Calendar year of arrival in Delhi

Year	Valid per cent
1972 to 1973	7.4
1974 to 1976	11.8
1977 to 1978	10.3
1979 to 1980	19.9
1981 to 1982	14.0
1983 to 1984	11.8
1985 to 1986	7.4
1987 to 1988	5.1
1989 to 1990	2.9
1991 to 1992	9.6
	100.0

Valid cases 136   Missing cases 48

Table A-2.14 Age at arrival in Delhi

Age (in years)	Valid per cent
10 to 14	5.4
15 to 19	30.4
20 to 24	31.0
25 to 29	17.4
30 to 34	7.1
35 to 39	5.4
40 and over	3.3
	100.0

Valid cases 184   Missing cases 0

Table A-2.15 Type of place of last residence

Type	Per cent
Village	97.3
Town	0.5
City	2.2
	100.0

(n = 184)

Table A-2.16 State of birth

State	Valid per cent
Bihar	28.3
Haryana	2.2
Madhya Pradesh	0.5
Orissa	0.5
Rajasthan	8.2
Tamil Nadu	3.8
Uttar Pradesh	45.7
West Bengal	10.9
	100.0

Valid cases 184   Missing cases 0

Table A-2.17 Percentage distribution of criteria migrants by
State of last residence

State	Valid per cent
Andhra Pradesh	0.5
Bihar	29.9
Haryana	2.7
Madhya Pradesh	0.5
Orissa	0.5
Rajasthan	7.6
Tamil Nadu	3.8
Uttar Pradesh	45.7
West Bengal	8.7
	100.0

(n = 184)

Table A-3.1 Duration of unemployment for those unemployed
before migration

Duration of unemployment (in days)	Valid per cent
1 to 7	1.9
8 to 30	10.3
31 to 60	21.5
61 to 90	17.8
91 to 120	13.1
121 to 180	23.4
181 to 240	8.4
241 to 300	2.8
301 to 360	0.9
	100.0

Valid cases 107   Missing cases 0

Table A-3.2 Duration of underemployment for those underemployed
before migration (in days)

Duration of underemployment	Valid per cent
300	12.5
365	50.0
730	25.0
1095	12.5
	100.0

Valid cases 8   Missing cases 2

Table A-3.3 Percentage distribution of respondents by the amount of total and cultivable land owned (acres)

Size-class (acres)	Total land		Cultivable land	
	Valid Per cent	Cumulative Per cent	Valid Per cent	Cumulative Per cent
Up to 0.49	7.7	7.7	15.4	15.4
0.50 to 0.99	14.3	22.0	17.6	33.0
1.00 to 2.49	33.0	54.9	28.6	61.5
2.50 to 4.99	23.1	78.0	25.3	86.8
5.00 to 7.49	12.1	90.1	7.7	94.5
7.50 to 9.99	7.7	97.8	4.4	98.9
10 and over	2.2	100.0	1.1	100.0
	100.0		100.0	

Valid cases 91   Missing cases 0

Table A-3.4 Leased-in land (in acres)

Size-class (acres)	Valid per cent	Cumulative per cent
Up to 0.49	10.9	10.9
0.50 to 0.99	23.6	34.5
1.00 to 1.74	27.3	61.8
1.75 to 2.49	7.3	69.1
2.50 to 3.49	20.0	89.1
3.50 to 4.99	3.6	92.7
5.00 to 7.49	5.5	98.2
10 and over	1.8	100.0
	100.0	

Valid cases 55   Missing cases 0

Table A-3.5 Size of single plot of leased-in land (acres)

Size-class (acres)	Valid per cent	Cumulative per cent
0.25 to 0.49	16.1	16.1
0.50 to 0.74	19.4	35.5
1.00 to 1.99	41.9	77.4
2.00 to 2.99	9.7	87.1
3 and over	12.9	100.0
	100.0	

Valid cases 31   Missing cases 0

Table A-3.6 Percentage of leased-in to owned cultivable land

Per cent	Valid per cent	Cumulative per cent
Up to 24	12.1	12.1
25 to 49	18.2	30.3
50 to 74	27.3	57.6
75 to 99	3.0	60.6
100 to 199	21.2	81.8
200 to 399	9.1	90.9
400 and over	9.1	100.0
	100.0	

Valid cases 33   Missing cases 0

Table A-4.1 Calendar month of pre-migration visit

Month	Valid per cent	Cumulative per cent
April	16.7	16.7
June	33.3	50.0
August	25.0	75.0
October	16.7	91.7
November	8.3	100.0
	100.0	

Valid cases 12   Missing cases 10

Table A-4.2 Calendar year of pre-migration visit

Years	Valid per cent	Cumulative per cent
1960 to 1970	10.0	10.0
1971 to 1973	25.0	35.0
1974 to 1976	5.0	40.0
1977 to 1980	25.0	65.0
1981 to 1984	15.0	80.0
1985 to 1988	10.0	90.0
1989 to 1992	10.0	100.0
	100.0	

Valid cases 20   Missing cases 2

Table A-4.3 Length of stay during pre-migration visit (in days)

Stay (in days)	Valid per cent	Cumulative per cent
1 to 7	23.8	23.8
8 to 30	28.6	52.4
31 to 180	33.3	85.7
181 to 365	14.3	100.0
	100.0	

Valid cases 21   Missing cases 1

Table A-4.4 First job in Delhi

Code	First occupation	Per cent	Cumulative per cent
1	Animal husbandry	0.5	0.5
2	Agricultural labour	1.6	2.2
3	Unskilled construction work (*beldari*)	33.2	35.3
4	Semi-skilled construction work	0.5	35.9
5	Other unskilled construction work	3.8	39.7
6	Helper/labourer in nongarment factory	8.7	48.4
7	Semi-skilled nongarment factory work	3.3	51.6
8	Helper/labourer in garment factory	2.2	53.8
9	Tailor	6.0	59.8
10	Other semi-skilled garment factory work	2.7	62.5
11	Craft and tradesperson	6.5	69.0
12	Shopkeeping	1.1	70.1
13	Shop worker	2.2	72.3
14	Vendor	3.8	76.1
15	Sweeper	7.6	83.7
16	Watchman/security guard	3.3	87.0
17	Peon	2.2	89.1
18	Hotel/restaurant /bar and related work	3.3	92.4
19	Domestic servant	2.2	94.6
20	Other service sector work	2.2	96.7
21	Others	3.3	100.0
		100.0	

Valid cases 184   Missing cases 0

Table A-4.5 Total duration of first job (in months)

Duration (in months)	Valid per cent	Cumulative per cent
Up to 0.23	7.6	7.6
0.24 to 0.50	5.4	13.0
0.51 to 1.00	4.9	17.9
1.01 to 3.00	15.8	33.7
3.01 to 6.00	15.2	48.9
6.01 to 12.00	13.6	62.5
12.01 to 36.00	14.1	76.6
36.01 to 72.00	10.9	87.5
72.01 to 108.00	2.7	90.2
108.01 to 180.00	7.1	97.3
180.01 to 240.00	2.7	100.0
	100.0	

Valid cases 184   Missing cases 0

Table A-4.6 Second job in Delhi

Code	Occupation	Valid per cent	Cumulative per cent
1	Animal husbandry	1.1	1.1
2	Agricultural labour	1.1	2.1
3	Unskilled construction work (*beldari*)	8.4	10.5
4	Semi-skilled construction work	6.3	16.8
5	Other unskilled construction work	2.1	18.9
6	Helpers/labourer in nongarment	6.3	25.3
7	Semi-skilled nongarment factory work	5.3	30.5
8	Helper/labourer in nongarment factory	9.5	40.0
9	Tailor	1.1	41.1
10	Other semi-skilled garment factory work	5.3	46.3
11	Craft and tradesperson	5.3	51.6
12	Shopkeeping	4.2	55.8
13	Shop worker	2.1	57.9
14	Vendor	5.3	63.2
15	Sweeper	8.4	71.6
16	Watchman/security guard	7.4	78.9
17	Peon	5.3	84.2
20	Other service sector work	4.2	88.4
21	Others	11.6	100.0
		100.0	

Valid cases 95   Missing cases 5   Inapplicable 84

Table A-4.7 Third job in Delhi

Code	Occupation	Valid per cent	Cumulative per cent
3	Unskilled construction work (*beldari*)	14.7	14.7
4	Semi-skilled construction work	8.8	23.5
5	Other unskilled construction work	2.9	26.5
6	Helper/labourer in nongarment factory	5.9	32.4
7	Semiskilled nongarment factory work	14.7	47.1
9	Tailor	5.9	52.9
10	Other semi-skilled garment factory work	8.8	61.8
11	Craft and tradesperson	2.9	64.7
12	Shopkeeping	2.9	67.6
14	Vendor	2.9	70.6
15	Sweeper	8.8	79.4
16	Watchman/security guard	2.9	82.4
18	Hotel/restaurant/bar and related work	2.9	85.3
20	Other service sector work	8.8	94.1
21	Others	5.9	100.0
		100.0	

Valid cases 34   Missing cases 5   Inapplicable 145

Table A-4.8 Fourth job in Delhi

Code	Occupation	Valid per cent	Cumulative per cent
3	Unskilled construction work (*beldari*)	11.1	11.1
4	Semi-skilled construction work	33.3	44.4
6	Helper/labourer in nongarment factory	11.1	55.6
12	Shopkeeping	33.3	100.0
		100.0	

Valid cases 9   Missing cases 5   Inapplicable 170

Table A-5.1 Reason for death (all sources used)

	Frequency	Valid per cent	Cumulative per cent
TB	1	12.5	12.5
'Illness'	5	62.5	75.0
Cancer	1	12.5	87.5
Heart attack	1	12.5	100.0
Total	8	100.0	

Table A-5.2 Locality during migrant resurvey in 2009

	Frequency	Valid per cent	Cumulative per cent
Balmiki Mohalla	3	4.3	4.3
Churia Mohalla (Tughlakabad)	3	4.3	8.7
Dakshinpuri	2	2.9	11.6
Harinagar Extension Part II (D-2/47), Jaitpur	1	1.4	13.0
Okhla Phase II	1	1.4	14.5
Subhash Camp	30	43.5	58.0
Sanjay Colony	29	42.0	100.0
Total	69	100.0	

Valid cases = 69   Missing cases = 2

Table A-5.3 Main activity of the respondents

	Frequency	Valid per cent	Cumulative per cent
Work for living	65	91.5	91.5
Sick/disabled	5	7.0	98.6
Other	1	1.4	100.0
Total	71	100.0	

Table A-5.4 Cross-tabulation of the sectors of the first city jobs with the sectors of the current city jobs

Main occupation 2009		First occupation in Delhi					Total
		Construction	Service	Factory	Shopkeeping and shop worker	Others	
Construction	Count	8	2	1	0	1	12
	Expected count	2.8	3.7	2.8	1.8	0.9	12.0
Service	Count	3	9	3	3	2	20
	Expected count	4.6	6.2	4.6	3.1	1.5	20.0
Factory	Count	1	1	8	1	0	11
	Expected count	2.5	3.4	2.5	1.7	0.8	11.0
Shopkeeping and shop worker	Count	1	4	3	6	0	14
	Expected count	3.2	4.3	3.2	2.2	1.1	14.0
Others	Count	2	4	0	0	2	8
	Expected count	1.8	2.5	1.8	1.2	0.6	8.0
Count		15	20	15	10	5	65
Expected Count		15.0	20.0	15.0	10.0	5.0	65.0

Pearson chi-square = 48.409 at degree of freedom = 16 and asymptotic significance 0.000
Cramer's V = 0.431 at approximate significance = 0.000

Table A-5.5 Kind of study or work learned

	Frequency	Valid per cent	Cumulative per cent
Land rejuvenation	1	16.7	16.7
Mechanic's work	1	16.7	33.3
Learned operating photocopy and printing machines	1	16.7	50.0
Making ovens	1	16.7	66.7
Work of a painter	1	16.7	83.3
Electrician's work	1	16.7	100.0
Total	6	100.0	

Table A-6.1 Data and cluster norms from k-means clustering

Sr. No.	Attribute Name	Data Norm	Cluster1 Norm	Cluster2 Norm
1	**ageatarr (years)**	**20 to 29**	**20 to 29**	**20 to 29**
	10 to 14	9 (5%)	3 (4%)	6 (7%)
	15 to 19	52 (34%)	27 (39%)	25 (30%)
	20 to 29	72 (47%)	34 (49%)	38 (45%)
	30 and over	19 (12%)	5 (7%)	14 (16%)
2	**polrdist**	**Rest of the country**	**Aohom**	**Rest of the country**
	1. Area of high migration (aohom)	63 (41%)	39 (56%)	24 (28%)
	2. Rest of the country	89 (58%)	30 (43%)	59 (71%)
3	**mostimp**	**In search of job**	**In search of job**	**In search of job**
	1. Village- job related negative factors	55 (36%)	23 (33%)	32 (38%)
	2. In search of job	75 (49%)	35 (50%)	40 (48%)
	3. City-job related positive factors	16 (10%)	9 (13%)	7 (8%)
	8. "Non-economic" (largely social but also 'natural') factors	6 (3%)	2 (2%)	4 (4%)
4	**age 2009**	**32 to 51 cohort**	**32 to 51 cohort**	**32 to 51 cohort**
	1. 32 to 51 cohort	99 (65%)	49 (71%)	50 (60%)
	2. 52 to 61 cohort	44 (28%)	19 (27%)	25 (30%)
	3. 62 to 76 cohort	9 (5%)	1 (1%)	8 (9%)
5	**read**	**Yes**	**Yes**	**No**
	Yes	88 (57%)	51 (73%)	37 (44%)
	No	64 (42%)	18 (26%)	46 (55%)
6	**school**	**Yes**	**Yes**	**No**
	1. Yes	83 (54%)	51(73%)	32 (38%)
	2. No	69 (45%)	18 (26%)	51 (61%)
7	**work_ybm**	**Yes**	**Yes**	**Yes**
	1. Yes	125 (2%)	54 (78%)	71 (85%)
	2. No	27 (17%)	15 (21%)	12 (14%)

8	**mainjob**	**Workers**	**Peasant**	**Workers**
	1. Peasants	44 (28%)	36 (52%)	8 (9%)
	2. Workers	61 (40%)	10 (14%)	51 (61%)
	3. Artisans, traders	20 (13%)	8 (11%)	12 (14%)
	8. Inapplicable (i.e., not working during year before migration)	27 (17%)	15 (21%)	12 (14%)
9	**hired**	**No**	**No**	**Yes**
	1. Yes	58 (38%)	8 (11%)	50 (60%)
	2. No	67 (44%)	46 (66%)	21 (25%)
	8. Inapplicable (i.e., not working during year before migration)	27 (17%)	15 (21%)	12 (14%)
10	**hirebase**	**Own business**	**Own business**	**Day**
	1. Day	35 (23%)	5 (7%)	30 (36%)
	2. Month	9 (5%)	1 (1%)	8 (9%)
	3. Year	8 (5%)	0 (0%)	8 (9%)
	4. Rest	6 (3%)	2 (2%)	4 (4%)
	8. Not working	27 (17%)	15 (21%)	12 (14%)
	88. Own business	67 (44%)	46 (66%)	21 (25%)
11	**whyquit1**	**Low income and associated reasons**	**Low income and associated reasons**	**Low income and associated reasons**
	1. Low income and associated reasons	62 (40%)	26 (37%)	36 (43%)
	2. Unemployment or underemployment	15 (9%)	4 (5%)	11 (13%)
	3. Incompatibility of skills and jobs in rural areas (for development of knowledge and skill according to urban labour market)	15 (9%)	5 (7%)	10 (12%)
	4. Family reasons	16 (9%)	9 (13%)	6 (7%)
	5. Inspiration from others/ own motivation	5 (3%)	4 (5%)	2 (2%)
	6. Rest of the reasons	12 (7%)	6 (8%)	6 (7%)
	8. Inapplicable (i.e., not working during year before migration)	27 (17%)	15 (21%)	12 (14%)
12	**unempld**	**Yes**	**Yes**	**Yes**
	1. Yes	89 (58%)	29 (42%)	60 (72%)
	2. No	30 (19%)	23 (33%)	7 (8%)

(Continued)

Table A-6.1 (Continued)

Sr. No.	Attribute Name	Data Norm	Cluster1 Norm	Cluster2 Norm
	3. Underemp	6 (3%)	2 (2%)	4 (4%)
	8. Inapplicable (i.e., not working during year before migration)	27 (17%)	15 (21%)	12 (14%)
13	**durunemp (in days)**	**Low unemployment**	**Inapplicable (Workers before migration but not unemployment, i.e., those were "fully employed")**	**Low unemployment**
	1. Low unemployment	45 (29%)	12 (17%)	33 (39%)
	2. Medium unemployment	32 (21%)	13 (18%)	19 (22%)
	3. High unemployment	18 (11%)	6 (8%)	12(14%)
	8. Inapplicable (not working during year before migration)	27 (17%)	15 (21%)	12 (14%)
	88. Inapplicable (Workers before migration but not unemployment, i.e., those were "fully employed")	30 (19%)	23 (33%)	7 (8%)
14	**ownland**	**Yes**	**Yes**	**No**
	1. Yes	80 (52%)	67 (97%)	13 (15%)
	2. No	72 (47%)	2 (2%)	70 (84%)
15	**oh_tenure**	**Inapplicable (for those operating no land)**	**Wholly owned and self-operated**	**Inapplicable (for those operating no land)**
	1. Wholly owned and self-operated	46 (30%)	41 (59%)	5 (6%)
	2. Partly owned and partly leased-in	30 (19%)	24 (34%)	6 (7%)
	3. Wholly leased-in	17 (11%)	3 (4%)	14 (16%)
	8. Inapplicable (for those operating no land)	59 (38%)	1 (1%)	58 (69%)
16	**oh_size**	**Inapplicable (for those operating no land)**	**Marginal(up to 2.47)**	**Inapplicable (for those operating no land)**
	1. Marginal (up to 2.47)	50 (32%)	38 (55%)	12 (14%)
	2. Small (2.48 to 4.94)	23 (15%)	14 (20%)	9 (10%)
	3. Semi-medium (4.95 to 9.88)	16 (10%)	12 (17%)	4 (4%)

	4. The rest (both medium *and* large) (9.89 and over)	4 (2%)	4 (5%)	0 (0%)
	8. Inapplicable (for those operating no land)	59 (38%)	1 (1%)	58 (69%)
17	**difflt**	**Yes**	**Yes**	**Inapplicable (those operating no land)**
	1. Yes	58 (38%)	38 (55%)	20 (24%)
	2. No	13 (8%)	10 (14%)	3 (3%)
	8. Inapplicable (those operating no land)	58 (38%)	0 (0%)	58 (69%)
	88. Inapplicable (cultivators whose harvest lasts yearlong or more)	23 (15%)	21 (30%)	2 (2%)
18	**famtype**	**Parental**	**Parental**	**Parental**
	1. Parental	111 (73%)	49 (71%)	62 (74%)
	2. Extended	20 (13%)	15 (21%)	5 (6%)
	3. Nuclear	18 (11%)	4 (5%)	14 (16%)
	4. Other	3 (1%)	1 (1%)	2 (2%)
19	**compare**	**Below average**	**Below average**	**Below average**
	1. Above average	9 (5%)	7 (10%)	2 (2%)
	2. Average	31 (20%)	21 (30%)	10 (12%)
	3. Below average	112 (73%)	41 (59%)	71 (85%)
20	**repmem**	**No**	**No**	**No**
	1. Yes	30 (19%)	19 (27%)	11 (13%)
	2. No	122 (80%)	50 (72%)	72 (86%)
21	**indebt**	**Yes**	**Yes**	**Yes**
	1. Yes	94 (61%)	37 (53%)	57 (68%)
	2. No	58 (38%)	32 (46%)	26 (31%)
22	**visit**	**No**	**No**	**No**
	1. Yes	46 (30%)	14 (20%)	32 (38%)
	2. No	106 (69%)	55 (79%)	51 (61%)
23	**famatt**	**Supportive**	**Supportive**	**Supportive**
	1. Supportive	111 (73%)	46 (66%)	65 (78%)
	2. Unsupportive	39 (25%)	23 (33%)	16 (19%)
	8. Inapplicable (No one else in the family)	2 (1%)	0 (0%)	2 (2%)

(Continued)

Table A-6.1 (Continued)

Sr. No.	Attribute Name	Data Norm	Cluster1 Norm	Cluster2 Norm
24	**support1**	**Family and relatives**	**Family and relatives**	**Family and relatives**
	1. Past savings; sale of property; loans	29 (19%)	8 (11%)	21 (25%)
	2. Family and relatives	75 (49%)	37 (53%)	38 (45%)
	3. Co-villagers	20 (13%)	12 (17%)	8 (9%)
	4. Diverse methods (friends; help with domestic work of urban contact; contractor; other source)	12 (7%)	5 (7%)	7 (8%)
	5. Inapplicable [(those who had 'job offer') + (those who did not have to wait for job)	16 (10%)	7 (10%)	9 (10%)
25	**fjindel**	**Construction**	**Factory**	**Construction**
	1. Construction	56 (36%)	14 (20%)	42 (50%)
	2. Service	36 (23%)	17 (24%)	19 (22%)
	3. Factory	38 (25%)	27 (39%)	11 (13%)
	4. Shop-keeping/shop worker	13 (8%)	7 (10%)	6 (7%)
	5. Others	9 (5%)	4 (5%)	5 (6%)
26	**channel1**	**Urbcontact**	**Urbcontact**	**Urbcontact**
	1. Jobbers	17 (11%)	5 (7%)	12 (14%)
	2. Urbcontact	99 (65%)	48 (69%)	51 (61%)
	3. Worksite	15 (9%)	8 (11%)	7 (8%)
	4. Chowk	14 (9%)	5 (7%)	9 (10%)
	5. Rest	7 (4%)	3 (4%)	4 (4%)
	8. Inapplicable	0 (0%)	0 (0%)	0 (0%)
27	**livevill**	**Yes**	**Yes**	**Yes**
	1. Yes	139 (91%)	61 (88%)	78 (93%)
	2. No	13 (8%)	8 (11%)	5 (6%)
28	**sjivill**	**Yes**	**Yes**	**Yes**
	1. Yes	137 (90%)	63 (91%)	74 (89%)
	2. No	15 (9%)	6 (8%)	9 (10%)
29	**paymeth**	**Daily**	**Monthly**	**Daily**
	1. Daily	66 (43%)	21 (30%)	45 (54%)
	2. Monthly	55 (36%)	36 (52%)	19 (22%)

#		Adverse factors associated with employment	Adverse factors associated with employment	Adverse factors associated with employment
	3. Piece work	9 (5%)	3 (4%)	6 (7%)
	4. Other Methods	11 (7%)	5 (7%)	6 (7%)
	8. Inapplicable (for those not working for wages)	11 (7%)	4 (5%)	7 (8%)
30	**endreason1**			
	1. Laying off	32 (21%)	16 (23%)	16 (19%)
	2. Adverse factors associated with employment	51 (33%)	19 (27%)	32 (38%)
	3. Positive factors (like taking another job or setting up business or completion of work training, etc.	31 (20%)	14 (20%)	17 (20%)
	4. Absenteeism	12 (7%)	6 (8%)	6 (7%)
	5. Other reasons	5 (3%)	4 (5%)	1 (1%)
	8. Inapplicable (those whose first job in Delhi has not ended)	21 (13%)	10 (14%)	11 (13%)
31	**ss_exist**	**Yes**	**Yes**	**Yes**
	1. Yes	97 (63%)	46 (66%)	51 (61%)
	2. No	55 (36%)	23 (33%)	32 (38%)
32	**cus_asu**	**Stayers**	**Stayers**	**Stayers**
	1. Stayers	105 (69%)	48 (69%)	57 (68%)
	2. Returnees	47 (30%)	21 (30%)	26 (31%)

References

GOI, Census of India (1961). *India: General population tables, Vol. 1, Pt. II-A (i)*. New Delhi: Registrar General and Census Commissioner, Government of India.

GOI (Government of India), Census of India (1961). *Vol. 1 India: Migration tables, part II-C (iii)*. New Delhi: Registrar General and Census Commissioner, Government of India, Government of India.

GOI, Census of India (1971). *Series 1-India, migration tables, part II-D (i)*. New Delhi: Registrar General and Census Commissioner, Government of India.

GOI, Census of India (1981). *Report and tables based on five percent data*. New Delhi: Registrar General and Census Commissioner, Government of India.

GOI, Census of India (1981). *Series 1-India, Part II B (i) Primary census abstract general population*. New Delhi: Registrar General and Census Commissioner, Government of India.

GOI, Census of India (1981). *Series-1, India; Migration tables, part V-A & B*. New Delhi: Registrar General and Census Commissioner, Government of India.

GOI, Census of India 1991 (1991). *Series-31, Delhi- provisional population totals, paper 1 of 1991*. Delhi: Director of Census Operations, Delhi, Government of India.

GOI, Ministry of Urban Development (1990). *Master plan for Delhi*. The Gazette of India (Extraordinary), No. 437. New Delhi: Ministry of Urban Development, Government of India.

Kundu, A. (1986). Migration, urbanisation and inter-regional inequality: The emerging socio-political challenge, *Economic and Political Weekly*, 21(46): 2005–2008.

Mohan, R. (1982). *The Morphology of urbanisation in India: Some results from the 1981 Census*. Paper presented in the seminar on Urbanisation and Planned Economic Development – Present and future perspectives, organised by the Centre for the Study of Regional Development, Jawaharlal Nehru University, New Delhi.

Ratnoo, H.S. (1987). *Migration, urbanisation and economic development: Rajasthan in the all India context (1961–81)*. Unpublished MPhil dissertation, Jawaharlal Nehru University, New Delhi.

Appendix G

Details relating to the reduced dataset

Preparing the dataset

Based on the data analysis during the preparation of the PhD work, the important variables were identified and a recoding scheme was employed on the basis of categories used for descriptions in the thesis (Ratnoo, 1994). The extensive data reduction exercise was carried out which resulted in thirty-eight variables in all, with several smaller categories submerged into larger categories. Out of these thirty-eight variables, five variables pertain to the fieldwork in 2009. The remaining thirty-three variables are from the fieldwork done in 1992. The list of variables along with their value labels is given in Table G1.

Table G1 List of variables in the reduced dataset

Sr. No.	Variables	Values	Value labels	Categories merged
1	Age at arrival in Delhi (in years) (ageatarr)	1	10 to 14	
		2	15 to 19	
		3	20 to 29	
		4	30 and over	
2	Area of last residence (polrdist)	1	Area of high out-migration (aohom)	*See Table A-1.5 showing area of high out-migration as specified by Mohan (1982)
		2	Rest of the country	
3	Most important reason of migration (mostimp)	1	Village- job related negative factors	Work was insufficient to support the family
				Nature of the work unsatisfactory
				Unemployment
				Irregularity of work
				Landlessness
				Poverty
				Economic difficulty
				Indebtedness
		2	In search of job	To learn skill
		3	City-job related positive factors	To seek better job/income
				Offered better job/income
				Bought land/business in Delhi
		4	'Non-economic' (largely social but also 'natural') factors	Family/social feud in the previous place of residence
				Caste violence/social oppression
				Family tragedy
				Natural calamities
				Other reasons
4	Age at the time of survey in 2009 (in years) (computed) (age2009)	1	32 to 51 cohort	
		2	52 to 61 cohort	
		3	62 to 76 cohort	
5	The ability to read in any language (read)	1	Yes	
		2	No	
6	Attended school? (school)	1	Yes	
		2	No	

7	Working for living during the year before migration? (work_ybm)	1	Yes
		2	No
8	What was your main job? (mainjob)	1	Peasants
			Agriculture
			Animal husbandry
			Grazing/Cow keeping
			Sharecropper
			Agricultural worker
		2	Workers
			Unskilled construction worker (*beldar*)
			Other unskilled construction sector worker
			Factory and mill worker
			Service worker
		3	Artisans, traders
			Tailor
			Other artisan and craftsperson
			Shopkeeper/vendor
			Others
		8	Inapplicable (i.e., not working during year before migration)
9	Were you hired? (hired)	1	Yes
		2	No
		8	Inapplicable (i.e., not working during year before migration)
10	Basis of hiring (hirebase)	1	Day
		2	Month
		3	Year
		4	Rest of the bases
			Harvest
			Season
			Piece work
			Other
		8	Inapplicable (not working during year before migration)
		88	Inapplicable (Working but not hired, i.e., those in own business)

(Continued)

Table G1 (Continued)

Sr. No.	Variables	Values	Value labels	Categories merged
11	First main reason group for leaving pre-migration job (whyquit1)	1	Low income and associated reasons	No land Insufficiency of land Low income Paid off debt To repay debt/was indebted
		2	Unemployment or underemployment	Skill not in demand there
		3	Incompatibility of skills and jobs in rural areas (for development of knowledge and skill according to urban labour market)	Irregularity / unpunctuality of payment Trouble with the employer Poor working conditions To take another job Apprenticeship/training over To learn skill/join training To set up business
		4	Family reasons	Family strategy Family size large Family social feud Tragedy/illness in the family Others lived here/were coming here
		5	Inspiration from others/own motivation	Wanted to move to another area Have not stopped (go during the season)
		6	Rest of the reasons	Laid off, no work Laid off, other reasons Job completed Could not continue study To get married Got married Pregnant Ill health/disability Caste/social oppression/violence Natural disasters Other reasons

No.	Question/Variable	Code	Value
12	Were you without work and wanting work before moving? (unempld)	8	Inapplicable (i.e., not working during year before migration)
		1	Yes
		2	No
		3	Underemployed
		8	Inapplicable (i.e., not working during year before migration)
13	Duration of unemployment (in days) (durunemp (in days))	1	Low unemployment (up to 90)
		2	Medium unemployment (91–180)
		3	High unemployment (181 and above)
		8	Inapplicable (not working during year before migration)
		88	Inapplicable (Workers before migration but not unemployed, i.e., those were "fully employed")
14	Did your family own any land? (ownland)	1	Yes
		2	No
15	Operational holding_ tenurial category (oh_tenure)	1	Wholly owned and self-operated
		2	Partly owned and partly leased-in
		3	Wholly leased-in
		8	Inapplicable (for those operating no land)
16	Operational holding_ size group (in acres) (oh_size)	1	Marginal (up to 2.47)
		2	Small (2.48 to 4.94)
		3	Semi-medium (4.95 to 9.88)
		4	The rest (both medium *and* large) (9.89 and over)
		8	Inapplicable (for those operating no land)

(Continued)

Table G1 (Continued)

Sr. No.	Variables	Values	Value labels	Categories merged
17	Difficulty in meeting family food requirement in off season (difflt)	1	Yes	Very difficult
				Difficult
				Not difficult
		2	No	Easy
				Very easy
		8	Inapplicable (those operating no land)	
		88	Inapplicable (cultivators whose harvest lasts a year or more)	
18	Family type (famtype)	1	Parental	Maternal
		2	Extended	Other
		3	Nuclear	
		4	Other	
19	Livelihood compared to other families in the village (compare)	1	Above average	Much higher than average
				Above average
		2	Average	
		3	Below average	Below average
				Much below average
20	Any family member in a representative body (repmem)	1	Yes	
		2	No	
21	Family in debt (indebt)	1	Yes	
		2	No	
22	Visited Delhi before migration (visit)	1	Yes	
		2	No	

23	Attitude of family towards migration (famatt)	1	Supported
		2	Worry
			Did not mind
			Opposed
			Fled/came without telling/consulting them
			Indifferent
	Supportive		Supported
	Unsupportive		Worry
		8	Inapplicable (no one else in the family)
24	First 'methods of support' group during the waiting period (support1)	1	Past savings
			Sold cattle/property in the village
			Loan
	Past savings; sale of property; loans	1	
		2	Support from family in village
			Brought food from the village
			Family members support in the city
			Relatives' support in Delhi
	Family and relatives	2	
		3	Friends' support in Delhi
		4	In lieu of help with domestic work (of urban contact)
			Contractor arranged it
			Other source (Did small work, bought essentials on credit from the shopkeeper, etc.)
	Co-villagers	3	
	Diverse methods (friends; help with domestic work of urban contact; contractor; other source)	4	
	Inapplicable [(those who had 'job offer') + (those who did not have to wait for job)]	8	
25	First occupation in Delhi (fjindel)	1	Unskilled construction work (beldari)
			Semi-skilled construction sector worker
			Other unskilled construction sector workers
	Construction	1	
		2	Vendors
			Sweeper
			Watchman\security guard
			Peon
			Hotel\restaurant\bar and related workers
			Domestic servants
			Other service sector workers
	Service	2	

(Continued)

Table G1 (Continued)

Sr. No.	Variables	Values	Value labels	Categories merged
		3	Factory	Helper\labourer in nongarment sector factory
				Semi-skilled nongarment sector factory workers
				Helper\labourer in garment sector factory
				Tailors
				Other semi-skilled garment sector factory workers
		4	Shopkeeping/ shop worker	Craft and tradespersons
				Shopkeeping
				Shop worker
		5	Others	Animal husbandry
				Agricultural labourer
				Others
		8	Inapplicable	
26	First 'channel' of recruitment (grouped) to the first job in Delhi (channel1)	1	Jobbers	Referrals
		2	Search efforts of urban contacts	Information from earlier settlers about 'impending recruitment plans'
				Search efforts of urban contacts
		3	Approaching factories, worksites, etc.	Gate hiring
				Approaching factories, worksites, shops and offices
		4	Chowk (market square)	
		5	Rest (institutional methods; setting up business; other methods)	Radio/television
				Newspapers
				Employment exchange
				Tried to set up business
				Other
		8	Inapplicable (for those who have not found the first job in Delhi)	
27	Would prefer to live in the village for same income? (livevill)	1	Yes	
		2	No	

28	Preparedness to do a similar job in the village (sjivill)	1	Yes
		2	No
29	Method of payment in the first job (paymeth)	1	Daily
			Casual, daily
			Regular, daily
		2	Monthly
		3	Piece work
		4	Other methods
			Season
			Weekly
			Fortnightly
			Annually
			Pocket money
			Other (like, 'according to the weight of scrap paper picked'; 'no work, no pay'; 'half the money received for the clothes stitched')
		8	Inapplicable (for those not working for wages)
30	First reason (group) for ending the first job in Delhi (endreason1)	1	Laying off
			Laid off, no work
			Laid off, factory\shop closed
			Laid off, other reasons
		2	Adverse factors associated with employment
			Quit, low income (quit, low piece rate; quit, didn't give pay raise)
			Quit, unpunctual payment\cheating
			Job was irregular; insecurity of job
			Quit, poor working conditions
			Ill health, disability (occupational accident\illness)
			Quarrel\dispute with the employer

(Continued)

Table G1 (Continued)

Sr. No.	Variables	Values	Value labels	Categories merged
		3	Positive factors (like taking another job or setting up business or completion of work training, etc.	Got promotion\regularisation Quit to take another job Completed/gave up apprenticeship/training Quit, to join training/to learn work Quit to set up business
		4	Absenteeism	
		5	Other reasons	Quit, other reasons (Season over; 'to do it in different way; 'didn't know the work'; 'quit, didn't match skill'; 'company was shifting to a distant place) Job completed To get married Pregnant Wanted to move to another area Other ('family feud'; 'chaos (Indira's death)'
		8	Inapplicable (those whose first job in Delhi has not ended)	
31	Squatter settlement (of 1992) existing or not? (ss_exist)	1	Yes	
		2	No	
32	Current updated status – all sources used (cus_asu)	1	Stayers	
		2	Returnees	
		3	Dead	
		9	Untraced (No clue cases!)	

References

Mohan, R. (1982). *The morphology of urbanisation in India: Some results from the 1981 census*. Paper presented in the seminar on Urbanisation and Planned Economic Development – Present and future perspectives, organised by the Centre for the Study of Regional Development, Jawaharlal Nehru University, New Delhi.

Ratnoo, H. S. (1994). *Socio-economic status, channels of recruitment and the rural to urban migration of labour: A case study of the squatter settlements of Delhi, India*. Unpublished doctoral thesis, University of London.

Appendix H

The four questionnaires and a letter format used during different stages of the study

The small-scale sample survey of inter-State rural migrants in Delhi 1992

Stage I

Questionnaire for all heads of household of the selected census blocks

Confidential

Unit Code No. _____

House _____

Locality _____

Date ———————

Time ——————————

Namaskar. I am a student. Earlier I was studying in Delhi. Now I am on scholarship in *vilayat* and doing this survey for my studies. This is about the people who have come from rural areas to Delhi for work. Would you mind answering some questions about your stay in Delhi?

Q1 Were you born in Delhi?

YES   NO

[IF ANSWER IS YES, SKIP TO Q7]

Q2 (a) Where were you born?

Village/Town/City _____
Tehsil _____
District _____
State/Country _____

(b) Was it a village, town or city?

Village
Town
City
Estate/Plantation
Other (specify_____)

(c) Did your mother always live there?

YES   NO

[If the answer is YES, skip to Q3(a)]

(d) Where did your mother normally live?

Village/Town/City _____
Tehsil   _____
District   _____
State/Country _____

(e) Was this a village, town or city?

Village
Town
City
Estate/Plantation
Other (specify_____)

Q3 (a) How long have you been in Delhi?

Months _____ Years _____

(b) Would you recall the month and year of your coming to Delhi?

Month _____ Year _____

Q4 How old were you when you moved to Delhi?

_____ Years

Q5 (a) Where did you usually live before you moved to Delhi?

Village/Town/City _____
Tehsil _____
District _____
State/Country _____

(b) What sort of place was this?

City
Town
Village
Estate/Plantation
Other (specify_____)

Q6 (a) Why did you move to Delhi?

(RECORD UP TO THREE: MARK IF REPLIES MATCH THE OPTIONS, NOTE IF DIFFERENT)

Transfer of place in old job
In search of a job
Work was insufficient to support family
Nature of work unsatisfactory
Bought land/business in Delhi
To seek better job/income
Offered better job/income
To get education for self
To get education for children
To get married
To accompany family
Family/social feuds in previous place of residence
Have other friends and relatives here
Poor amenities in previous place of residence
Other (specify_____)
Don't know

(b) Which of these reasons was the most important?

_____

Q7 (a) How old are you?

_____

Q8 (a) Can you read in any language?

YES   NO

(b) Can you write in any language?

YES   NO

(c) Did you go to school?

YES   NO

[IF ANSWER IS NO, SKIP TO Q9]

(d) How long were you at school?

_____

Q9 (a) Are you married?

YES   NO

IF YES,

(b) Do you have any children?

IF YES, HOW MANY AND WHAT ARE THEIR AGES

_____

_____

Thanks for your kind cooperation.

REQUEST TO THE MIGRANT HEAD OF THE HOUSEHOLD TO BE INTERVIEWED AGAIN

Q10(a) Would you please be kind enough to give me half an hour to talk to you about how you came to Delhi?

YES   NO

[IF ANSWER IS NO, SKIP TO Q10(C)]

IF YES,

(b) Can we talk now?

YES   NO

[IF ANSWER IS YES, SKIP TO STAGE II QUESTIONNAIRE]

(C) Is it possible any other time, today or any other day?

Date _____

Time _____

The small-scale sample survey of inter-State rural migrants in Delhi 1992

Stage II

Questionnaire for the migrant head of the household

Confidential

Unit Code No. _____

House _____

Locality _____

Date————————————-

Time————————————

Namaskar. It is very kind of you to agree to spend some more time with me.

As I mentioned earlier, I would like to know more about how you moved to Delhi.

(Wait for reaction. If there is any spontaneous remark or reflection, note it. Otherwise, move on to questions if the respondent is ready.)

First, some questions on what happened in the year before you came to Delhi. Imagine that you are in your village (name the village) in the year****. The questions that I am about to ask you all relate to that one year.

Q1.What was your **main** activity?

[Listen to the reply and note what is said instead of reading the list]

1. Work for living   **[SKIP TO Q3]**
2. Housework
3. Attending school
4. Sick/disabled
5. Retired
6. Other (specify_____)

Q2 Did you work?

YES   NO

[IF ANSWER IS YES, SKIP TO Q3]

(b) Did you want to work?

YES   NO

[IF ANSWER IS YES, SKIP TO Q4;

IF ANSWER IS NO, SKIP TO Q5]

Q3 If you were working during that year, then:

(a) What was your main job?

Occupation _____

What kind of work did it involve?

_____

(b) Were you hired?

YES   NO

[IF ANSWER IS NO, SKIP TO (d)]

(c) Were you hired by the day, by the week, by the month or on any other basis?

1. Day
2. Week
3. Month
4. Year
5. Harvest
6. Season
7. Piece work
8. Other (specify_____)

[SKIP TO (e)]

(d) If it was your own family business and you are not doing it now, please tell me, if after your departure:

(1) Did they hire, or arrange with, somebody to replace you?

YES   NO   DON'T KNOW

(e) What was the **main** reason you stopped working?

1. Have not stopped
2. Quit, low income
3. Quit, poor working conditions
4. Quit, to take another job
5. Quit, to set up business
6. Laid off, no work
7. Laid off, other reasons
8. Job completed
9. Ill health, disability

10. To get married
11. Pregnant
12. Paid off debt
13. Completed/gave up apprenticeship/training
14. Wanted to move to another area
15. Other (specify_____)

(f) Were you without work and wanting work for any time before you moved?

YES   NO

IF YES, for how long?

Weeks _____ Months _____

(g) Besides your main work, what other work did you do in those 12 months?

[IF ANSWER IS NONE, SKIP TO (h)]

1. Occupation _____
What kind of work did it involve? _____
2. Occupation _____
What kind of work did it involve? _____
3. Occupation _____
What kind of work did it involve? _____

(h) For about how many months, in all, did you work?

Months _____

[IF NONE, SKIP TO Q4]

[SKIP TO Q5]

Q4 **If you did not work, but wanted to, then:**
(a) How long were you without work?
Never worked **[SKIP TO Q5]**

Months _____
Years _____

(b) What sort of work had you been doing before you stopped?

1. Main occupation _____
2. The kind of work it involved _____

Now, I want to ask you some questions on landholding, cultivation and livestock in that year.

Q5 Did you have any livestock?

YES   NO

[IF ANSWER IS NO, SKIP Q6]

(b) Which and how many?

_____

_____

_____

(c) Did you sell any livestock or its product in the 12 months before your leaving the village?

YES   NO

Q6 Did your family own any land?

YES   NO

[IF ANSWER IS NO, SKIP TO Q10]

(b) How much was the total land?

_____acres

(c) How much of it was cultivable?

_____acres

[IF ANSWER IS NONE, SKIP TO Q10]

(d) Was it one plot?

[IF ANSWER IS YES, SKIP TO f]

(e) How many pieces?

_____

(f) How much of it was irrigated?

_____ acres

Q7 Did you cultivate all of your (cultivable) land?

YES   NO

[IF ANSWER IS YES, SKIP TO Q8]

(b) How much of it did you cultivate?

_____acres

(c) How much of it was irrigated?

_____acres

Q8 Did you employ any labour?

YES   NO

Q9 Did you lease-out any land?

YES   NO

[IF ANSWER IS NO, SKIP TO Q10]

(b) How much?

_____ acres

(c) Why did you have to lease-out?

Q10 Did you lease-in any land?

YES   NO

[IF ANSWER IS NO, SKIP TO NEXT SECTION]

(b) How much did you lease-in?

_____ acres

(c) Was it one plot?

YES   NO

[IF ANSWER IS YES, SKIP TO e]

(d) How many pieces?

_____

(e) How much of it was irrigated?

_____acres

Now, some questions on the harvest in that year:

[IF ANSWER TO Q6 AND Q10 IS NO, SKIP TO Q15]

Q11 How many harvests did you take in that year?

1. One
2. Two
3. Three
4. Four
5. More than four

Q12 Did you sell any produce in the market?

YES   NO

[IF ANSWER IS NO, SKIP TO Q13]

(b) What proportion of your total agricultural output did you sell that year?

1. All
2. More than half
3. Half
4. More than one-third
5. One-third
6. More than one-fourth
7. One-fourth
8. Less than one-fourth

Q13 Approximately how many months did your food grain harvest last in terms of home consumption?

_____ months

If less than 12 months,

(b) How difficult was it to fulfil the family's food requirements in the off-season?

1. Very difficult
2. Difficult
3. Not difficult

4. Easy
5. Very easy

If difficult,

(c) Did you have to borrow because of this?

YES   NO

Q14 Do you have a rough idea of how much livelihood (in *anna* terms) the family gained from different sources?

1. Cultivation of your own land
2. Leasing-out
3. Leasing-in
4. Other source (specify_____)

Now, some general questions.

Q15 Did you live in a parental family or in a joint family or a nuclear family?

1. Parental
2. Extended
3. Nuclear

Q16 How would you describe your family's economic position before you came to Delhi?

Q17 How good was your livelihood compared to other families in your village?

1. Much higher than average
2. Above average
3. Average
4. Below average
5. Much below average

Q18 Did people turn to your father for advice?

Q19 Was any member of your family in any representative body like the *pan-chayat*, cooperative society, etc.?

YES   NO

Q20 Was your family in debt?

YES   NO

[IF ANSWER IS YES, SKIP TO Q21]

(b) Did people owe money to your family?

YES   NO

Q21 Did you have any electricity connection?

YES   NO

[IF ANSWER IS NO, SKIP TO Q22]

(b) Did you have any of these and if YES, how many:

1. Fridge
2. Fan
3. Television
4. Any other gadget(s)

Q22 Did your family have the following?

If YES, how many

1. Tractor
2. Scooter
3. Motorcycle
4. Three-wheeler
5. Water pump engine
6. Well
7. Horse
8. Bullocks
9. Bullock cart
10. Cycle
11. Radio

[IF THE RESPONDENT CAN READ, SKIP TO Q23 (b)]

Q23 Could anyone in your family read in any language?

YES   NO

(b) Did you get any daily newspaper?

YES   NO

(c) Did you get any magazine?

YES   NO

[IF HE/SHE DOES NOT HAVE ANY CHILDREN, SKIP TO Q25]

Q24 Did your children go to school?

(b) Did your children have books?

Now, some questions on how you moved to Delhi and what you knew about jobs before you came here.

Q25 Did you visit Delhi before you came to settle here?

> **YES   NO**
>
> **[IF THE ANSWER IS NO, SKIP TO Q26]**

(b) Did you visit often?

> **YES   NO**
>
> **[IF ANSWER IS YES, SKIP TO (f)]**

(c) When was it?

Month _____ Year _____

(d) What was the purpose of your trip?

(e) How long did you stay in Delhi during that visit?

Days _____
Months _____

[SKIP TO Q26]

(f) What used to be the reason for visiting Delhi so often?

Q26 Did you know somebody in Delhi before you moved here?

> **YES   NO**
>
> **[IF ANSWER IS NO, SKIP TO Q27]**

(b) Whom did you know?

(i)_____
(ii)_____
(iii)_____

(c) What did he/she (they) do for work?

(i)_____
(ii)_____
(iii)_____

(d) Did you get any information or advice from him (them) before you came?

(i)_____

(ii)_____

(iii)_____

Q27 Were you offered a job before you came?

YES   NO

[IF ANSWER IS YES, SKIP TO Q34]

Q28 What did you know about the chances to get work in Delhi before you moved here?

Q29 Did you know about job vacancies before you came?

YES   NO

[IF ANSWER IS NO, SKIP TO Q30]

(b) Did you know about a particular job vacancy for which you were qualified?

YES   NO

[IF ANSWER IS NO, SKIP TO Q30]

(c) What job was this?

(d) What work did it involve?

(e) Who told you about it?

Q30 What was attitude of your family to your migration to Delhi?

1. Did not mind
2. Supported
3. Opposed
4. Indifferent
5. Other (specify_____)

(b) How?

Q31 For how long were you in Delhi before you **started** looking for a job?

1. Have not started   **[SKIP TO Q33]**
2. Days _____

Months_____

(b) If you did not start looking for a job immediately, what were you doing?

(c) What methods did you mainly use for searching for work?

1. Jobbers
2. Private employment agency

3. Referrals
4. Information from earlier settlers about 'impending recruitment plans'
5. Radio
6. Newspapers
7. Employment exchange
8. Search efforts of urban contacts
9. Gate hiring
10. Approaching factories, worksites, shops and offices
11. *Chowk* (market square)
12. Tried to set up business
13. Other (specify_____)

Q32 How long after your arrival did you start working?

Days _____
Months _____
Year_____

Q33 How did (do) you support yourself during this waiting period?

1. Past savings
2. Loan
3. Support from family in village
4. Friends' support in Delhi
5. Relatives' support in Delhi
6. Other source (specify_____)

Now, some questions about your first job in Delhi:

Q34 What was your first job in Delhi?

Occupation_____
What kind of work did it involve?_____

Q35 Through which channel did you get this job?

1. Jobbers
2. Private employment agency
3. Referrals
4. Information from earlier settlers about 'impending recruitment plans'
5. Radio
6. Newspapers
7. Employment exchange
8. Search efforts of urban contacts
9. Gate hiring
10. Approaching factories, worksites, shops and offices
11. *Chowk* (market square)
12. Tried to set up business
13. Other (specify_____)

Q36 What else did you do?

1. Occupation _____
What kind of work did it involve?_____
2. Occupation _____
What kind of work did it involve?_____
3. Occupation _____
    What kind of work did it involve?_____

Q 37 If you could earn the same income in your village, would you prefer to live there?

YES   NO

[IF ANSWER IS YES, SKIP TO (c)]

(b) What is the reason for it?
(c) Suppose you get a similar job in your village, would you be prepared to do it?

YES   NO

[IF ANSWER IS YES, SKIP TO Q37]

(d) Why not?

Q38 **If you were working for wages,** how were you paid?

1. Season
2. Casual, daily
3. Weekly
4. Monthly
5. Annually
6. Piece work
7. Other (specify_____)

Q39 For how long did you remain in your first job?

1. Still in job **[SKIP TO Q40]**
2. Years_____
Months_____
Days_____

[ASK MONTHS ONLY IF LESS THAN ONE YEAR]

(b) What was the main reason for ending that job?

1. Have not stopped
2. Quit, low income

3. Quit, poor working conditions
4. Quit, to take another job
5. Quit, to set up business
6. Laid off, no work
7. Laid off, other reasons
8. Job completed
9. Ill health, disability
10. To get married
11. Pregnant
12. Paid off debt
13. Completed/gave up apprenticeship/training
14. Wanted to move to another area
15. Other (specify_____)

Q40 Looking on balance, why did you come?

The small-scale sample survey of inter-State rural migrants in Delhi 2009

Stage III

(Resurvey)

Questionnaire for the neighbour/relative/ friend/ community leader in Delhi of the migrant heads of household who were interviewed in 1992

Confidential

Reference information of the small-scale sample survey of inter-State rural migrants conducted in Delhi in 1992

Migrant Code No. _____

Name of the head of the household _____

House _____

Locality _____

Date _____

Time _____

Information about village before migration

Village _____

Tehsil _____

District _____

State _____

Confidential

Unit Code No. _____

Name of the information provider _____

Relation with the migrant head of the household _____

House _____

Locality _____

Telephone number _____

Date ————————————-

Time ————————————

Namaskar. I teach in the University at Rohtak and am located at the Jawaharlal Nehru University these days for survey research. About 17 years back, I conducted a survey for my research studies that was about the people who have come from rural areas to Delhi for work. At that time I talked to *Shri*. . . . . (Name of the migrant head of the household) residing in. . . . . (Name of the locality) concerning how he came to Delhi.

I wish to conduct a further survey about it.

(Wait for reaction. If there is any spontaneous remark or reflection, note it. Otherwise, move on to questions if the respondent is ready.)

Would you please be kind enough to answer a few questions about the present residence of *Shri*. . . . . ?

(Wait for reaction. Otherwise, move on to questions if the respondent is ready.)

Q1 Do you know *Shri*. . . . . of. . . . .(village) who used to reside in. . . . .(Name of the locality) 17 years back?

> **YES   NO**
>
> **[IF ANSWER IS NO, SKIP TO Q5]**

Q2 Does he still live in. . . . . (Name of the locality)?

> **YES   NO   DON'T KNOW**
>
> **[IF ANSWER IS NO, SKIP TO Q3]**
>
> **[IF ANSWER IS DON'T KNOW, SKIP TO Q5]**

(b) Do you know where he lives now?

> **YES   NO**
>
> **[IF ANSWER IS NO, SKIP TO Q5]**

(c) Please tell his abode in the locality.

> House _____
> Locality _____
> Telephone number _____

Q3 Do you know where he lives now?

> **YES   NO**
>
> **[IF ANSWER IS NO, SKIP TO Q5]**

> Village/Town/City _____
> *Tehsil* _____
> District _____
> State/Country _____

Q4 Could you give his address and telephone number?

YES　NO

[IF ANSWER IS NO, SKIP TO Q5]

(b) Please tell.

Address _____

_____

_____

Telephone _____

[If the whereabouts have been obtained, skip to the end of the questionnaire]

Q5 Do you know anyone from whom his whereabouts can be found?

YES　NO

[IF ANSWER IS NO, SKIP TO THE END OF THE QUESTIONNAIRE]

(b) Please tell about that person

Name _____
Address _____

_____

_____

Telephone _____

You have been very kind to spare time for me.

The small-scale sample survey of inter-State rural migrants in Delhi 2009

Stage IV

(Resurvey)

Questionnaire for a reinterview with those migrant heads of household who were interviewed in 1992 and retraced in Delhi in 2009

Confidential

Reference information of the small-scale sample survey of inter-State rural migrants conducted in Delhi in 1992

Migrant Code No. _____

Name of the head of the household _____

House _____

Locality _____

Date _____

Time _____

Now in Delhi:

House _____

Locality _____

_____

Date ———————-

Time ———————

Telephone number _____

Namaskar. Perhaps you remember that when I conducted a survey for my studies 17 years back in the year 1992, you told me how you moved to Delhi. I would like to talk to you in that context.

(Wait for reaction. Otherwise, move on to questions if the respondent is ready.)

Q1. After I conducted your survey 17 years back, have you usually lived in Delhi itself?

YES   NO

[IF ANSWER IS YES, SKIP TO Q3][1]

Q3 What is your **main** activity these days?

[Listen to the reply and note what is said instead of reading the list]

1. Work for living   **[SKIP TO Q5]**
2. Petty help to the family
3. Unemployed
4. Housework
5. Attending school
6. Apprenticeship/training
7. Sick/disabled
8. Retired
9. Other (specify_____)

Q4 Do you work?

YES   NO

[IF ANSWER IS YES, SKIP TO Q5]

(b) Do you want to work?

YES   NO

[IF ANSWER IS YES, SKIP TO Q8;

IF ANSWER IS NO, SKIP TO Q6]

Q5 **If you are working, then:**

(a) What is your main job?

Occupation _____
What kind of work does it involve?

_____

(b) Do you do any other work along with this main job?

YES   NO

IF YES, THEN WHAT *OTHER* DIFFERENT JOBS YOU DO AND WHERE?

(i)_____
(ii)_____
(iii)_____

Q6 What else did you do after our last meeting 17 years back in the year 1992? Please tell in chronological order.

[IF ANSWER IS NONE, SKIP TO Q. 7]

1. Occupation _____
What kind of work did it involve? _____
For how long a period? _____ Years _____Months

What was the reason for ending it?

1. Have not stopped **[SKIP TO Q 7]**
2. Got promotion\regularisation
3. Quit, low income
4. Paid off debt
5. Quit, unpunctual payment\cheating
6. Job was irregular
7. Went to village\absenteeism
8. Quit, poor working conditions
9. Health, disability
10. Quarrel\dispute with the employer
11. Quit, to take another job
12. Completed/gave up apprenticeship/training
13. Quit, to join training/to learn work
14. Quit, to set up business
15. Quit, other reasons
16. Laid off, no work
17. Laid off, factory\shop closed
18. Laid off, other reasons
19. Job completed
20. To get married
21. Pregnant
22. Wanted to move to another area
23. Other (specify_____)

Q 6 (2)

2. Occupation _____
What kind of work did it involve? _____
For how long a period? _____ Years _____Months

What was the reason for ending it?

1. Have not stopped **[SKIP TO Q 7]**
2. Got promotion\regularisation
3. Quit, low income
4. Paid off debt
5. Quit, unpunctual payment\cheating

6. Job was irregular
7. Went to village\absenteeism
8. Quit, poor working conditions
9. Health, disability
10. Quarrel\dispute with the employer
11. Quit, to take another job
12. Completed/gave up apprenticeship/training
13. Quit, to join training/to learn work
14. Quit, to set up business
15. Quit, other reasons
16. Laid off, no work
17. Laid off, factory\shop closed
18. Laid off, other reasons
19. Job completed
20. To get married
21. Pregnant
22. Wanted to move to another area
23. Other (specify_____)

Q 7 Is the main job that you are doing now the same that you were doing at the time of our meeting 17 years back?

YES   NO

(b) **If 'Yes'**, then what has changed in it?
(c) **If 'No'**, then how is it different from the job that you were doing 17 years back?

[SKIP TO Q. 9]

Q 8 **If you are not working but want to, then:**
(a) How long have you been without work?

Have not stopped   **[SKIP BACK TO Q3]**
Months _____
Years _____

(b) What kind of a job did you do before you stopped?

Main occupation _____
The kind of work it involved _____

Q 9 Did you study or learn work during the past 17 years?
If YES, then what (different things) did you study or learn?

1. _____
2. _____

3. _____

Q 10 . . . . years back, you moved from your village. . . . . to Delhi.

At that time, looking on balance, why did you come?

Format of the letter sent to the *Sarpanches* of the villages of origin of the migrants who could not be traced in Delhi in 2009

By Registered Post

To   Dated

Honourable *Sarpanch*/Village president

Village

Post Office/Tehsil/Thana/Police Station

District

State

Subject: **Request for information on the present residence of** *Shri*_____ **of your village (age about**_____ **years)**

Hon'ble Sir/Madam,

I conducted a survey in Delhi for my studies about 17 years back in the year 1992. This survey was about those living in Delhi who had migrated to Delhi from rural areas. During that survey I had interviewed *Shri*_____ _____of your village.

Now, for research study only, I am doing a resurvey of those whom I had then interviewed in Delhi. For this purpose, I need their current address/telephone number. I would be most grateful if you could kindly write the address and/or telephone number of the above-mentioned person (or that of such a person who can give information I am seeking) on the enclosed sheet, put it into the pre-stamped envelope bearing my address and deposit it at the earliest at a post office.

Regards,

Yours faithfully

(Himmat Singh Ratnoo)

Address:

Telephone:. . . . .

Mobile No.:. . . . .

E-mail:. . . . .

Migrant Code No.. . . . .

(For the Researcher) . . . .

Name: *Shri* . . . .

Village: . . . .

Current address:. . . . .

. . . .

. . . .

. . . .

. . . .

Telephone:. . . . .

Other information:

Note

1 In almost all the cases, the answer to Question 1 of the Stage IV questionnaire was 'Yes' and, hence, the questionnaire has been truncated to skip to Question 3.

Index

Page numbers for figures, maps, and tables are in italics.

accumulation 3−6
active labour army 4, 119
advice, pre-migration 54, 61−4, 115, 119
Africa 7
age, of migrants 40−1, 110, 113−16, 121, 142, *175*, *177*
agricultural: incomes 134; output *45*; sector 74, 119−20
Agricultural Census of India 41−2
agriculturists 32−7, 41−8, 147−50
Allahabad, India 135
all-India Agricultural Census 120
All India Report on Agricultural Census 1980−81 (AIRAC) 41−2
Ambedkar Nagar, South Delhi 27
Andhra Pradesh, India 134
Anhui Province, China 127
Annamalai (Narayan) 117n1
apartheid 126
area explanation 30−2
artisans 33−4, 107
Asia 6
asymmetry of information 11
attributes and variables 158−60
Australia 7
Azadpur Railway station 140
Azadpur-Wazirpur industrial area, North Delhi 140
Azamgarh, India 134

Bairoch, P. 6
Ballia, India 134
Banerjee, B. 10−11, 25
Bangladesh 126
basti 114−15
Basti, India 134

beldari (unskilled construction work) 63, 78, 99
Bengali Camp 27, 91
Bengali language 140−1
Berry, A. 6
Bhattacharya, P. 8−9
bicycles, ownership of 81
Bihar, India 15, 18n7, 29−31, 133−4
Bihar State Legislative Assembly 125
birth, state of *177*
Black, R. 125−6
Bogue, D. 132
Bombay, India 10, 119
Borjas, G. 12
borrowing 30
Bose, R. 14, 132
Breman, J. 1, 9−12, 17n3, 118−19, 126
Britain 122
Buchanan, D. 10, 118−19
bullock cart drivers 33
bungalow resident (*kothiwala*) 69

capital accumulation 3−6
capitalism 2−5, 11, 118
case study, background of 1−22
caste 37, 50
census blocks 25−7, 28n6, 140−1, *173*
Central Bihar, India 15, 29−31, 120, 134−5, 157
centralisation 4
child labourers 85
children, of migrants 65, 81, 142
Chile 9
China 9−10, 115, 119, 126−7
chi-square testing 30, 35, 39−40, 49−52, 72, 81, 93, 112

chowk (market square) 68, 71
city economies 115
class 2–3, 11, *34*
classical political economy 1–6, 11–13,
    115, 118
clean-ups 115
clustering 30, 105–10, 120, 156–8,
    186–90
Cole, W. 9, 17n4
concentration 4
conditional selectivity 12
construction sector: characterization
    of migrants in 109; distribution of
    jobs in *92, 96*; as entry point 73, 78;
    occupational mobility in *93, 94*
construction workers 33, 52, 113
contacts, pre-migration 60–2, 66, 71
Contreras, D. 122
counter-magnets 122
crafts sector 74
Cramer's V 105–6
credit markets 11
credit worthiness 30
criteria migrants: death of 89–91, *183*;
    defined 17; demographic profiles of
    142; occupational status and mobility
    of 91–9, 142–3; pre-migration
    socioeconomic status of 29–56; reasons
    for migration by *83*; residency of 144;
    selection of 25–7; statistical tables
    regarding *173–91*; whereabouts of
    88–9, 144–6
Crook, N. 10
crops, number of 44–5
cultivable land 147–52, *179–80*
current jobs *184*

daily employment 34
Dandekar, V. 14, 133
Dasgupta, P. 125
data collection 141–2
data-mining techniques 156–62
dataset, preparation of 193, *194–202*
day labourers 107
DDA (Delhi Development Authority)
    23–4, 137–8
death, of criteria migrants 89–91, *183*
debt 46, 51, 113–17, 121
decentralisation 9, 126
decision-tree method 111–17, 120–1,
    157–62
deficient agglomeration 10
Delhi Administration 137

Delhi Administration, Bureau of
    Economics and Statistics: *Report of the
    Committee on Poverty Line in Delhi* 138
Delhi Development Authority (DDA)
    23–4, 137–8
Delhi, India: age of arrival in *177*; choice
    of 2, 15; data collection in 23–8; debt
    of rural migrants to 46; duration, of stay
    in *175*; *jhuggie jhonpari* clusters in *173*;
    jobs in 72–80; migration to 10–11, 14,
    131–6; mobility and 142–3; month
    and year of arrival in *176*; population
    pressure and 123; retrospective on the
    process of migration to 102–4
Delhi Municipal Corporation 24
demand-pull forces 5–6, 134
Demographic Research Centre of the
    Institute of Economic Growth,
    New Delhi 27n1
density criterion 138–9
Deoria, India 134
deprivation 29–30, 120, 124
developing countries 6–10, 13, 115,
    122–7
disability 91–2
discount rates 9, 17n4
disguised unemployment 34
distress migration 124
diversity 10
domestic servants 33
dualistic models 12
dual markets 9, 122
Duesenberry, J. 12
durable items, ownership of 49, *50*
duration: of first jobs 75–6, *181*; of stay
    in Delhi *175*; of unemployment and
    underemployment *178*
Dyson, T. 7

East Delhi, India 138–9
Easterners (*poorbias; poorvees*) 30, 107–9
Eastern Uttar Pradesh, India 15, 29–31,
    120, 134–5, 157
ecliptic nodes 112
Economic Census of the Union Territory
    of Delhi 138
economic status *32*, 50–3
education 49–50, 62–3, 107, 138,
    142, *175*
Eighth Five Year Plan of India 123
electricity 49
Ellis, F. 1, 11, 118, 122–3, 127
Emergency, The 59–60

employment: agencies 71–2; exchanges
68; generation of 123; growth
133; levels of 37–40; months of,
before migration *40*; nature of 34;
pre-migration and 32–41, 107–9;
reason for leaving 35–7; security, of 34
England 3
entrepreneurship 33
Europe 6, 119
excess migration 10
expected frequency problem 72
expulsion *see* recruitment *versus* expulsion
hypothesis

factory sector 74, 78, *92*, 109, 113;
distribution of jobs in 96, *97*;
occupational mobility in *94*
factory workers 33, 52
Faizabad, India 135
families: attitudes to migration of 63–5,
119, 121; economic position of 53;
livelihood comparisons between 109;
reasons for leaving employment and 37;
support of 67–8
farm operators 10–11
fathers, status of 53–4
Fay, M. 7
FDI (foreign direct investment) 124
Fei, J. 17n2
female-male ratio 24, 133
female migration 135n1
fifth jobs 80
first jobs 73–8, 113–17, 120–1, *153–5*,
181, *184*
floating population 126
Food and Supplies Department Circles 137
food output and requirement 45–6
foreign direct investment (FDI) 124
formal sector 9
fourth jobs 80, *183*
Fox, S. 10
fragmentation 150
free labourers 5

gain ration 112–13, 159
garment sector 52, 62
Gazipur, India 134
gender, of migrants 142
gender selective migration 24
generalising case study 16
Gillmore, R. 122
Gini coefficient 12–13, 112
go-betweens 121

Gorakhpur, India 135
Gould, W. 7
Gregory, P. 17n3
growth centres 122
growth rates, of income and
employment 133
Gupta, R. 23

Harris, J. 7–13
Harris, N. 1, 10–11, 118, 122–3, 127
Harris–Todaro model 8–11, 104
harvest employment 34, *35*
harvests: months of food from *46*; number
of before migration *44*
Haryana, India 132
heads of household 26–7, 142
health, over time 91–2
Hindi language 140
hired workers 34, *35*, 107
holistic approach 1
Hoselitz, B. 6–7, 11, 117–22, 135
hukou system 126
Hume, D. 2–3

idle period, job search and 66
IDSMT (Integrated Development of Small
and Medium Towns) 122–4
income: differentials 121; exclusiveness
of 47–8; expectations 121; inequality
10–13; levels, of agriculturists 42–4;
sources of 46–8, 64–5; in villages 80–1
indebtedness 115–17, 121
index of poverty and recentness of
migration 25, 139
Indian Parliament 125
Indonesia 126
industrial sector 5
industry, role of 10
industry/urban ratio 7
informal sector 8–9, 14, 17n3, 133
informal training 62
information and advice, pre-migration 54,
61–4, 115, 119
information, asymmetry of 11
information gain 160
in-migration 132
Institute for Socialist Education 24, 138
insurance markets 11
Integrated Development of Small and
Medium Towns (IDSMT) 122–4
integrated social science approach 1, 13
internal migration 13, 125, 157, *163–72*
internal nodes 112–13

inter-State migration 14–15, 18n6, 131–6, *171–2*
interviews 140–2, *174*
intra-sector distribution 93–7
involuntary self-employment 9
irrigation 150–1
ISSP (1995 International Social Survey Programme) 12–13

jhuggie jhonpari clusters 25, 137–8, *173*
jhuggies 24–5, 140
jhuggi jhompari areas 114–15
job allocation rules 9
jobbers 68, 71
jobs: change of 78–80, *153–5*; changes in 99–100; differences between 100–1; pre-migration 107–9; in villages 80–2
job search 11, 65–72, 82–4

k-means clustering 105–6, 156–8, *186–90*
Kolkata, India 125
kothiwala (bungalow resident) *69*
Kundu, A. 132

labour demand 5–6, 15–16, 85, 120–2, 134
labourers 47, 107–9
labour transfer 2–6
Lall, S. 10
land, insufficiency and scarcity of 14, 35, 133
land–labour ratio 6–7
landlessness 2, 10–11, 35, 52, 85
land ownership 10–11, 17, 41–2, 52, 109, 147–52
last residence, state of *178*
Latin America 9
leaf nodes 112–13
leasing-in 17, 42–5, 109, 147–52, *179–80*
leasing-out 47–9, 81, 147–52
Lee, E. 6
Lenin, V. 5, 118
less developed country (LDC) 6–7
Lewis, W. 5–7, 17n1–2
liberalisation policies 123
Liebig, T. 12
listing survey 25–7
literacy 49–52, 107, 142
livelihood categories 51–2
livelihood comparisons 109
livestock, ownership of 48–9
location, of migrants 89–91, *183*

long-distance migration 132
longitudinal social science approach 11–13
lottery 9, 91, 121
luck, in job search 68–9

machine learning 157–8
Madhya Pradesh, India 134
Maharashtra, India 125, 132
Mahatma Gandhi National Rural Employment Guarantee Act (MNREGA) 124–5
Malaysia 126
male migration *163–72*
Mallick, S. 14
man–land ratio 119–20
manual workers 122
manufacturing sector 119
marital status, of migrants 142, *175*
market square (*chowk*) 68, 71
Martin, K. 17n1
Marxist political economy 1–6, 13, 118
Marx, K. 3–5, 11–12, 115
Master Plan for Delhi 138
Mazumdar, D. 7
Mehrotra, G. 132, 135n1
Mexico 126
Micevska, M. 12–13, 118
Middle South Asia 7
migrants: age of 40–1, 110, 113–16, 121, 142, *175*, *177*; children of 65, 81, 142; discovering and characterising groups of 105–10; marital status of 142, *175*; social positions of 12, 50–2; stay or return dichotomy and 111–17; *see also* criteria migrants
migration: channels of 110; classifications of 135n1; distress 124; excess 10; internal 13, 125, 157, *163–72*; long-distance 132; process of 57–87; retrospective on the process of 88–104; return 1, 11–15, 111–21, 132–3, 160–72; socioeconomic status before 29–56, 115;
mill workers 33
Misra, G. 23
missing migrant respondents 145–6
'Mission Statement & Guidelines' (Smart Cities Mission) 125
Mitra, A. 14, 133
MNREGA (Mahatma Gandhi National Rural Employment Guarantee Act) 124–5

mobility 4–5, 30, 91–9, 118, 127, 132, 142–3
Mohan, R. 15, 30, 134–5, 144
monthly employment 34
mortgage income 47
Mukherji, S. 14
Mumbai, India 11, 125
Municipal Corporation of Delhi 137–8
Mycielski, J. 12–13, 118

Narayan, R.: *Annamalai* 117n1
National Capital Region (NCR) of India 89, 123
National Capital Region Planning Board 123
National Commission on Urbanisation (NCU) 122–3
National Rural Employment Guarantee Act 125
natural disasters 37
naukari (service job) 41, 81
negative selectivity 12–13
neo-liberal reforms 124
Nepali language 141
New Delhi Municipal Committee 24
newspaper job searches 68, 72
1981 Population Census 135n1
1995 International Social Survey Programme (ISSP) 12–13
1991 Census 135n2, 135n4
Ninth Plan 123–4
nonagricultural workers 32–7
non-Eastern (*non-poorvee*) migrants 30, 107–9
non-*poorvanchalis* 120
nonworkers 40–1, 102
North America 3
North and Central Bihar, India 15, 29–31, 120, 134–5, 157
North Delhi, India 140
null hypothesis 23

off-season food requirements *46*
Okhla Industrial Area 27
Opal, C. 7
operational holdings 41–3, 119–20
Orissa, India 134
Oucho, J. 7
out-migration 14–15, 29–32, 110, 132–3, 144, 157, *172*
overpopulation 119–20
over-urbanisation 6–10, 13, 117–21, 135

panchayat 50–2
partition 132
payment, method of 74–5, 109
peasants 2, 33–7, 52, 107, 120
Peru 126
pessimistic model 2, 5–13, 120
phi coefficient 93, 105–6
piece-meal employment 34–5
place of birth (POB) 149
place of last residence (POLR) 135n1, 149, *177*
policy approaches 122–7
poorbias/poorvees (Easterners) 30, 107–9
poorvanchalis 120
population: density 138–9; growth 134–5, 138; pressure 123; spatial distribution of 126
population/college ratio 138
post-mercantilism 2
post-migration factors 120–1
poverty 133, 138–9
poverty hypothesis 7, 16, 29, 110, 119–20, 133–5
Poverty Reduction Strategy Papers (PRSPs) 125–6
predicting attributes and variables 111–13, 158–60
pre-migration: contacts 60–2, 66, 71; family attitudes and 63–5; information and advice 54, 61–4, 115, 119; jobs 107–9; job search 65–72; knowledge 62–3; noneconomic considerations 80–2; reasons for migration 82–8; socioeconomic status 29–56, 115; unemployment 109; visits 58–60, *180*
Preston, S. 7
primary relations 61
private employment agencies 71–2
productivity 4, 122
property income 47
PRSPs (Poverty Reduction Strategy Papers) 125–6
Puentes, E. 122
pull factors 5–6, 134
Punjab, India 10–11
push migration 6, 13–16, 29, 72, 119–24, 133–5

questionnaires 140, 204–30

radios, ownership of 81
radio/television job searches 72
Rajasthan, India 10–11, 18n7, 133

Ranis, G. 17n2
rate of accumulation 3
Rath, N. 14, 133
rational migration 9
ration cards 125, 137
Ratnagiri, India 10, 119
Ratnoo, H. 18n7
*ray*a 54
recruitment 16, 37, *70–1*, 116, 119–20, 123–4
recruitment *versus* expulsion hypothesis 13–16, 27, 118–19, 157
rectangular nodes 112
referrals 72
relative deprivation 1, 9–15, 30, 118–19, 124
repeat migration 11
Report of the Committee on Poverty Line in Delhi (Delhi Administration, Bureau of Economics and Statistics) 138
representative sampling 15–16
reserve army of labour 4–5, 115–19
resettlement colonies 23
resurvey, location during 89–91, *183*
return migration 1, 11–15, 111–21, 132–3, 160–2
Revenstein, E. 17n2
Ricardo, D. 3–4
risk aversion 9
root nodes 112–13
rural areas, class differentiation in 2–3
rural development 124–6
Rural Labour Inquiry 46, 51
rural-urban apartheid 126
Russia 5

Sabates-Wheeler, R. 125–6
Sabot, R. 6
sampling 15–16, 23–8
Sanders, R. 9, 17n4
Sanjay Colony 27
Sarpanches 144–6
school attendance 49–51, 142, *175*
seasonal employment 34–5
secondary relations 61
second jobs *79, 182*
sectors: cross-tabulation of *184*; of first jobs 73–4, 121; move across 93; of second and third jobs *79*
sector-wise distribution 92
security, of employment 34
self-cultivation 150
self-employment 9, 34, 74, 107, 124
Selod, H. 10

semi-skilled workers 78
service job (*naukari*) 41, 81
service sector 73–4, 78, *92*, 113, 119; distribution of jobs in *96*; occupational mobility in *94*, 95
service workers 33, 52
seventh jobs 80
Shahdara Zone of the Municipal Corporation of Delhi 138
Shalizi, Z. 10
shame 81–2, 87
shopkeepers 33, 47, *92*
shopkeeping sector 81, 95–8
sickness 91–2
silhouette widths 157
Sixth Five Year Plan 122
sixth jobs 80
Skeldon, R. 125–6
skills 62–3, 101
Smart Cities Mission: 'Mission Statement & Guidelines' 125
Smith, A. 3–4
social factors 80–1
social science approach 1, 11–13
sociocultural status 49–50
socioeconomic status 29–56, 115
Sousa-Poza, A. 12
South Africa 126
South Delhi Zone, India 24–7, 138–9
spill-over migration 16, 133
squatter settlements 113–120, *173*; age of heads of households in 142; choice of 23–5; estimating percentage of 137–8; index for selection of 139; resurvey in 145–6
Stark, O. 1, 9, 12–13, 118
status: categories 52; consciousness 81–2; indicators of 48–50, 115; occupational 32–41, 91–9, 107–9
stay or return dichotomy 113–17, 160–2
Subhas Camp 27
subregional analysis 134–5
sub-sectoral level, job changes at *153–5*
subsequent jobs 78
subsidiary jobs 33
subsistence sector 5
Sultanpur, India 134
support, methods of 67–9
Suri, P. 23, 138
surplus labour 4–5, 8, 44–5
sweepers 33, 99

tailors 35–6
Tamil language 141

Tanzania 126
TCPO (Town and Country Planning Organisation) 123
teashop workers 33
television job searches 72
Tenth Plan 124
Thailand 126
third jobs 79, *182*
Third World 7–9, 13, 17n3
Todaro, M. 7–13, 117, 122
Todaro model 9–10, 121–2
Todaro paradox 10–11
too big city syndrome 122–3
total relative deprivation (TRD) 12
Town and Country Planning Organisation (TCPO) 123
traders 33–4, 107
tradespersons 74
traditional pessimistic model 2, 5–13, 120
training 62
translations 140
transmigration 126
TRD (total relative deprivation) 12
two-sector model 7–10
two-stream migration models 9
2009 resurvey 27, 89–91, *183*
2001 population census 124
2013 UN report 125–6

UIDSSMT (Urban Infrastructure Development Scheme for Small and Medium Towns) 124
underemployment 8, 34–6, *178*
unemployment 3, 8–10, 35–6; disguised 34; duration of *39*, 121–2, *178*; levels of 37–40; over time 102; pre-migration 109
United Nations 10, 25, 125–6
United States 7, 122

unskilled construction work (*beldari*) 63, 78, 99
untouchability 50
UN/UNFPA workshop 123
urban bias 10, 117, 121
Urban Infrastructure Development Scheme for Small and Medium Towns (UIDSSMT) 124
urbanisation 13, 118–19, 122–7, 131–5
Uttar Pradesh, India 10–11, 15, 18n7, 30, 133–4

vacancies, knowledge of 62–3
Varanasi, India 135
variables 111–13, 158–60, 193, *194–202*
vending 81
village, jobs in 80–2
visits, pre-migration 58–60, *180*
voluntary self-employment 9

Waddington, C. 125–6
wage labour 33–5, 107, 124
wages 3–9, 52
waiting period 66–9, 72, 119
WEKA data mining software 112–13, 156–8
West Bengal, India 132
Williamson, J. 122
Winters, A. 125–6
World Bank 6

Xiamen, China 126

Yamuna river 25
Yap, L. 121–2
years since migration *176*

Zachariah, K. 132

For Product Safety Concerns and Information please contact our EU
representative GPSR@taylorandfrancis.com
Taylor & Francis Verlag GmbH, Kaufingerstraße 24, 80331 München, Germany